PHILIP COGGAN

The Last Vote

The Threats to Western Democracy

PENGUIN BOOKS

PENGUIN BOOKS

Published by the Penguin Group
Penguin Books Ltd, 80 Strand, London WC2R ORL, England
Penguin Group (USA), Inc., 375 Hudson Street, New York, New York 10014, USA
Penguin Group (Canada), 90 Eglinton Avenue East, Suite 700, Toronto, Ontario, Canada M4P 2Y3
(a division of Pearson Penguin Canada Inc.)
Penguin Ireland, 25 St Stephen's Green, Dublin 2, Ireland (a division of Penguin Books Ltd)
Penguin Group (Australia), 707 Collins Road, Melbourne, Victoria 3008, Australia
(a division of Pearson Australia Group Pty Ltd)
Penguin Books India Pvt Ltd, 11 Community Centre, Panchsheel Park,
New Delhi – 110 017, India
Penguin Group (NZ), 67 Apollo Drive, Rosedale, Auckland 0632, New Zealand
(a division of Pearson New Zealand Ltd)
Penguin Books (South Africa) (Pty) Ltd, Block D, Rosebank Office Park,
181 Jan Smuts Avenue, Parktown North, Guateng, South Africa 2193

Penguin Books Ltd, Registered Offices: 80 Strand, London WC2R ORL, England

www.penguin.com

First published by Allen Lane 2013
Published in Penguin Books 2014
001

Copyright © Philip Coggan, 2013

The moral right of the author has been asserted

Typeset by Jouve (UK), Milton Keynes
Printed in Great Britain by Clays Ltd, St Ives plc

A CIP catalogue record for this book is available from the British Library

978-0-718-19727-8

www.greenpenguin.co.uk

To Sandie, for making my life so wonderful over the last 15 years

Contents

Preface and Acknowledgements

Financial journalists write about companies, markets and economics. But in the last few years, it became clear that the debt crisis which broke in 2007 was having a much broader impact – on politics and on society. This was clearly brought home as governments throughout the developed world fell from office and, in some cases, as technocrats became prime ministers. As my last book argued, high debt levels create a conflict between creditors and debtors, in which the former try to safeguard their capital and the latter try to reduce the burden of debt servicing. These issues raise tricky battles for democracies as well as for economic policy – should creditors be paid off if the result is a loss of wealth for ordinary citizens? Or do countries need the goodwill of creditors if they are to prosper in the long run?

Democracies are struggling to deal with these problems. The 'bargain' between politicians and voters is that the former generate a continually rising standard of living for the latter. But after 2007 developed economies seem to have stopped growing. Elected leaders have to deal with the demands of the markets on the one hand and the hopes of the voters on the other, all at a time when politicians are staggeringly unpopular. All this inspired me to look back at the early debates about democracy, and I found that the issues that concern us today also worried Plato, Aristotle and the American founding fathers. In turn, that made me worry that democracy might be more fragile than most people assume. I hope that this book can make a small contribution to promoting democratic reform. If I can only start readers thinking more deeply about some of the issues concerned – for example, the balance between minority and majority rights, between economic efficiency and political accountability or the role that democracy can play in dealing with issues that cut across national borders – this book will have achieved something. As the footnotes and bibliography will show, there has been much work by excellent authors in these areas.

This book has also been inspired by the tremendous experience of working at *The Economist* for the last seven years, and thanks are once again due to John Micklethwait and Daniel Franklin for allowing me to pursue this project while writing my regular articles. There can be few better places to work. It should be emphasized that the views expressed are all my own, and should not be taken as *The Economist*'s leader line. That said, I benefited enormously from the advice of Edward Carr and Andrew Palmer, who read through drafts of my book.

At Penguin, thanks must go to Georgina Laycock for commissioning me again, to Thomas Penn and Patrick Loughran for seeing this book through to publication, and to Richard Mason for his thorough copy-editing.

Finally, I thank my family, Sandie, Helena and Catherine, for their patience while Dad disappeared into the study to read another old book, or to rewrite a chapter for the fifth time. Their love and support kept me going.

Philip Coggan, May 2013

Introduction

Democracy perishes by two excesses, the aristocracy of those who govern, or the contempt of the people for the authorities which it has itself established.

Maximilien de Robespierre

Don't vote. It only encourages them.

graffiti

Democracy seems to be enjoying a moment of triumph. Almost half the world's population now lives in a democratic state:[1] the 'Arab spring', the series of revolts that began in Tunisia in December 2010, may add more countries to the total. Many believe that rising prosperity will eventually force China into the democratic camp.

But in the countries of Europe and North America where modern democracy first took root, the picture seems much less healthy. Voter turnout has fallen; politicians are held in low esteem; support for extremist parties is on the rise. The financial crisis that began in 2007 has raised some troubling questions about the ability of developed countries to maintain an economic model based on a combination of high social spending, complex tax codes and volatile financial markets. Nearly 70 years of economic activism, first with fiscal policy (the balance of tax and government spending) and then with monetary policy (the level of interest rates and the amount of money in the economy), has left most Western nations with huge debts, near-zero interest rates and sluggish growth.

Furthermore, democracy seems to be failing to live up to one of its main attractions: the ability to deliver higher living standards for the ordinary person. Instead, it seems to be rigged in favour of a few groups that receive preferential treatment from the government, such as the banks or multinational corporations. Those groups fund the political parties and, in some cases, take a direct place in government. Each citizen may have an equal vote; few believe that each citizen has equal influence.

Just at the moment when politicians are dealing with the tricky issues of slow growth, budget deficits and an ageing population, they find they have staggeringly low public support. In January 2013 a survey of Americans found that Congressmen and Congresswomen were less popular than cockroaches and traffic jams.[2] A YouGov opinion poll in January 2012 found that 62% of Britons agreed with the statement that 'politicians tell lies all the time – you can't believe a word they say'.[3] Turnout in national elections has been falling since the 1970s in many countries of the Western world; recent turnout levels are around a fifth lower than those of four decades ago. Voters are even less willing to trek to the polls for local elections or for the European Parliament.

The cynicism of voters in the developed world is, in part, the result of a series of scandals that have shown politicians willing to cheat on both their expenses and their spouses, and to break the solemn promises they made to voters before their election. Many people also have the feeling that, in practice, there is little difference between the main parties; that, however citizens vote, policies will not change. Like the creatures at the end of George Orwell's *Animal Farm* gazing at the oppressive humans and the supposedly sympathetic pigs, the voters can no longer tell the difference.

As a report on European right-wing voters noted:

> The sense that many of the key discussions take place behind closed doors where parties hash out compromises, among a tight circle of people who have often been to school and to university together . . . can easily fuel the feeling that the prevailing modus operandi is not so much a consensus as a stitch-up.[4]

In Europe, support for the main parties has ebbed away in favour of single-issue parties, some serious, some frivolous and some plain nasty. Neo-fascists, complete with swastika-like symbols and 'Heil

Hitler' salutes, managed to gain seats in the Greek Parliament on a programme of mining the borders to prevent immigration.

The disillusionment of voters is fed by the way that politicians are portrayed in the media. Long gone is the age of deference in which journalists addressed political leaders as 'sir' and reported their words with reverence. When our leaders are not mocked on comedy shows, they are denounced as traitors or crooks on talk shows. Nowadays we save our reverent tones for film stars and musicians, at least until we get bored with them too. Like Basil Fawlty, the hotel manager in John Cleese's classic comedy, we seem to have no middle ground; either we fawn over those in the public eye or we treat them with appalling rudeness.

Our hostility towards our leaders does not help them govern. Think about whether you yourself would like to take the decisions that our leaders have to make every day; do they send troops to a struggling country like Mali, risk being sucked into an endless war, only to be accused of being bloodthirsty meddling fools? Or do they stand aside (as the West did in Rwanda), only to be accused of callous racism? Would you want your expenses and tax details examined in fine detail, your appearance and taste in clothing mocked, your children photographed and bullied? If not, how can we expect to recruit good people into politics?

As if the press and TV are not bad enough, the Internet is a haven for conspiracy theorists and trolls, who can use the anonymity of the Web to spew abuse without comeback. Sometimes it seems as if it is no longer possible for reasonable people to disagree reasonably; unpopular views on the part of a politician are often automatically taken as a sign of corrupt motives or moral turpitude.

Our modern democratic mechanism is a long way from the Athenian ideal of civilized people discussing issues in an open forum. In some ways, this is a good thing; the Athenians excluded women and slaves from voting. Direct participation is also much harder to organize in a society where voters number in their tens of millions, not a few thousand. Modern societies delegate their decisions to elected representatives. But even those representatives have passed control to another set of unelected experts, such as central bankers, who have enormous power over the economy. We have a system not just of delegation but of double delegation.

Double delegation means that the democratic rights of citizens of the developed world are more restricted than they might think. Constitutions and laws have been written to protect the rights of minorities against tyrannical majorities. Countries join international bodies, and sign conventions and treaties, that limit their ability to pass certain laws or behave in certain ways. Being a member of the European Union, for example, means that voters in Britain or Spain cannot stop the citizens of other EU countries from migrating to their countries. International courts can overrule domestic Parliaments, as when the European Court of Human Rights told the British government it could not deport the terror suspect Abu Qutada.

It is possible, of course, to justify all these individual instances of the voters being overruled. International agreements are needed if global issues are to be tackled; history suggests that the rights of minorities can be oppressed in individual countries, so legal rights are needed. In theory, of course, a democracy can vote to withdraw from all these obligations.

Nevertheless, there is a mismatch between the modern notion of democracy as an ideal and the modern practice of restricting democracy's scope in a wide range of areas. Is democracy the best system of government, or is it not? How do we decide as a society which issues are fit for democratic decision-making and which are not? If we need central banks to decide the level of interest rates, do we need other experts to decide on the right level of taxes and spending? If voters are not competent to decide on the big economic issues of the day, what are they competent to decide about? Once democracy ceases to be an absolute right, and becomes one factor to be balanced among many, it is easy to see how it can be undermined further.

HISTORY AS A MOVING WALKWAY

Are all these problems overstated? Most people will probably say that these problems are nothing out of the ordinary; politics is a long series of crises that we muddle through in the end. Over the long run, the natural trend of society is towards democracy. Twenty years ago, in his influential book *The End of History and the Last Man,*[5] Francis

Fukuyama suggested that liberal democracy had won the ideological battle; it (not communism) was the final stage of historical development.

But history is not like the moving walkways at an airport, bearing passengers relentlessly towards their destination. Sometimes, the forward progress can be rudely interrupted. For much of history, most of mankind was ruled by monarchies or hereditary elites. It was not until the mid to late eighteenth century that any society regarded Athenian democracy as a model to be imitated.

It is easy to think that because most Western countries have been democratic in living memory, they will always remain so. But history can be capricious. In the mid-1980s most people thought that Eastern Europe would be communist for the foreseeable future. By the early twentieth century, the Hapsburgs had been dynastic rulers for more than six hundred years and the Romanovs for four hundred; yet by 1918 both had been swept away. Where citizens had the choice, democracy gained adherents because it seemed much more appealing than monarchies or one-party states. But as Samuel Huntington said, 'democracy is a solution to the problem of tyranny but not necessarily to anything else'.[6]

In his last book,[7] the late Tony Judt wrote that 'Few in the West today can conceive of a complete breakdown of liberal institutions, an utter disintegration of the democratic consensus.' But Northern Ireland's history in the twentieth century shows that democracy can become unworkable if the community is sufficiently divided. A built-in Protestant majority, bolstered by gerrymandered constituencies and a link between property ownership and voting, discriminated against Catholics, particularly in employment. The result was a civil rights campaign, British Army involvement, a surge in terrorism and suspension of rule by the Belfast Parliament. And former Yugoslavia provides a horrifying recent example of how communities that had lived side by side for centuries could start killing each other.

Indeed, the history of democracy has been a series of 'two steps forward, one step back'. In the 1920s and 1930s many European countries slipped back into authoritarianism in the face of economic distress. The Great Depression appeared to indicate that liberal capitalism had failed to guarantee jobs and prosperity for all and that a planned economy was required; countries had to choose between communism and right-wing authoritarianism as practised by Mussolini, Franco or, most malignly, Hitler.

Even in the 1970s, as the post-war boom decayed into stagflation (high unemployment and rising prices), Western democracy appeared to totter. Under the 1970–74 Heath government, Britain suffered five states of emergency, complete with power cuts and strikes, along with bombings by the IRA. Abroad, terrorists were active in Greece, West Germany, Italy and Japan, while the leader of the free world, President Richard Nixon, resigned in 1974 before he was impeached. Willy Brandt, the West German chancellor, feared that 'parliamentary democracy in Western Europe could disappear in 20 or 30 years'. The *Financial Times* commentator (now Sir) Samuel Brittan gave a speech in which he said that 'liberal representative democracy' had proved incompatible with excessive economic expectations on the part of the public and the pursuit of group self-interest.[8] In a febrile atmosphere, there was open speculation about a British military coup and the Labour prime minister, Harold Wilson, fretted about MI5 plots against him. The experience of Chile, where Salvador Allende, the elected left-wing president, was overthrown in 1973 by the armed forces under General Augusto Pinochet, was a chilling omen for the left. Peregrine Worsthorne, a *Telegraph* columnist, wrote that, faced with the threat of communism, 'I hope and pray our armed forces would intervene to prevent such a calamity as efficiently as the armed forces did in Chile.'[9]

That democracy survived the turmoil of the 1970s does not mean it will necessarily pass the current test. Democracies did not emerge as the dominant system after an intellectual debate between competing models; they evolved through a process of political give and take.

When democracy started to gain ground in the last half of the nineteenth century, it was a response to the rising power of the 'ordinary people' as they moved away from the farms to the cities and factories, workplaces where they could mingle and demonstrate. The vote was granted by the ruling classes of the nineteenth and early twentieth centuries as a way of buying off the ordinary citizen and heading off the danger of revolution.

The 'liberal democracies' that were created respected property rights as well as the individual franchise; after the Russian Revolution of 1917, this placed them in stark contrast with the communist world, where economic equality was deemed more important than voting rights. Liberal democracies are not just concerned with the vote. They have a free press, competing political parties, an independent judiciary and (to varying degrees) guaranteed rights for minorities. Citizens are free to complain and to demonstrate; to write books and to make art that lampoons those in power.

But whereas most citizens welcome these rights, that is not all they want. Right from the start, those who campaigned for democracy saw it as a means to an end, rather than an end itself; as a way of getting more rights for themselves as workers and a bigger share of national GDP (Gross Domestic Product). Some thinkers have viewed this bargain in cynical terms. In the 1940s the American political scientist Joseph Schumpeter regarded democracy as a competition for power between members of the elite who were offering the equivalent of bribes to the electorate.[10]

The recent rise in inequality, particularly marked in America and Britain, has been accompanied by a huge gain in wealth for those who work in the financial sector, which many voters believe has not been accompanied by significant economic improvements (unlike, say, the success of the technology sector). Indeed, the main result of finance's dominant position in the economy has been a banking crisis that required taxpayer bailouts to keep the financial elite in business. The natural temptation is to wonder whether different systems might have delivered better outcomes. The Occupy protests that emerged in late 2011 may not have generated a coherent political platform but they nevertheless articulated a genuine sentiment; that the 1% had benefited at the expense of the 99%.

Then there is the authoritarian impulse. Early states developed as a way of giving their citizens a form of physical security against the risk of robbery or murder by wandering raiders, and from invasions by rival states. The bargain (admittedly more implicit than explicit) was that the political rights of citizens were subordinate to the needs of national security. Even in modern times it is striking that, during wars or in the aftermath of the terrorist attacks of 11 September 2001, citizens seem willing to see their political rights curtailed in the name of security. Age-old privileges, like protection against imprisonment without trial, have been eroded; taboos against the use of torture have been weakened.

We can slide back if we are not careful. The 'war on terror' can be used to justify ever more intrusive measures by the state – phone-tapping and e-mail surveillance, for example. In seeking to safeguard our democracies we may dilute the qualities that make them special.

This is not just the view of this author. In September 2012 the *Independent*, a British newspaper, launched a reform campaign with the slogan 'Our Democracy is Desperately Sick',[11] while the *Financial Times* columnist Gideon Rachman wrote that 'Democracy is the loser' as Europeans battled to save their currency.[12] *The Economist* Intelligence Unit's 2011 report on the subject was headlined 'Democracy under Stress'. The United Nations Research Institute for Social Development decreed that 'technocratic styles of policymaking pose a threat to democracy'.[13]

This book is designed as a wake-up call. It is natural for those of us who have lived our adult lives in peaceful Western democracies to become blasé about the benefits of the system and cynical about the motives of our rulers. This cynicism is not entirely misplaced; special interests have too powerful a voice in our system. But we have not fought hard enough for reform.

Let me start by making three points clear, to avoid any possible misinterpretation. This book contains much analysis of the flaws within democracy, *but it is not an argument against democracy*. I agree with Churchill that 'democracy is the worst form of government except for all the others that have been tried'.

As citizens of the developed world in the twenty-first century, we should appreciate our luck, even if we do not vote and could not pick our local member of Parliament or Congress out of a line-up. We are living in an age when we have the chance to throw out our rulers in a peaceful way; for most of history, this option was not available. In the developing world, many citizens would love to have a freedom equivalent to ours. The remaining autocracies and one-party states do not respect the rights of their citizens and are marked by corruption that outstrips the petty scandals of expense claims and back-door funding of candidates that can dominate media coverage of politicians in Europe and the United States.

Second, this book does not parrot the agenda of the left or the right. There will be arguments that conservatives nod their heads at and there will be chapters that appeal to the centre-left. But the book is not a call for the abolition of the welfare state, or the end of free trade or the nationalization of the banking sector. It argues that the cumulative effect of left-wing *and* right-wing policies has landed us in this mess.

Third, this book is not predicting the arrival of a new Hitler or Stalin. It is true that there are some modern parallels with the 1930s, which were marked by a retreat from democracy as European economies struggled. But this does not mean that we will all turn into fascists and communists or that Europe will descend into war.

Nevertheless, plenty of unpleasant outcomes are possible. People may continue to vote, but in elections that change nothing, because the result is preordained. This is already the case for many voters in first-past-the-post electoral systems in America and Britain, where very few seats change hands. If you are a Democrat in Alabama, or a Conservative in Wales, your vote is effectively wasted. No doubt this is one of the factors behind the decline in turnout in many countries: the feeling that one's vote is wasted.

Even countries with systems of proportional representation do not solve this problem. Voters cast their ballots but the government is formed in behind-the-scenes negotiations between party leaders; the resulting coalition may be one that few voters ever envisaged. It may also pursue policies that are a compromise between the manifestos of two parties, and thus disliked by both sets of voters. The effect is to sever the connection between the individual voter and the actions of government.

The developing world has long been plagued by sham votes, in which polls are held but the outcome is known in advance; the form of democracy is observed but the substance is ignored. The danger is that the developed world too will start to slip down this same path and jaded voters will not care enough to stop the decline.

A long-standing problem is money. In America, elected politicians spend much of their time in office raising funds for the next election; in the case of the House of Representatives, this occurs every two years. As a result, politicians can become beholden to the interest groups that finance them; this can also be true in Europe, where left-wing parties rely on the trade unions and right-wing parties depend on business.

But Western nations in general are also becoming dependent on foreign creditors. This restricts the range of economic policies they can follow; if they adopt the 'wrong' policies, they will lose access to finance. They may then be forced into the hands of fellow governments or official creditors like the International Monetary Fund. Those creditors may then insist on policy changes before they lend more money.

This phenomenon is not new. Britain's disastrous Suez invasion of 1956 was cut short when President Eisenhower threatened to withdraw support for the pound. In the early 1980s the French president François Mitterrand was forced to change his socialist programme after the franc came under pressure in response to his programme of nationalization. It is clearly anti-democratic that creditors can veto the decisions of voters, although, equally, countries have no right to demand that others lend them money. Many nations are currently struggling to deal with this dichotomy.

The relationship between voters and foreign creditors points to a much broader question. As a universal model, the nation state is a relatively modern phenomenon. Historically, individuals owed their allegiance to their tribe, their feudal lord or their city. Medieval Italy was a combination of monarchies and city states; Germany was a patchwork of principalities until its reorganization, first by Napoleon and then by Bismarck. African national boundaries were imposed on their citizens by colonial powers. The Versailles settlement after the First World War created a raft of new nations out of the ashes of the Austro-Hungarian monarchy. At the same time, voting rights were extended to nearly all men (and some women) in recognition of the efforts of citizen soldiers between 1914 and 1918 and, in part, to head off a repeat of the revolution that had brought the Bolsheviks to power in Russia in 1917.

The nation state and democracy thus developed in tandem. The existence of a national Parliament was a symbol of a nation's freedom. For good or ill, voters made their decisions at the level of the nation state; for example, their representatives imposed tariffs on foreign goods or reduced defence expenditure. In the post-1945 era, many economic decisions were national; stimulus programmes were implemented to reduce unemployment, for example, or incomes policies to combat inflation.

In the second half of the twentieth century, to the extent that nation states faced a challenge to their authority, it was from minorities within their borders. The broad principle of the Versailles settlement, as enunciated in Woodrow Wilson's 'Fourteen Points', was that people 'should be accorded the freest opportunity to autonomous development' – in other words, a people should have the right to rule themselves.[14] But the population of Europe was not neatly divided into homelands of ethnic and religious groups, occupying lands that were neatly delineated by natural boundaries like rivers or mountains. Even the vast migrations that marked the end of the Second World War (as the German state disintegrated and its citizens fled eastern Europe) still left a lot of geographical and ethnic untidiness elsewhere in Europe – the long-standing division of Northern Ireland between Catholic and Protestant, the Basques in northern Spain and so on.

In some cases, it took decades (and much blood) before nation states reached a deal with their minorities, based on devolution and power-sharing, and not all disputes have been settled. Even now, there are pressures for independence in regions such as Catalonia (in Spain). By themselves, these campaigns are a sign that the nation state is losing its appeal now that it can no longer appear to deliver the steadily rising incomes that it managed in the post-1945 era.

And while some voters demand more local power, the modern economy has become globalized, with the fate of the European and American consumer dependent on decisions made, for example, in Beijing. Multinational companies may choose to place their production plants in the country with the lowest wages or taxes and to boycott those nations with policies that are not business-friendly; as already noted, international investors can follow the same approach.

The free flow of goods and capital means that a stimulus package in one country might see most of the benefits flow overseas; hand every American $1,000 and many might spend the proceeds on a flat-screen TV from South Korea. Furthermore, there are plenty of non-economic problems like climate change or terrorism or pandemic flu that now require global coordinated action. The actions of one nation – damming a river, polluting the ocean – will have an effect on its neighbours.

International problems demand international solutions. At this point, democracy struggles to find its role. Yes, the leaders of democratic countries have a voice in global decisions, but so do the leaders of autocratic ones. International decision-making is not conducted on a democratic basis; for historic reasons, certain countries on the United Nations Security Council have the power of veto, for example. But if decisions were to be made on a democratic basis, how would that work? Would the citizens of India and China be allowed to outvote (because they are more populous) the citizens of Europe and North America?

These are complex issues. At their heart is the question of legitimacy; citizens of modern democracies may grumble about the laws of their country but, by and large, they obey them because they recognize that such laws have been passed in a 'fair' way. Citizens appreciate that they need some system for passing laws to regulate their collective conduct and majority rule seems the fairest way of doing so. Pre-modern societies worked on the assumption that a wise monarch, or the socially superior classes, knew what was best for the nation or that society's laws were an expression of God's will (still the theory behind sharia law today). Today's Western voters are generally unconvinced about the appeal of rule by God or King. For legitimacy to work, voters in the developed world have to feel they have a genuine stake in the making of those laws and that the process is not biased against their group.

Clearly, however, very few voters are involved in, or even aware of, the process by which such laws are actually passed. Modern democracy involves a fair degree of delegation; we elect representatives who make decisions on our behalf. Voters merely have the right to throw the bums out if they do not like the outcome.

RISE OF THE TECHNOCRATS

In the last fifty years or so we have taken the process of delegation one stage further. Elected representatives pass on the responsibility for many policies to experts or technocrats. This may be a sensible way for treating complex issues; we would rather that medicines are approved by bodies like the Food and Drug Administration than by politicians or public vote. But it does raise a question of legitimacy; what is the dividing line between policy areas voters can control and those they can't?

Global decision-making is another example of double delegation and one where accountability is even more difficult. The danger is that power passes to a kind of permanent technocracy, consisting of central banks or international bodies like the International Monetary Fund (IMF) or World Trade Organization (WTO). In a full technocracy, we would still vote but our opinions would be meaningless; the real decisions would be made elsewhere.[15]

The European Union is a case in point. It is a bold experiment in international cooperation, with citizens moving freely across national borders and a common currency, the euro, with its own central bank. But decision-making at a 27-state level has been extremely fraught, as the financial crisis has shown. The EU has a democratic deficit. While there is a common Parliament, voter turnout is much lower than at the national level and the powers of the elected representatives are severely circumscribed. Economic integration has been a top-down rather than a bottom-up process, with the leaders of France and Germany tending to push the process forward. When voters have opposed EU projects, such as the referenda on the Lisbon treaty on political integration, they have been told to vote again. Hostility to the high-handedness of Brussels (where the EU bureaucracy is based) has grown, and not just in traditionally eurosceptic Britain.

The Economist Intelligence Unit gives countries a democratic score based on five categories: the electoral process and pluralism; civil liberties; the functioning of government; political participation; and political culture. In 2011 it found that seven countries in Western Europe, and eleven in Eastern Europe, had a decline in their score. The UK and the US now lag behind Uruguay (and are only just ahead of Costa Rica) on its measure.[16]

Global issues can be governed by international law, of course. But what gives international law legitimacy? Just as at the national level, international judges are unelected; their decisions can frustrate the will of the majority of one country's citizens. A current example is the demand by the European Court of Human Rights that Britain give prisoners the vote – a view rejected by 63% of Britons questioned in an opinion poll.[17] However, history suggests that the will of the majority may need to be constrained if minority rights are to be protected. Who, however, is to decide how that boundary is to be drawn? The result of judicial independence can be a feeling in the general population that yet another elite is able to override the views of ordinary citizens.

The sense that the really big decisions – economic, legal, environmental – are made outside national borders and outside democratic processes may only add to the contempt that voters feel for their domestic leaders. In their electoral rhetoric, leaders may promise change; but in office, they cannot deliver it even if they try. A January 2012 poll[18] of Britons found that a small plurality (47% to 39%, with 14% don't knows) believed that the British government had largely lost its power to make decisions about the country's future.

The economic slowdown that began in 2007 has also weakened the appeal of elected leaders. As an obvious example, in 2011 Italy and Greece turned to technocrats, in the form of Mario Monti and Lucas Papademos respectively, to run their countries. In both cases, their appointments were relatively brief. They were brought in to do the dirty work when elected politicians failed in their task. Silvio Berlusconi, who came to office in Italy promising reform, did not deliver it, and the country was one of the slowest-growing economies in the world in the first decade of the twenty-first century.

The appeal of technocrats is that they have received some training in another field – law or economics – as opposed to a politician, who may have spent all of his (or her) career in a party machine. But it is worth remembering that technocrats are capable of huge errors – such as their supervision of the financial system – and that there is no universally agreed theory of economics for them to rely on.

At least a technocracy is a more palatable alternative than the concentration of power in the hands of a business tycoon, such as Berlusconi, who used his newspapers and TV to shore up his support and to undermine his challengers. He was eventually forced out of office by the financial crisis, and the views of Germany and France, rather than by the Italian voters; indeed, his attempted comeback in the February 2013 election showed that almost a third of Italians still supported him.

One only has to look to Russia to see a more malign version of the 'big man' phenomenon: the long rule of Vladimir Putin. The outward trappings of democracy have been maintained; for a while President Putin even stood aside for Dmitry Medvedev and accepted the (notional) secondary rule of prime minister to meet the constitutional niceties. But it was no surprise when he was re-elected president in 2012. Many opponents were simply intimidated out of challenging him; those who did risk a campaign laboured under a huge disadvantage in terms of finances and media coverage.

Perhaps strong men will emerge in other countries, promising to sweep away the old elites. The appeal of the outsider is a familiar historical theme, dating back to Cincinnatus, who was recalled from his farm in 458 BC to defend Rome from invasion but who then resigned his office (returning the symbolic fasces, or bundle of sticks) after he had succeeded in his task. In recent memory, Dwight Eisenhower, a five-star general and Supreme Allied Commander towards the end of the Second World War, was elected President of the United States in 1952, while Charles de Gaulle was recalled to the French leadership in 1958 in the middle of the Algerian crisis. In the aftermath of a war, military men are seen to be the ones with the 'right stuff'; now it is economists and central bankers who seem to be the men of the hour.

Many politicians define themselves as being against the established elite, even when they appear to come from within it. The essence of Margaret Thatcher's appeal was her status as the common-sense middle-class housewife, battling the inefficient social democratic consensus that had landed Britain in its mid-1970s economic mess. In America, Sarah Palin burst onto the scene in 2008 when she was nominated as the Republican vice-presidential candidate, and earned a brief blaze of popularity as a plain-speaking outsider who could connect with ordinary voters. Herman Cain, a former pizza magnate, had a similarly short-lived burst of fame in the 2012 US primaries. The appeal of Palin and Cain came in part because they did not use the same tired political language as the existing leadership, although in both cases it was quickly demonstrated that their simple language was in large part due to their failure to have studied the policy options in any significant detail.

The success of Beppe Grillo, a comedian, in getting 25% of the vote in the Italian elections of February 2013 showed the willingness of voters to support a party outside of the mainstream. One day, an outsider may sweep into power and argue that we need not bother with the arcane and boring processes of Parliamentary democracy any more. Who needs politicians when they have so obviously failed? That was the nature of the appeal of Mussolini in Italy or Franco in Spain; men of action who swept away the squabbling and corrupt political elites. A similar rationale was used to justify military takeovers in Latin America in the 1970s and is still used in Africa today.

Perhaps all this seems outlandish. After all, in 2012, we have seen power pass peacefully in France from Nicolas Sarkozy to François Hollande, and the world's most powerful country, America, has seen more than 120 million citizens vote in the presidential election. How can such a system possibly disintegrate?

But think of a democracy not as the inevitable result of historical processes, but merely as one system of government, which may be as perishable as any other. Athenian democracy was replaced, at times, by tyrants; the Roman Republic was replaced by emperors and the Empire itself eventually crumbled.

As they have developed, democracies have been plagued by a number of questions. Who should vote? Who should rule, and how much latitude should those rulers have? How should the votes be counted? On what scale should a democracy be organized; local, regional, national or even global? What rights should a minority have? Are there other factors (equality or justice, say) that should take priority over democracy? The answers to these questions have been different at different times and our understanding of the term 'democracy' has changed as a result.

Democracy's modern success may be the source of its weakness. When populations rebelled in the nineteenth century, as in the European revolutions of 1848, they fought against the established powers, which were absolute monarchies; democracy was the weapon of change. Now it is democracy that is the old order. For those who feel that the economic system is failing, the switch from Sarkozy to Hollande (or Gordon Brown to David Cameron) may seem insufficiently radical. For those who were opposed to the Iraq war, the failure of politicians to respond to the peaceful protests against it was equally alienating.

In short, there may be significant parts of the population who feel the current regime lacks legitimacy; on the left, because politicians have failed to stop rising inequality or military adventures; on the right, because politicians have failed to stop immigration or the transfer of power to international bodies. And then there are religious or ethnic minorities who feel alienated because of the West's 'war on terror'. Of course, there will always be dissatisfied groups within society but these will be outweighed by the broad mass of people who are content with the status quo. Lose that support and the system will really be under threat. And that is why the current widespread contempt for politicians is so disturbing. Democracies thus face 'top-down' threats, as power shifts from the nation state to multinational bodies and international creditors, and 'bottom-up' threats, as voters, disillusioned by their apparent powerlessness and disappointed in their leadership, are tempted by the extremes.

This book will attempt to deal with all these themes, starting with how the idea of democracy was criticized by thinkers for much of history. I will then ponder the evidence of its growing unpopularity, declining voter turnout and public attitudes to politicians; look at the history of how modern democracy came into being; and examine the economic problems faced by modern democracies. Then it will be time to look at the rise of extremist parties; at the way the modern media and the Internet are polarizing the political debate; and at how democracies are willing to erode liberties in the face of terrorism. Chapter 9 will be devoted to the continent where democracy looks most threatened – Europe – before I turn in Chapter 10 to the main issues in America, inequality and the control of the rich over democratic funding. The penultimate chapter will look at the power of unelected bodies and attempt to frame the theoretical and practical issues facing democracy today. And, finally, Chapter 12 will look at ways we might be able to refresh democracy; the solutions may require a change in the attitude of individual citizens. We must re-engage with our political system. The fault lies not with our politicians alone, but in what we have asked them to do in our name.

I

A Turbulent History

This city is free and ruled by no one man
The people reign, in annual succession
They do not yield the power to the rich
The poor man has an equal share in it.
                              Euripides, *The Suppliants*

While we tend to think of our democratic traditions as starting in
Athens more than two thousand years ago, the Athenian democracy
was quite different from our own system. Only male citizens had the
vote; not women and definitely not slaves. The democracy took place
in an assembly, which every citizen had a right to attend. The agenda
for each meeting was drawn up by a council of 500, with members
chosen by lot; an executive of 50 was formed from that 500 and a
chairman (again selected by lot) from within that 50.

Taking part was seen as a citizen's duty. According to the historian
Thucydides, the orator Pericles said that 'we alone regard the man who
takes no part in public affairs, not as one who minds his own business,
but as good for nothing'. This was government, town-hall style, with
citizens (many of whom knew each other) debating the issues of the
day. We don't have many records of how the system worked, but pre-
sumably the Athenians suffered from the same irritations as those of
us who attend modern-day meetings: pompous windbags, nit-picking
timewasters, and a tendency for the first few items on the agenda to be
debated at length, whereas the last few are dashed through because
everyone wants to go home.

Modern democracy doesn't look much like the Athenian version, at
least at the national level. Public participation is not merely confined to

voting; citizens write to their elected representatives, participate in opinion polls, join political parties, post comments on websites, sign petitions and take part in protests and marches. Occasionally, they may be asked to vote on a specific issue in a referendum.

But it is hard to disagree with the academic John Dunn when he writes:

> If ancient democracy was the citizens choosing freely and immediately for themselves, modern democracy, it seems, is principally the citizens, very intermittently, choosing under highly constrained circumstances, the relatively small number of their fellows who will from then on choose for them.[1]

It is safe to say that an ancient Athenian would struggle to recognize our current system as akin to his ancient democracy. Indeed, for much of the time between the fall of Athens in 338 BC and the late eighteenth century, the term 'democracy' was treated as a dirty word. Its origins are from the Greek words *demos* (meaning 'people') and *kratein* (meaning 'power'). But philosophers often treated 'demos' as meaning 'mob' rather than 'people' and believed that democracy played its role in the eventual downfall of Athens. As the historian Jennifer Tolbert Roberts has pointed out in an analysis of the ancient literature on democracy,[2] commentators at the time tended to be critical rather than enthusiastic; neither Plato nor Aristotle wholly believed in the concept. These criticisms fell into various categories.

THE IRRATIONAL CROWD

One concern was that, in a public meeting, the crowd would be convinced by the best orator, rather than by the best arguments; indeed, the term 'demagogue' was devised for someone who could manipulate the masses in this way. Thucydides wrote that the Athenian *demos* was 'irrational, unreasonable and easily swayed by emotion'. Plato said that, in a democracy, 'Popular acclaim will attend on the man who tells the people what they want to hear rather than what truly benefits them.' Both Plato and Aristotle thought that this tendency would cause democracy to slide into tyranny; had either philosopher been around during the rise of Mussolini, they might have cited him as evidence for their case.

Some believed that democracy caused the Athenians to indulge in foreign policy adventures, as they were swayed by the chance for conquest. (In modern times, of course, many have argued that democracies are *less* likely to go to war, at least with each other.) The fact that the Athenian Republic was eventually conquered (by Philip of Macedon, the father of Alexander the Great) and was eclipsed by the Roman Republic has led to a lot of *post hoc ergo propter hoc* analysis – Athens was a democracy, therefore it must have been the system of democracy that caused its decline. Some argued, by contrast, that democracy made Athens too pacifist, in contrast with the more authoritarian (and highly militaristic) Sparta. But Athens operated as a democracy for almost two hundred years, winning many naval and military battles in its time; it lasted a lot longer than communist rule in Eastern Europe, for example.

The Roman statesman Cicero decreed that 'Greece in ancient times, once so flourishing in its wealth, dominion and glory, fell through this single evil, the excessive liberty and licence of its meetings.' Some believed that democracy caused Athenian leaders to dither, unlike the decisive Spartans; others that money which should have been spent on defence was diverted to fripperies like the arts.

Modern critics hold that democracies can also be manipulated through the means of advertising or biased reporting on TV and in newspapers. If public opinion can be swayed by a marketing campaign, then politicians are not really responding to the wishes of 'the people', but to the beliefs of those with the deepest purses. Regrettably, the use of 'attack adverts' in American election campaigns is widespread and virtually compulsory: candidates know that their opponent will take every opportunity to slander their own record, so they get their attack in first. The victor may not be the candidate with the best policies but rather with the best ad men.

RULE OF THE STUPID

Being philosophers, Plato and Aristotle showed disdain for what modern-day snobs would call 'the great unwashed'. It made no sense to them that the ignorant and the illiterate should have the same voice in affairs as the educated. Aristotle was more balanced in his views than Plato; he felt it was reasonable for ordinary people to be involved in decisions, but only in a limited way. Their views needed to be balanced by wiser, more distinguished heads and by laws that could not be overridden by popular vote. Aristotle wrote:

> It is necessary that the freemen who comprise the bulk of the people should have absolute power in some things; but as they are neither men of property, nor act uniformly upon principles of virtue, it is not safe to trust them with the first office of state, both on account of their iniquity and their ignorance.[3]

Aristotle tended to use the metaphor of the family, with the wise father having to control the children (the people). Plato used a different analogy – that everyone has a specialized role in society. Cobblers make shoes, builders construct houses and, by extension, there are some people who are simply more suited to rule.

In *The Republic*, Plato expressed some praise for democracy, having one of his characters describe it as 'the most attractive of all societies' because of the associated liberty and freedom of speech. He also appreciated the fact that a democracy 'doesn't mind what the habits and background of its politicians are, provided they profess themselves the people's friends, they are duly honoured'. Plato compared a state to a ship, saying that 'If one chose ships' captains on grounds of wealth and never gave a poor man a command, even if he was a better sailor, you would have some pretty bad navigation.'

However, Plato worried that individuals in a democracy would 'live from day to day, indulging the pleasure of the moment'. In the long run, he feared that 'an excessive desire for liberty at the expense of everything else is what undermines democracy and leads to the demand for tyranny. A democratic society in its thirst for liberty may fall under the influence of bad leaders.' Plato concluded, therefore, that not everyone who wanted to rule should be allowed to do so: 'The state whose prospective rulers come to their duties with least enthusiasm is bound to have the best and most tranquil government, and the state whose rulers are eager to rule the worst.'

Plato's ideal state would be ruled by special people known as the guardians, trained since childhood for the role and uninterested in wealth or dynastic advancement. These guardians would take the broader view of society's good; in essence, they would be philosophers like Plato himself. Even with the guardians, he worried that an individual might be 'swamped by the flood of popular praise and blame and carried away with the stream till he finds himself agreeing with popular ideas of what is admirable or disgraceful, behaving like the crowd or becoming one of them'.[4]

Nothing like Plato's scheme has ever been tried in practice, although plenty of later rulers have claimed guardian status as 'father of the nation', taking the tough decisions on behalf of us little people. And many later philosophers took it for granted that ordinary people were too stupid to rule.

The nineteenth-century English philosopher John Stuart Mill is generally considered to be the very epitome of the Victorian liberal, and was a proponent of free speech and author of the classic *On Liberty*, which propounded the theory that individuals should be free to do what they like unless they harm others. But even he had worries about the effect of one person, one vote (not one man, one vote; Mill was an early advocate of female suffrage). In his *Considerations on Representative Government* he wrote that, 'No arrangement of the suffrage, therefore, can be permanently satisfactory in which any person or class is peremptorily excluded – in which the electoral privilege is not open to all persons of full age who wish to obtain it.' But his very next sentence begins 'There are, however, certain exclusions . . .' For a start, Mill thought that nobody should be able to vote without 'being able to read, write and I will add, perform the common operations of arithmetic'.[5] His answer, being a liberal, was universal education so that people could acquire these skills and thus could vote. But he was clear that education should come first.

Present-day voters might share the great man's opinion. A YouGov poll found that a small plurality (45% versus 39%) thought those who failed a basic test of literacy and knowledge of British democracy should be barred from voting.[6]

TYRANNY OF THE POOR

Ancient Athens was marked by a division between a landowning elite and a much broader mass of the poor (not to mention the slaves). The philosophers took it for granted that democracy would lead the poor to take advantage of the rich. Aristotle wrote that democracy 'was a regime of naked group interest, unapologetically devoted to serving the many at the expense of the wealthier, the better, the more elevated, the more fastidious or virtuous'. Plato in *The Republic* worried that democratic leaders would 'rob the rich, keep as much of the proceeds as they can for themselves and distribute the rest to the people'. If the rich responded to being plundered, they will be 'accused by their rivals of plotting against the people and being reactionaries and oligarchs'.

This fear was still around in the eighteenth century when the founding fathers of the American Republic (many of them wealthy individuals) considered the structure of their government. John Adams worried about 'the eight or nine millions who have no property ... usurping the rights of the one or two millions who have'. He fretted that 'debts would be abolished first; taxes laid heavy on the rich and not at all on the others and at last a downright equal division of every thing be demanded and voted'. James Madison wrote in 1787 that:

> A pure democracy, by which I mean a society of a small number of citizens, who assemble and administer the government in person, can admit of no cure from the mischiefs of faction ... Hence it is, that such democracies have ever been spectacles of turbulence and contention; have ever been found incompatible with personal security, or the rights of property; and have, in general, been as short in their lives as they have been violent in their deaths.[7]

Madison also feared that full Athenian-type democracy would lead to a 'rage for paper money, for an abolition of debts, for an equal division of property, or for any other improper or wicked project'.[8] He distinguished democracy from a republican system in which the voters delegated decisions to elected representatives who would 'refine and enlarge the public views' and who could govern an area larger than a city state.

By the end of his life, Madison had been proved wrong. The individual states had abolished property qualifications for voting by the mid-1820s; although the hoi polloi could vote, private property continued to be respected. Alexis de Tocqueville, the great chronicler of American democracy, suspected that the US had big advantage in this respect; it had a huge amount of land to give away as it expanded westwards, some of it confiscated from the native population. There was enough property to go around without confiscating the property of the rich.

Back in Britain, John Stuart Mill thought that people should not vote unless they paid income (not sales) taxes. 'The assembly that votes the taxes, either general or local, should be elected exclusively by those who pay something towards the taxes imposed,' he wrote. 'Those who pay no taxes, disposing by their votes of other people's money, have every motive to be lavish and none to economise.'[9]

He further added that those who received parish relief, the Victorian equivalent of unemployment benefit, should also be excluded: 'He who cannot by his own labour suffice for his own support, has no claim to the privilege of helping himself to the money of others.'

This theme has been echoed by modern conservatives who believe that the welfare state has created a client base for bigger government. In 2012 Mitt Romney, the Republican candidate for US president, was secretly recorded at a fund-raising dinner saying, 'There are 47 percent of the people who will vote for the president no matter what. These people are with Obama because they're dependent upon government, see themselves as victims, think government has a responsibility to care for them, and think they are entitled to health care, to food, to housing, you name it.'

At the heart of these issues is the question of the origins of individual wealth; is wealth entirely the result of an individual's effort or is it derived, to some extent, from collective investment? The ancients, rather like modern conservatives, tend to view private wealth as a sign of individual virtue, skill or effort. Social democrats argue that most people are educated by the state and take advantage of public goods, notably infrastructure. President Barack Obama also got into murky waters by talking of the roads and bridges that enabled individual businessmen to get their goods to market. 'You didn't build that,' he said, the grammatical slip (replacing 'those' with 'that') allowing his opponents to accuse him of denigrating all entrepreneurs: 'We built it' was a slogan at the 2012 Republican Convention.

If one regards wealth as purely the result of individual effort, then taxes represent confiscation by the state, as well as a disincentive to individual effort. But if one views the provision of public goods as a necessity, then all incomes are potential sources of revenue; it is thus a political decision as to which items are excluded (or preferentially treated) in tax policy.

The original drive towards a wider suffrage was that the people who paid the taxes should have a say in how they were spent; the Parliamentarians in the English Civil War battled on this issue, and of course the American colonists argued for 'No taxation without representation'. But it is easy to forget that the corollary – no representation without taxation – was also believed by many. As recently as the late 1980s, Margaret Thatcher pushed through a reform of British local taxation – the poll tax, as it became known – in the belief that local councils took money from middle-class ratepayers and doled it out to the rest who made no contribution. She too was echoing Mill, since he had argued that the answer to his tax/representation problem was to levy a *per capita* charge on everyone. The average citizen would thereby become more watchful about how his money was spent.

In the late nineteenth century, of course, these arguments were turned on their head. A crucial impetus behind democracy was the belief among the mass of citizens that the vote would lead to an improvement in their living standards. And, as we shall note in Chapter 10, the period after the Second World War, when the Western nations re-emerged into democracy, was marked by a rise in living standards for the poor and a narrowing of wealth and income gaps with the rich. But we shall also see that some modern democracies today look more like tyrannies of the rich than tyrannies of the poor, with income and wealth inequality increasing, and the beneficiaries using their wealth to buy access to politicians.

TYRANNY OF THE MAJORITY

A variant of the economic argument is that a democratic system allows the majority to lord it over the minority – any minority. One reason why Plato may have been so hostile towards democracy is that it put his teacher and idol, Socrates, to death. That was an example of a democracy suppressing a free thinker – the brilliant outsider who spoke uncomfortable truths. Communist countries, which claimed to be democracies, pursued a similar course.

Modern philosophers have struggled with this idea as well. A democratic society might be more tyrannical than a medieval monarch because the individual would come under pressure from his neighbours to conform to society's standards. In ancient times, if a man paid his taxes and did not rebel or conspire against the government, he would probably be left alone by the ruling powers. In modern times, individuals are subject to a whole range of laws that are designed to constrain their behaviour – from the requirement to wear a seat belt when driving to the ban on smoking in public places. We are free to play a part in choosing our government, we are not free to disobey the law, and we are less free to pursue an eccentric lifestyle than we would have been under, say, Louis XIV of France or George III of Britain.

The majority is not necessarily right just because it is a majority. Most people believed that the sun went round the earth even after Nikolaus Copernicus established the opposite in the sixteenth century; a 2007 poll found that 66% of Americans believed that God created man at some point in the last 10,000 years, even though scientists have believed no such thing for ages (Darwin's *The Origin of Species* was written in 1859).[10] Some nineteenth-century philosophers believed that a democracy would be, by its nature, intellectually stultifying, particularly compared with the freedom of thought afforded the Victorian gentleman.

But there is a much broader democratic problem than that of the persecuted intellectual. Any state might include a minority – ethnic, religious or cultural. The rights of those minorities are dependent on the goodwill of the majority, unless they are protected in law. Even then, the dilemma is not solved. Either the majority has the right to abolish or dilute such laws (in which case the minority's rights are theoretically under threat and democracy is undermined) or they do not have the right (in which case the system is not fully democratic).

Attempts can be made to balance the rights of majority and minority. The classic example is the US Constitution. The House of Representatives is the popular assembly, with seats allocated (roughly) in proportion to the population of the individual states. But the upper house (Senate) has two senators per state – giving Alaska the same weight as California. And the president is elected, not by a numerical majority, but through an electoral college with each state having its own weight; the system allowed George W. Bush to beat Al Gore in 2000, even though the latter received more individuals' votes overall.

This system emerged as part of the deal whereby the 13 original states agreed to pool their sovereignty; at the time, the smaller states worried that their power would be swamped by the larger ones. But it was also a way of restraining the democratic impulse. 'The senate,' wrote James Madison, 'derives its appointment indirectly from the people.'[11] Until the early twentieth century, senators were appointed by state legislatures rather than being directly elected. The idea was to free senators from the pressure of the madding crowd; George Washington supposedly said that 'we pour legislation into the Senatorial saucer to cool it'.[12]

Madison was keen on a balance of power within government, arguing that 'the society itself will be broken into so many parts, interests and classes of citizens, that the rights of individuals, or the minority will be in little danger from interested combinations of the majority'.[13] However, by creating these checks and balances, he did not seem to consider that a minority might be able to use its veto power in oppressive fashion. One of the most notable uses of the Senate's rights (the filibuster and other procedural delays) was to frustrate the efforts to give civil rights to the African American population in the first half of the twentieth century. In that case, a minority of senators (those from the southern states) used their power to oppress a minority of the population. Until Lyndon Johnson, no national politician had the courage to force a change through the system.

Europeans often find there is a contrast between the fairly liberal Americans they meet (who often hail from coastal states like New York and California) and the right-wing tone of American national politics. They forget that the middle of the country (the heartland, as it is known) has a much more conservative bent. Does the electoral system give those states an edge, and thus tilt America to the right? In 2010 the smallest 25 states had 50.75 million residents, or around a sixth of the total population. But they controlled half the Senate. As of October 2012, the Democrats had 28 senators from the smallest states (including two independents who caucus with them), the Republicans just 22. In the 25 states with the largest populations, the two parties had an equal number of senators. So in this case, it was the Democrats who owed their majority to the small-state bias.[14]

It may be that a democracy works best where the population is homogeneous, as voters in ancient Athens evidently were. Problems certainly arise when there is a minority within a state who would like to live in their own, or another, state; or when the majority population of a state treat a minority as second-class citizens (as African Americans were treated by many of the state's legal structures until the 1960s). Since that episode, America has been strikingly successful in incorporating its various minorities within the government, including its first African American president. Europe has been less successful on this score; it might be a long wait before we see the first Muslim European prime minister.

Robert Dahl is perhaps the pre-eminent modern writer about democracy. He argues that all governments impose rules that impinge on the rights of individuals, but democracy is less likely to do harm than the alternatives. Indeed, modern states tend to consist of multiple competing interests, what he calls a polyarchy. These interests are able to form coalitions that prevent any one interest from becoming dominant. For example, attempts to persecute one religious minority may raise alarm among other faiths; big business can often rely on small businesses in their campaigns against high taxes or regulations; and so on.

Mr Dahl has been broadly right so far, but a polyarchy still requires a broad acceptance of the legitimacy of the state. Regional minorities may demand independence and will not be satisfied by the compromise of devolution. Nor is it really clear how far the process of secession can go; what if the Orkney and Shetland islands rejected Scottish independence, for example? The islands are certainly geographically distinct from the mainland and surely have the same right to self-determination as, say, the Seychelles.

The existence of Northern Ireland, which many non-Britons regard as an anomaly, derives from this problem. In 1921, at the end of the Irish War of Independence, the Protestants in the north rejected going along with the rest of Ireland to become independent from Britain because it would have made them a minority within a Catholic state; in the process, of course, they created a Catholic minority within their own province. In such circumstances, the definition of democracy becomes hazy. Who then has the right to vote? If all of Ireland had been able to vote on the status of the north in 1921, it would have been included with the south. If all of Britain had voted, the south of Ireland might not have been given independence (although this vote would have been impossible to enforce). If just the Catholics of Northern Ireland had voted, their counties and towns might have joined the south, creating an odd patchwork construction.

People do not live in neatly defined geographic areas. One answer – to have a state divided into two non-contiguous parts – has been tried, but the results have often not been happy; Pakistan and East Pakistan (now Bangladesh) from 1947 to 1971 and the post-1918 creation of Germany and East Prussia both created great difficulties. The modern example of the Palestinians – split between the West Bank and Gaza – is another example. States work best when their borders are well defined.

It is ever more difficult these days to define what nationhood means. Most nations in the developed world can no longer be categorized as the home solely of a particular religious or ethnic group. A multicultural society presents problems which the ancient Athenians did not have to consider. If nothing unites the people – save allegiance to the national football team – how will society cope when it faces a moment of stress?

THE ILLUSION OF RULE

As already noted, our current system of democracy does not operate like Athens. In a world where most states have many millions of citizens, we could hardly follow any other approach. We delegate decision-making to elected representatives. John Stuart Mill probably encapsulated the rationale when he wrote that 'since all can not, in a community exceeding a single small town, participate personally in any but some very minor portions of the public business, it follows that the ideal type of a perfect government must be representative'.[15]

Not everyone would accept this as ideal. What we have today could be described as more like 'government by politician' rather than (in Abraham Lincoln's words) 'government by the people'. In his book *Capitalism, Socialism and Democracy*, Joseph Schumpeter argued that 'democracy does not mean that the people actually rule in any obvious sense of the terms "people" and "rule". Democracy means only that the people have the opportunity of accepting or refusing the men who are to rule them.'[16] In Schumpeter's view, elite groups compete to secure the vote of the populace by offering promises to voters. This can create complex economic problems, as we shall see in Chapter 5.

There is a further flaw – sometimes even elected representatives do not control many aspects of our lives. If the Athenian model of democracy involved citizens voting directly on issues that concerned them, and the Madisonian model involved us delegating those decisions to representatives, we seem to have reached a third level, in which our elected representatives often delegate their decisions to outside experts. Technocratic democracy, or double delegation, makes it even more difficult for voters to be sure that their occasional vote will translate into actual changes in policy. It is not just a matter of 'throwing the bums out'; we have to rely on the bums to throw the other bums out.

Those of us who live in the European Union must obey laws passed by the European Parliament, where each country's representatives are vastly outnumbered. If we are dissatisfied with the job being done by the European Council of Ministers, or the European Parliament or the European Commission, we can do nothing but change our own representatives on that body. But they may also be supporting the policies we desire, only to be outvoted by the representatives of other countries. We may pass laws in our domestic Parliament only to have them ruled invalid by the European Court of Human Rights. We may seem to block imports on moral or health-related grounds, such as hormone-treated beef from American cows, and find that our objections are ruled invalid by the World Trade Organization.

THE WRONG TYPE OF VOTING

Within the confines of representative democracy, any system of translating votes into seats has its flaws. In a first-past-the-post system, small parties may be under-represented or on occasions a party might win without having a majority of the popular vote (indeed this has been the case in most British elections). In a system of proportional representation, who governs is decided by bargains between parties, not by voters; small parties, because they hold the swing seats, can have too much power.

The Greeks would not have considered a single vote, cast once every four or five years, as democratic participation. It hardly suggests that political decisions have the wholehearted support of the population, nor does it encourage the average person to involve himself or herself in the issues. Nineteenth-century enthusiasts thought of democracy as a form of moral improvement for the population and therefore allowed ordinary people to take part in political events, but merely marking a piece of paper is token participation at best.

In a liberal democracy, of course, we still have freedom of speech and citizens are at liberty to express their opinion in a wide range of ways. Politicians for their part may or may not be influenced by them. Should rallies, petitions, letter-writing campaigns and the like be treated as a fair reflection of popular opinion? Some would argue that for every one person who has the energy to go to a rally, another ten people passively support the cause. But it is dangerous to make this presumption. A well-organized letter-writing campaign may make an issue more prominent than its place in the *average* voter's mind.

Take, for example, the British pro-hunting demonstrations in 2004. These were well attended and illustrated that a significant portion of the population was against a ban. Anti-hunting demonstrations were less well attended but equally passionate. Should the relative size of the crowd count? Or should broader public opinion (in favour of a ban by around two to one) be the primary guide? The issue was not clear-cut, especially as many voters seemed to disapprove of the amount of Parliamentary time absorbed by the issue. Does the strong opinion of one person whose life is deeply affected by the issue count for more than the weak opinions of three others who have only a shallow interest in the subject? In practice, that does seem to be the case, although, as we shall see when we look at economic issues in Chapter 5, the results may be unfortunate.

Direct democracy could deal with some of these problems. We could vote in referenda, or one day via the Internet. But this approach too has its flaws, as California, which has a very high level of referenda-driven, direct democracy in its legislative mix, has shown. It is hard to reduce complex issues down to a simple question; only those with an interest in the outcome may be motivated to vote, or to campaign in favour of their desired result; different votes may result in incompatible outcomes, for example against higher taxes, in favour of higher spending and a balanced budget. (In the case of California, this has made the prospect of a balanced budget near impossible, of course, and a number of governors have taken the fall for the electorate's decisions in this regard.)

A further problem with referenda, noted by the pollster Peter Kellner,[17] lies round the issue of framing. In a survey, one group was asked whether they thought the BBC licence fee was value for money at £145 a year; they said No by a margin of two to one. A second group was asked whether the licence fee was good value at 40p a day; they said Yes by the same margin. The two amounts are identical. In the Californian system, referendum or proposition questions can often be posed in convoluted form, making it difficult for the unwary voter to know precisely what he or she is being asked to approve.

And the difficulties don't stop there. Another issue polled by YouGov concerned the idea of a £1 million salary cap; most people approved of the idea. But the choice of £1 million was entirely arbitrary. It is not clear whether people had thought £1 million was the ideal sum or whether they just approved of the general idea of a cap; they might have said Yes to £2 million or £500,000. (This is another framing issue. If British male voters were asked 'Would you like to see the Premiership lose all its foreign football stars?', most would surely say No. But that is what a £1 million salary cap would entail.)

POLITICS IS LESS IMPORTANT THAN ECONOMICS, OR RELIGION OR FREEDOM

This criticism of democracy comes in various forms. The first is the idea that there are more important issues concerning the governance of a nation state than the ability to vote. The best-known example in the nineteenth and twentieth centuries was communism. Communists annexed the word 'democracy' for the title of some of their states but argued that the true meaning of the word was rule by the working class, and that all other systems were 'bourgeois' and a fig leaf to disguise exploitation of the masses. The freedom to vote is less important than the right to earn a decent standard of living.

The initial phase of communism, as it emerged in Russia after 1917, was quite democratic. Factories and military units were run by committees of workers and soldiers, or soviets; hence the state's name, the Union of Soviet Socialist Republics. But this system proved rather too messy for the liking of Lenin and the other Russian leaders. There was no guarantee that the workers and soldiers would see things in the same way as the Bolshevik Party, which represented a very small proportion of the Russian population. The bold democratic experiment was effectively suspended, initially on the plausible grounds that the Russians were facing a civil war, with Western powers supporting the rebellion by 'white' forces.

But even when the whites were defeated, the freedom of the soviets was not restored; sailors from the naval fortress at Kronstadt argued in 1921 for new elections to the soviets which they felt did not 'express the wishes of the workers and peasants'. They also argued for freedom of speech and of assembly. In a true workers' paradise, these rights should have been easy to grant; instead the sailors were attacked by some 60,000 soldiers and the rebellion was crushed.

With the tortuous logic that was to go on to mark their 70-year rule, the communist leadership argued either that the workers were not ready for democracy or that (a wonderfully Orwellian touch) since the interests of the working classes were crystal clear, there was no need for free discussion; the best policy for the working class was what the Communist Party determined it to be. By definition, any dissenters from this view were clearly counter-revolutionaries, capitalist roaders, bourgeois degenerates or Western spies (the insulting adjectives changed over time). The best thing for the country would be economic growth and such growth required central planning, not local control. As Lenin said, 'Industry is indispensable, democracy is not.'[18] In an ironic twist, he also presaged the modern theme that policy is best left in the expert hands of technocrats. 'This marks the beginning of that very happy time when politics will recede into the background, when politics will be discussed less often and at shorter length, and when engineers and agronomists will do most of the talking,' he said in 1920.

The atrocities committed in the name of communism – the forced deportations, the show trials, the labour camps, the dissidents held in mental hospitals – are too well known to need repeating here. But there is still a respectable point of view that political and economic equality need to be more closely linked.

In his standard work on democracy,[19] David Held argues that true democracy involves not just equal rights to vote but equal rights to participate. These are restricted, in his view, by current social policies. Equal participation would require, for example, more investment in childcare, so women can take part; more investment in education, so more people can be informed about the issues; and might involve the curtailment of the rights of some groups, such as corporations and religions, to control the policy agenda. Mr Held's vision does seem to assume that everyone wants to live in Sweden; the only true democracy, in his view, seems to be one with a high level of social care and government involvement in the economy.

The second criticism is that religion, or morality, is more important than democracy. In the West, this idea can be traced back to the Emperor Constantine in the fourth century, who proclaimed Christianity the religion of the Roman Empire. Many subsequent monarchs claimed religious authority as the basis for their rule (divine right); the coronation of the British sovereign is still a religious occasion (and the Queen is head of the Church of England). If the monarch derives his or her authority from God, then citizens have no business disputing their decrees. Islamic fundamentalists would also claim that the rules of human conduct are set down by Allah in the form of sharia law; such rules cannot be overridden by the votes of mere mortals.

While we may have abandoned the idea of divine right in the West, regular clashes between democracy and religious doctrine occur. These issues may not be resolvable by compromise. For those who believe that abortion is murder, for example, then the only acceptable level of abortions is zero. The views of voters (or, in the US, the Supreme Court) do not enter into the matter. In Scotland, the Catholic

Church has argued against the legalization of gay marriage, saying that it is not for the state to define the terms for what was originally a religious rite; there have been battles in Catholic countries on other issues such as divorce.

On similar grounds, some environmentalists would argue that there must be some constraints on human activity, regardless of what the voters want, in the long-term interests of the planet and the other species that share it with us. Indeed, they would argue that current voters owe a debt to future generations, who will suffer the consequences of our thoughtlessness. (Ironically, right-wing Republicans in the US, who tend to dismiss the idea of global warming, make a similar point about debt; we should not burden our children with the consequences of our profligacy.)

The final anti-democratic argument comes from the anarchists. To them, any state is oppressive because the government has the ability to control the actions of the individual; it doesn't really matter whether the rules have been voted on or not. While the popular picture of an anarchist is of a bearded revolutionary, a similar argument is expressed by the libertarians of the right. In Ayn Rand's novel *Atlas Shrugged*,[20] the elite citizens of the world, led by John Galt, revolt against the state and go off to live in their own community, leaving the rest of society to collapse.

Whether or not they agree with these specific criticisms, many people would accept the underlying point; that democracy is a means to an end, rather than an end in itself. There may be higher goals – justice, racial and sexual equality, freedom from want, freedom from fear, freedom of speech, freedom of religion – that are not met in a democracy. Indeed, many people in the developing world would regard Britain as the ultimate hypocrite for trumpeting its democratic traditions at home while denying the same rights to citizens of its empire for centuries, and would tar America with the same brush for its willingness to prop up brutal dictators, provided that they were supportive in its various wars, cold or otherwise. And, of course, these objections apply to the ancient Athenians themselves, who talked of democracy while owning slaves and were happy to conquer other cities when required.

THE CASE FOR THE DEFENCE

Having spent such a long time on the criticisms, what is the case for the democratic defence? The most obvious point to make is that similar objections can be made to other systems. Many a monarch has lost his throne in foreign military adventures, such as Tsar Nicholas II or Kaiser Wilhelm II. Dissenters are more likely to be crushed by autocratic regimes than by democracies; lobby groups (such as the Army) have even more influence in autocracies; an aristocracy is rule by the rich and so on. We cannot expect any system to be perfect; the main requirement is that it be better than all the others.

Even if one accepts the proposition that the general, let alone specific, knowledge of many voters is very limited, that is still not a good reason for denying them the vote. Many a monarch has been ignorant, while communist leaders such as Stalin and Mao Zedong pursued incredibly destructive economic policies under the influence of their misguided ideology.

Moving to a technocracy would not solve the dilemma. First, experts disagree on many of the issues that confront society, and even the consensus may change its mind – think of how nuclear power has fallen in and out of favour, for example. This is not like putting Newton's Third Law of Motion to a democratic vote. Plato's argument that there is some higher 'moral' knowledge, which only a few can attain, seems very tenuous. Indeed, anyone who claimed to be morally superior to the rest of humanity would rightly be regarded with suspicion. What was common behaviour in Athenian times would be considered highly immoral today, and vice versa. There is no suggestion in *The Republic*, for example, that Plato had any problems with the existence of slavery.

Second, voters are not generally deciding the minutiae of policy – they are choosing representatives to make those decisions on their behalf. There is no reason to suppose that the average voter is a poor judge of character, provided a free press exists that can provide critical analysis of the individual candidates.

Third, if countries were to entrust these decisions to an intelligent elite – the 'guardians' envisaged in Plato's *Republic* – it would be naive to think that decision-making would be entirely disinterested. Guardians might intrigue against each other, or would battle to keep their status. They might look askance at citizens who campaigned against the whole concept of guardianship. They might hope to pass their status on to their children – although Plato had an elaborate system for avoiding this, a kind of stud farm in which children were raised collectively. (To modern eyes, the idea has nasty echoes of a 'master race'.) The history of modern strongmen like Joseph Mobutu of Zaire or Anastasio Somoza of Nicaragua is the history of kleptocracy, of the leader using his power not in the best interests of his people but systematically to loot the state on the behalf of his family and his cronies.

The theoretical issues are all very well but it also seems clear in practical terms that democracies are superior. The democratic West delivered a higher standard of living, as well as more freedom, than the communist East. It is surely no coincidence that democratic ideas re-emerged strongly in the late eighteenth and early nineteenth centuries, to be followed by the most rapid economic growth the world had ever seen. The US is the most successful economic and political nation on earth and it has been built on (broadly) democratic principles. Conversely, a Europe dominated by monarchies and dictatorships plunged into two calamitous twentieth-century wars; since 1945, a democratic Western Europe has lived in peace and prosperity.

But the key point in favour of democracy is a fundamental one. For all its faults, it is the system most likely to look after the interests of the broad mass of people. In a liberal democracy, with a free press and independent judicial system, a government cannot act in too dictatorial a fashion without being subject to censure and ultimate dismissal. To quote John Stuart Mill once again: 'The rights and interests of every or any person are only secure from being disregarded when the person interested is himself able, and habitually disposed to stand up for them.'[21]

2

The Grand Disillusion

Representative institutions are of little value, and may be a mere instrument of tyranny or intrigue, where the generality of electors are not sufficiently interested in their own government to give their vote.

John Stuart Mill,
Considerations on Representative Government, 1861

We are in fact drifting towards a political system in which a combination of modern technology, mendacious journalism and angry voters will undermine representative democracy.

Peter Kellner,
president of the polling group YouGov, 2012

A Welsh cricket pavilion in late autumn is normally a deserted place. But the Malpas club in Newport, South Wales, should have been unusually active on 15 November 2012: it was acting as a polling station for the election of a local police commissioner. Three officials sat all day and waited patiently for voters to arrive, but not a soul turned up. The no-show at Malpas turned out to have been part of the lowest turnout ever recorded – less than 15% – in a British election.

There were clear reasons for the low turnout. The post of police commissioner was a new one and there had been little publicity about the election; moreover, candidates had not been given the funds to send leaflets to the voters. As a result, voters had few ways of choosing between them. But the Malpas case was just an extreme example of a worrying long-term trend: a decline in voter turnout across many established democracies.

That is a worry for those who believe in the health of democracy. The rationale behind representative democracy is that voters should choose the people who make the laws that govern them. Elections confer legitimacy upon governments – and, indeed, police commissioners. If participation in the electoral process is in constant decline, then the government's legitimacy must surely start to suffer. In its annual report on democracy, *The Economist* Intelligence Unit remarked: 'Without [this] broad, sustaining participation, democracy begins to wither and becomes the preserve of small select groups.'[1]

It is, in some senses, a mystery that people bother to vote at all. There is a modest amount of inconvenience; trekking to a polling station in all weathers, and fitting that trip into a busy schedule that involves work, childcare and home entertainment. Even applying for a postal vote requires a bit of organization. The chances that an individual voter will have an impact on the overall outcome are vanishingly small; even at the local level, the margin between victory and defeat is usually measured in hundreds of votes. One could imagine a husband and wife, say, travelling to the polls to vote for opposite sides, cancelling out each other's effort.

There is slightly more reason to vote in a system that uses proportional representation (PR) than in the first-past-the-post system used in the United Kingdom and the United States. Depending on the system being used, voters might find that their second-preference vote counts towards the winning candidate's total or that their vote might help their favoured party get seats at the national level. Even so, it is hard to imagine the individual vote of Joe or Josephine Bloggs being the one out of all the millions that sends a candidate to Parliament.

So why do we bother? For many people, voting feels like a civic duty, their part in maintaining a free society. There may be a lingering consciousness that the right to vote was hard fought for, a sentiment that can only be reinforced by the sight of pro-democracy demonstrations in Egypt or Iran. Another reason for voting is, perhaps, group solidarity: a sentiment akin to cheering for your local football team. Although supporters know their individual chants cannot be heard by the players, home teams do perform better because of the crowd's roar. Early political parties were organized on the grounds of class or religion; by voting, we contribute to our own group having a say in decision-making and (just as important) help ensure that our clan is not dominated by rival groups.

In the case of a young democracy, one would also expect turnout to be high. People are excited by the novelty of voting for the first time and anxious to express their opinion after being denied that option in the past. Any restriction in the franchise implies that the excluded are second-class citizens; that they have less ability to make political decisions and are less worthy of respect. Removing this stigma was one of the aims of the Suffragette movement before the First World War. And the Suffragettes were right: men did once put forward the argument that women were too emotional to vote, and that their interests could be adequately represented by their husbands (a minority of men still believe this). Similarly, the Jim Crow rules in the American south were a deliberately discriminative attempt to deter African Americans from voting.

Democracy has often come into being when citizens, and large sections of the ruling elite, have grown disenchanted with the old regime, whether it be a monarchy or a communist dictatorship. New voters may have had specific grievances that they wanted to see addressed: more job security, greater individual liberty, and so on. Meanwhile, supporters of the old regime may have been motivated to vote to prevent their rights and privileges from being undermined. Group solidarity, on both sides, would therefore often have been high. Over time, however, these motivations towards solidarity are diluted. Most governments involve a compromise between various interest groups; some desires are satisfied, others are disappointed. Voters soon realize that you can't always get what you want. And the maths also sinks in: their votes are very unlikely to make a difference.

Figure 2.1 shows the rolling five-year average[2] of turnout in Parliamentary elections across the Western democracies since the Second World War. (A five-year average shows the trend, smoothing out the effect of years when only a small number of countries had polls.) Since some countries make voting compulsory, there are two lines – one for all countries, and one for those without compulsion. For the first part of the post-war era, the trend is remarkably consistent. Around eight out of ten eligible citizens exercised their vote. Nowadays, only around seven out of ten people bother to vote, with the proportion bumped up slightly by including the likes of Australia, where voting is still compulsory.

In countries where voting is optional the decline in voter participation starts to emerge in the mid-1970s,[3] and in the late 1980s for the compulsory-voting countries. In retrospect, it may seem ironic that the decline started just as liberal democracy was triumphing over communism. But perhaps the collapse of the Soviet Union, in weakening the threat to democracy, also weakened the desire of voters to maintain their regular commitment to the electoral process. Perhaps working-class voters lost their faith in socialism as a result: the 1990s saw the rise of left-of-centre politicians, such as Bill Clinton and Tony Blair, who were perfectly happy with the free-market system. During the 1980s, right-of-centre politicians like Margaret Thatcher and Ronald Reagan had also made a conscious appeal to aspirational working-class voters, believing that spreading home ownership was one way of securing support for property rights. This may have caused

Figure 2.1 Voter turnout in developed world (five-year rolling average)

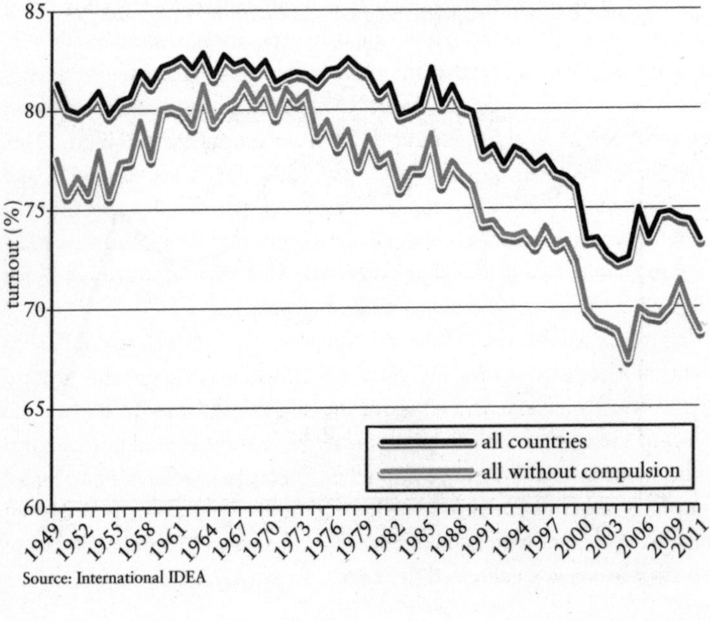

Source: International IDEA

voters to switch to the conservative cause, or at least to feel less committed to the working-class camp and thus less inclined to show solidarity by voting.

From the 1990s onwards, elections seemed less like a clash between opposing world views (at least in economics; the US now struggles instead with the cultural divide between the religious right and the secular liberals in its domestic politics) and more like a choice between rival teams of managers. Which politician seems most competent to look after the economy? It is an important issue, but not one that inspires the same degree of passion as the old class-centred contests.

One can see a similar pattern in the turnout numbers for US Presidential elections (Fig. 2.2). Almost 96% of registered voters turned out in the 1964 election, which pitted Lyndon Johnson against Barry Goldwater, but the trend has been steadily downwards. Despite the youthful enthusiasm for Barack Obama in 2008, turnout was only 70%. Many young people registered to vote but a lot of them failed to make it to the polls. Only 57.5% of those of voting age actually turned out on the day.

Figure 2.2 US Presidential election turnout, 1964–2008*

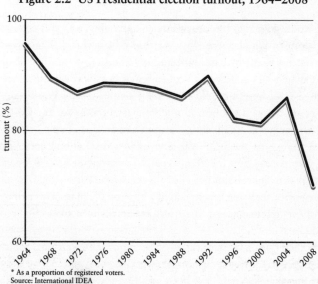

* As a proportion of registered voters.
Source: International IDEA

Figure 2.3 UK election turnout, 1945–2010

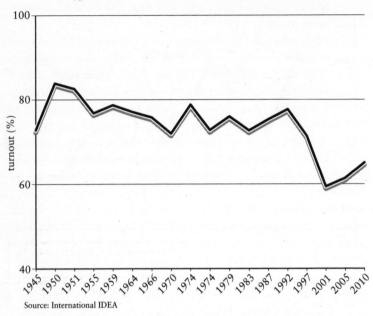

Source: International IDEA

In Britain (Fig. 2.3) voter turnout peaked in the 1950 and 1951 elections, both of which were close-run battles between a Conservative Party led by Winston Churchill and a Labour Party under Clement Attlee, which had achieved a vast range of post-war reforms, including the establishment of the National Health Service. Working-class identification with Labour and middle-class support for the Conservatives was very strong. By 2005, turnout had dropped by 20 percentage points: thanks to the Iraq War, enthusiasm for Labour under Tony Blair was weak, but the Conservatives proved even less popular. Although turnout rebounded a little in the 2010 election, the long-term trend was not really changed; David Cameron came to power to form a coalition government on the third-lowest turnout since the Second World War.

In France (Fig. 2.4), around eight in ten of the electorate could be relied upon to turn out in almost every election up to 1973; since then, however, the trend has been steadily downwards, hitting 57%

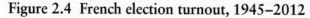

Figure 2.4 French election turnout, 1945–2012

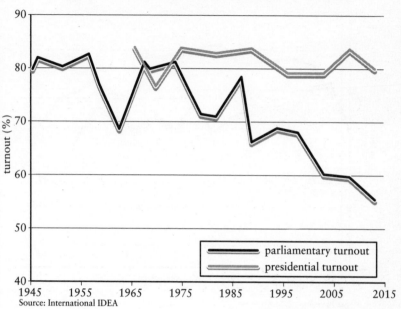

Source: International IDEA

for the Parliamentary elections of 2012.[4] The German figures (Fig. 2.5) may have been distorted by the impact of unification after 1990, but there has nevertheless been a loss of enthusiasm in the last decade: the 2009 turnout was 20 percentage points below its peak in 1972.

The legitimacy problem for governments elected on low turnouts is exacerbated in countries which use a first-past-the-post system. This is designed to give a majority to the party with the highest share of the vote, even if its overall share is less than 50%. In the 2005 British election, for example, Labour's 35% vote translated into 55% of the seats. But on a turnout of just 61.3% of the electorate, that meant only 21.5% of those of voting age backed the government.

Although this low turnout may have resulted from disillusionment after the invasion of Iraq in 2003, there was even less enthusiasm for the other parties than for Labour. Nevertheless, it was hard to feel that Labour had much of a mandate in the face of such public indifference. To make things worse, power passed from Tony Blair to

Figure 2.5 German* election turnout, 1949–2009

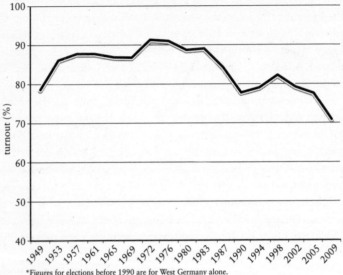

*Figures for elections before 1990 are for West Germany alone.
Source: International IDEA

Gordon Brown in 2007 without even a leadership election in the Labour Party. After a brief honeymoon, Mr Brown's tenure in office was dogged by a hostile press, which harped on the unelected nature of his rule.

DON'T CARE, WON'T VOTE

Turnout is almost always much higher in national elections than in local ones, or indeed in polls for the European Parliament; in Britain, turnout for the EU elections has never been higher than 40%. Even in pro-European Germany, turnout for the 2009 European Parliament elections was just 43%. People are generally less aware of the name of their European Parliament representative than of their national representative in their domestic Parliament; they are also less aware of what the European Parliament does.

In short, voters are more willing to turn out if they feel the contest matters. This means that closely fought polls tend to arouse bigger turnouts; the decline in the US Presidential poll numbers was briefly halted in 1992, for example, when there was a three-way contest. US mid-term Congressional elections get a lower turnout, not just because there is no Presidential poll but because incumbents are so rarely defeated. British turnout was higher in the close-fought 2010 election than in the easy Labour victories of 2001 and 2005.

Even if you start out enthusiastically exercising the vote, the novelty can soon pall, particularly should the choice of candidates not be to your liking. The 1991 Louisiana governor's elections pitted Edwin Edwards, a politician long dogged by allegations of corruption, against David Duke of the Ku Klux Klan. Louisiana voters had a sense of humour about the affair – a popular bumper sticker read 'Vote for the crook: It's important' – but it was nevertheless pitiful that no better candidates could be found for an office of such potential importance. Edwards won, but in 2002 he went to jail on racketeering charges.

Even when the candidates are from the mainstream, voters might like some but not all of their views; British voters who were fiscally conservative but socially liberal would have struggled with a choice between Margaret Thatcher and Labour's Neil Kinnock, for example. American voters might like the economic views of a Republican candidate but be repelled by his views on women's rights.

Alternative candidates may be available, but in first-past-the-post systems they have little chance of success if they are not from the main two or three parties. The American system remains dominated by the two main parties: third-party candidates may occasionally appear but their chances are limited. Ross Perot, the technology billionaire, received 19 million votes in 1992 (19% of the total) but failed to carry a single state, thereby receiving no votes in the electoral college. The main impact of Ralph Nader, who ran for office several times, may simply have been to deny the presidency to Al Gore in 2000.

British voters have been more willing to shift away from the main parties, despite the built-in bias of the system. In 1951 the Conservative and Labour parties received almost 96% of the total vote; by 1974 their combined share had fallen to 75%, and by 2010 it was just 65%. Even with the Liberal Democrats included, the share of the three main parties in 2010 was its lowest since the Second World War. That low share meant that, for the first time since the war, the parties were forced to form a coalition.

Systems of proportional representation, by contrast, give more incentives for voters to favour third parties. In the first national election in the united Germany, the two main parties, the Christian Democrats (with their Bavarian sister party, the CSU) and the Social Democrats, received 77% of the vote. But in the 2010 election their combined vote share was just under 57%.

The two-stage nature of the French electoral process has led to a very fractured vote. In the first round of the 2012 Presidential elections, the top two candidates (Nicolas Sarkozy and François Hollande) received just 56% of the vote; another six candidates (including the far left and right) got more than 1%. In the legislative elections that followed in June, 11 parties got more than 1% in the first round. The decline in influence of the mainstream parties is not always encouraging on the evidence of recent decades; as we shall discuss in Chapter 6, it has often been accompanied by gains for extremist groups.

Democracies come in many forms. The political scientist Arend Lijphart[5] distinguishes between 'majoritarian rule', where one party runs the government, and 'consensus rule', where the government is run by coalition. The latter result is, of course, much more likely to result from proportional representation, whereas first-past-the-post systems are more likely to produce majorities. The arguments for and against PR are quite well known. The system gives voters more of a chance to express their real view, instead of forcing them to choose between the lesser of two evils in the form of the two main parties. For example, voters may be conservative on fiscal issues and liberal on social ones, making it difficult to choose between Republicans and Democrats in the US or between Labour and Conservatives in Britain (although David Cameron has been attempting to move the Tories in a more socially liberal direction). Under PR, fewer votes are wasted; even if your vote does not help a local candidate to win, it may ensure that the party is represented at the national level. That may encourage voter turnout.

However, the effect of PR is to create a multiplicity of parties, and that can make it difficult to form a government. Belgium was run by a caretaker administration between April 2010 and December 2011 because the various parties could not agree. Admittedly, Belgium is something of a special case because of the linguistic split between the Flemish (Dutch-speaking) and Walloon (French-speaking) populations. But it also took six weeks to form a Dutch government in the autumn of 2012 because the two main parties debated the extent of austerity measures.

Lijphart finds that countries with coalition governments tend to spend more (5.3% of their GDP on average) on social welfare than do majority governments. Perhaps this is because each party in the governing coalition has a price for entry – a reward for the social groups that supported it. But he does not find that countries with consensus governments are ineffective in economic terms; indeed, they have slightly better records on inflation and unemployment than their majoritarian equivalents.

Where third parties multiply, a different democratic problem emerges: any government will usually be formed of a coalition of two or more parties. Such a coalition will be something for which no citizen explicitly voted. Nor can voters be certain that, if the situation changes at the next election, some of the same politicians will not return to power in a different combination. In Germany, the Free Democrats were a perpetual part of the government from 1969 to 1998, despite receiving a small share of the popular vote; they switched sides in 1982 from the Social Democrats to the Christian Democrats.

All this is profoundly unsatisfying to voters in a world where, as consumers, they have become used to the idea of choice. If it is possible for Starbucks to serve a non-fat soya latte with an extra shot, why can't the consumer choose a tailor-made electoral candidate? Of course, there is a problem of aggregation here; if 60 million Britons decided to order a collective coffee, the ultimate concoction would probably not be satisfying for any of them. But understanding that problem doesn't make the outcome any better for the individual.

It is clear that people are willing to engage with the political issues when the cause is politically compelling. The February 2003 demonstrations against the imminent Iraq War were some of the largest protests in history: 800 cities around the world staged rallies, with those in London, Barcelona and Rome attracting 1 million attendees each. Of course, this display of public enthusiasm had no practical effect whatsoever, something that may only have increased popular cynicism towards the democratic process.

TURNED OFF, SO WE WON'T TURN OUT

Cynicism certainly seems to run high in Britain these days. A YouGov report[6] of January 2012 found that only 24% of Britons thought that Parliament debated issues of public concern in a sensible and considered way; only 16% thought it reflected the full range of people and views of the British electorate; 15% thought it represented the interests and wishes of people like themselves; and just 12% thought it understood the daily lives of people like themselves. Those polled believed MPs paid more attention to the views of people who run large companies, civil servants in Whitehall and the EU and the owners of tabloid newspapers than they did to their actual voters.

The YouGov poll also asked voters what they thought of their local MP. Helpfully, this repeated a question posed in 1954 by Gallup. Whereas in 1954, 38% of the electorate believed their representative was doing a good job, only 15% of voters today believe the same thing.

Disturbingly, 62% of those polled agreed with the statement that 'politicians tell lies all the time. You can't believe a word they say.' This proportion rose to 80% or more among voters who supported the fringe parties – the UK Independence Party (UKIP), the Greens and the British National Party (BNP) – indicating that disillusionment may be a significant factor in those parties' appeal. Nor is this necessarily a matter of ignorance on the part of voters: 57% of those who watch political programmes like the BBC's flagship current affairs show *Newsnight* agree with the above statement.

The British Social Attitudes Survey conducts polls after each general election and asks people whether they 'trust British governments of any party to place the needs of the nation above the interests of their party'. In 1987, 47% trusted governments almost always or most of the time. But the proportion has fallen steadily, hitting 20% by the 2010 election.[7]

The 2012 YouGov poll also found that 58% of the electorate agreed that it didn't make much difference who won the election, since the parties were virtually identical. Again, this view is more common among supporters of the fringe parties. Only a small majority of voters polled (43% versus 38%) opposed the idea that politicians should simply be replaced by technocrats, as they have been in Greece and Italy recently. Slightly more of those polled preferred rule by referendum to Parliamentary rule. But despite all these criticisms, 63% of those polled thought that 'for all its faults, Britain's democratic system is one of the finest in the world'.

Similar opinions can be found elsewhere in Europe. A feeling that Italy's politics were beset by corruption was a big factor behind the success of Beppe Grillo's Five Star movement in the 2013 election. In France, a Socialist government swept into power in 2012 promising to punish the rich with a 75% tax rate. But in March 2013 Jerome Cahuzac, the budget minister and the man responsible for tackling tax fraud, was forced to resign after admitting that he had hidden money in an offshore account. In the wake of the scandal, President François Hollande ordered all ministers to reveal their wealth; eight, including the president himself, had assets worth more than €1 million. By that stage, Mr Hollande's popularity had fallen further and faster than any president in the history of the Fifth Republic.

GOING DIRECT

Perhaps there is an alternative. Some argue that direct democracy may be the answer to inspire voters. The modern version of democracy settled for the most part on a representative model because, for any settlement larger than a small town, gathering all the citizens in one meeting place was clearly impractical. But the Internet allows a large number of people to communicate simultaneously and referenda allow voters to express their opinion on a wide number of issues.

A referendum turnout can be high if the issue is posed on the same day as a national poll. But when Britain held only its second-ever national referendum in 2011 on the same day as elections for local councils, the turnout was only 42%. (Ironically, the issue was whether to switch to a PR system.) Nearly 40 local elections in the UK were recently held on the issue of directly electing mayors: the average turnout was just over 30%. The danger of a low turnout in a referendum is that the most motivated voters may simply be the ones most directly affected: those that might benefit from the tax break or subsidy being proposed, for example. To avoid this problem, some EU countries insist on minimum turnout levels being achieved before a proposition can become law.

The experience of California, the US state which uses referenda most frequently, does not inspire hope. Holding a referendum is an expensive business: proponents are required to collect signatures from the public within a window lasting just 150 days. That requires them to hire signature-gatherers, who hope to persuade passers-by to support the initiative. The cost can vary between 10 and 20 cents a signature to several dollars as the deadline approaches.[8] That creates an incentive to forge or invent the required names. It also clearly gives an advantage to the corporate sector and the wealthy when conducting campaigns, subverting the premise that democracy returns power to the people.

Referenda questions can also be phrased in such a complex way that people may not be sure which way to vote (e.g. 'Shall the City of Elmhurst have the authority to arrange for the supply of electricity for its residential and small commercial retail customers who have not opted out of such a program?').[9] And the initiatives that lie behind each question have become longer and longer. In the 1980s and 1990s they averaged 1,000–3,000 words; in 2006 two measures ran to more than 17,000 words apiece.[10]

The decline in voter turnout has been accompanied by another phenomenon: falling membership of political parties. In the early 1950s the combined membership of the British Conservative and Labour parties was almost 10 million people. True, around 6 million of those members were trade unionists who had chosen not to 'opt out' of paying their membership fee via their union dues. Inertia accordingly played its part. However, given the very high popular vote for Labour at this period, it would be fair to say that trade unionists did have a strong loyalty to the party. Conservative Party membership may have had a social, as much as a political, role: it was a place where young middle-class people, such as Margaret Roberts – the future

Mrs Thatcher – could meet potential spouses. The modern twenty-something has more options for socializing.

By 2012 the three main parties had a combined membership of fewer than 500,000: around half the membership of the Royal Society for the Protection of Birds.[11] Membership had fallen from 20% to 1% of the population.[12] Elsewhere, the only two Western European countries in which party membership has risen over the last 30 years are Greece and Spain, both of which emerged from dictatorship in the 1970s.[13]

As the political scientist Robert D. Putnam notes in his book *Bowling Alone*, decline in political party membership may reflect a broader decline in collective activity.[14] Membership of all sorts of American social organizations, from tenpin bowling leagues to bridge clubs, has fallen since the 1960s. Putnam also found a 42% decline, between the early 1970s and early 1990s, in the number of people who had worked for a political party. This may relate to the greater variety of home entertainment, from cable TV to computer games; more benignly, it may also result from the greater willingness of modern fathers to spend more time with their children.

At this point, your author should make a confession. As a young man in the early 1980s I joined the British Liberal Party. This was a typically Groucho-esque[15] decision, in that it was driven more by dislike for the two big parties than it was by enthusiasm for the Liberal programme. The smarter long-term move appeared to be to join the Social Democrats, a breakaway group from Labour that was rising fast in the polls. Eventually, the two minor parties merged to become the Liberal Democrats.

At the time, however, the Liberals looked like being completely eclipsed by the Social Democrats. Indeed, the party was so short of members that, when I phoned to ask about joining, I was also asked to become the candidate in the forthcoming council elections. Foolishly, perhaps, I accepted on the grounds that first, it might be an interesting experience, and second, since my youth, I had maintained the romantic notion of becoming an MP.

The experience acted as an effective inoculation against political activity in later life. Those who dream of entering politics might fondly imagine delivering an impassioned speech to an adoring crowd, like

Barack Obama after an election victory. Instead, local-election activity is all about stuffing leaflets through doors and (much worse) knocking on those doors to canvass. One needs the tough skin of a door-to-door insurance salesman to pull this off; personally, I sympathized with the homeowners because I resented anyone knocking on my own door. The last straw was a sweet old lady who, on hearing my party designation, said 'Liberals? Ah yes, Mrs Thatcher, I'll vote for you.' Naive honesty led me to attest that Mrs Thatcher was in fact a Conservative. 'Don't worry, dear, I never liked her' came the reply.

Shortly after, I gave up canvassing as a pointless job and deservedly came ninth out of 11 candidates in the poll. Indeed, the Conservatives won all three seats in my ward because of their sudden popularity in the aftermath of the Falklands War, an issue completely removed from the bin collections and cracked pavements that are the stuff of local politics.

IGNORING THE ISSUES

Information is also a barrier to political engagement. Politics can be highly complex and understanding the issues can feel at times like a full-time job. Yet misinformation often seems to spread faster than the truth. When presented with a list of California's four largest-spending categories and asked to choose the highest spender, only 22% of Californian voters chose the right answer (schools) while 41% chose prisons – in fact the smallest of the four. In a phenomenon familiar to students of behavioural finance, the more confident respondents were about their answer, the less right they were likely to be. Unsurprisingly, a 2010 poll found that fewer than half of Californians had confidence in the ability of their fellow voters to make policy decisions.[16] Opinion polls also found that fewer than a third of Americans could identify the length of Congressional and Senatorial terms (two and six years respectively) or knew the number of votes needed to overcome a Senate filibuster (60). Two years after the Bush tax-cut programme of 2001, half of Americans could not remember the changes.[17]

Neither are voters encouraged to understand the issues. Indeed, many people find politics boring because politicians and economists talk in a jargon that is hard to penetrate. When they talk about spending cuts, they focus on the need to eliminate 'waste'. We can all agree that waste needs to be eliminated but it is hard to identify what that waste actually consists of; the vast bulk of spending goes on items, such as pensions and education, which most people would regard as essential. Similarly, cutting foreign aid will barely make a dent in the deficit, even if one accepts that foreign aid is in principle a bad idea. While those on the right talk of eliminating waste, those on the left talk of eliminating tax evasion, or of increasing taxes on the rich. Again, these might be good things in and of themselves and will raise a few billion. But when the deficit is measured in the hundreds of billions (and the overall debt in the trillions), such measures will not solve the problem. If tax rates are high enough, the rich will simply change their behaviour (or their domicile) to avoid them.

Turning to taxes, the big revenues tend to come from income or other taxes levied directly on the payroll, or from sales taxes such as VAT. These are the taxes that most voters tend to pay. More than 80% of US federal revenue comes from income or payroll taxes.[18] There is no national sales tax, but some 40% of state and local revenue comes from this source.[19] In Britain, almost half of all revenues come from income tax and national insurance contributions, with another quarter coming from VAT and excise duties on fuel, alcohol and tobacco.[20] In short, it is impossible to eliminate a substantial deficit without either raising taxes on the broad mass of people or cutting services or benefits that are enjoyed by a substantial number of people. Political debate often fails to make this clear.

David Romer, an American economist, concluded that 'voters' incentives to understand difficult policy issues are minimal. As a result, they – understandably – rely on intuition, superficial impressions and emotion in their political decisions.'[21]

The economist Mancur Olson suggested that the typical citizen is rationally ignorant about public affairs.[22] Only certain professions such as lobbyists, academics and journalists will find it worthwhile to make a study of such subjects. In practice, of course, a wider proportion of the public will be interested. Politics, rather like cricket, will attract a certain type of 'knowledge addict': for some of us, election night is rather like the FA Cup Final or the World Series.

This would not be a great problem if such voters' errors were distributed randomly. But the ill-informed tend to vote differently from those voters who have acquired the political basics, and they vote differently in a predictable way. The libertarian economist Bryan Caplan says that the ill-informed tend to have a number of biases: they dislike free-market policies; they underestimate the benefits of interaction with foreigners; and they are pessimistic, usually believing that the economy is getting worse.[23] People don't want to have such prejudices challenged because that would force them to accept that they had been wrong in the past. Rather, 'people want to learn about the world without sacrificing their world view'.

A less cynical analysis is provided by Peter Kellner of YouGov, who says that voters divide into two types: positional and valence (terms from psychology used to denote a subject's emotional appeal).[24] A proportion of voters will make their decision based on positional issues – economics, immigration, abortion, and so on. These voters will tend not to switch their votes between elections, and will tend to be more interested in politics than most.

The valence voters are the swing voters who decide elections. They judge parties not so much by their policies but by whether the leaders appear likeable, competent and in touch with the voter's life. This is the 'regular guy' test, sometimes expressed as the candidate with whom you would most like to share a beer. American Presidential elections often throw up these kind of choices: the easy-going Reagan versus the preachy Carter, the folksy Clinton versus the patrician Bush senior, the relaxed Bush junior versus the uptight Gore. This test doesn't apply in all elections, let alone all countries: few Britons would pick Margaret Thatcher as a beer-drinking companion. But Tony Blair was a self-styled 'pretty straight kind of guy' in a sense that his successor, Gordon Brown, could never be. In France, Nicolas Sarkozy lost the 2012 Presidential election in part because voters didn't like his flashy, impetuous style.

But the gap between character and policy can lead to some strange voting patterns. In America, writers on the left have argued that working-class voters have been distracted from voting in their economic interest. Instead, right-wing politicians have persuaded them to cast their vote on the basis of cultural issues, such as gun rights, homosexuality and abortion.[25] Larry Bartels wrote:

Millions of citizens believed that the federal government should spend more money on a wide variety of programs, that the rich are asked to pay too little in taxes and that growing economic inequality is a bad thing – but they simultaneously supported policies whose main effects have been to reduce the tax burden of the rich, constrain funding for government programs and exacerbate growing economic inequality.[26]

If Americans have seemingly voted to the right of their underlying economic views, Britons may have voted to the left of their views on social issues. In 2005 the British Conservative Party shifted to the right with slogans such as 'It's not racist to believe in limits on immigration' and 'Are you thinking what we're thinking?' They were trying to deal with a specific problem. When voters were shown details of Conservative policies, they agreed with them. But they lost enthusiasm the moment they were told that they were Conservative proposals: the reputation of the Tory party as the 'nasty party' (a classic valence issue) was too strong.

One British fringe party, the UK Independence Party, has performed well in local elections and elections for the European Parliament, when voters don't care much about the outcome, but much less well in general elections. Its flagship proposal – withdrawal from the EU – is popular, as is its opposition to immigration. But when the Conservatives try to adopt UKIP issues as their own, they risk appearing obsessive. Obsession suggests extremism – and, for 'valence voters', extremism is a quality that turns them off.

This may be why the developed world has been lucky so far. Voters will protest against the mainstream parties but they will – if only at the last minute – resist giving power to extremists. Nevertheless, there are no grounds for complacency. The rise of extremist parties is just one element in the decline in electoral legitimacy, along with the fall in turnout and the contempt in which many politicians are held. Governments do not just have to worry about what happens at the ballot box; they need to worry about what happens on the streets.

3

The Triumph of an Idea

*We cannot count on historical forces to ensure that democracy
will always advance or even survive, as the long intervals in
which popular governments vanish from the earth remind us.*
Robert Dahl, *On Democracy*, 2000

When Athens fell to the Macedonians in the fourth century BC, the
broad idea of democracy was pretty much killed off for centuries to
come. While the Roman Republic had some democratic elements,
these vanished when Augustus ushered in imperial rule in 27 BC. After
the fall of Rome in the fifth century AD, European history over the
next few hundred years witnessesd a confusing series of invading
tribes which swept across the continent and settled in various areas,
only to be replaced in turn by other invaders.

We can pick up the story of democracy with the Vikings, who had
assemblies called 'tings' in an outdoor forum (a field surrounded by
stones), which sound rather like ancient Greek assemblies. The oldest
Parliament in the world, Iceland's Althing, founded in AD 930,
developed from this tradition. However, while Scandinavian countries
are seen by some as the model of a modern social democracy, there is
little sign that other countries ever followed the example of the Viking
parliaments.

The Italian city states of the Middle Ages represent a more influential stage of democratic development. Rather than being ruled by
hereditary monarchs, they were governed by ruling councils, made up
of the better-off citizens of the time. Scale seems to be important; as
with Athens, it was more feasible to have a democratic element in a
city state than in a large nation like France or England. The Italian

cities did not believe in 'one man, one vote' and they modelled themselves more on the Roman Republic than on the Athenian system. The idea was more that the wealthy citizens should run the government than that the average person should have the vote. As the historian Quentin Skinner has written: 'It would be highly anachronistic to suppose that, even in their heyday, the city-republics ever thought of themselves as upholders of democratic government. During the first century of their development, the very term democracy was virtually unknown.'[1] Nevertheless, the Italian cities did have elections, which were open to male householders with taxable property who met the requirement of birth or residency. The underlying principle was that, if a government taxed its citizens, then those who actually paid the taxes should have a say in how they were spent.

The tax-paying principle was also applied to the initial democratic experiments of later years. Even the United States of America started with a property qualification for the vote. A property-based democracy looks rather dubious to modern eyes, giving the poor no say at all. But it was a start. Similarly, the first English Parliament emerged in the thirteenth century with the nobles, and the better-off citizens, demanding the right to be consulted by the king. Again, the early Parliamentarians would have been horrified at the idea that the vote might be extended universally, and to both women and men. But the principle of consultation, once established, could be extended.

Finance was the fatal weakness of the monarchies. To wage wars and run their courts, monarchs needed to raise taxes; the commercial classes increasingly demanded to be consulted about how those taxes were raised or how the money would be spent. Charles I clashed with Parliament over taxes, thereby helping to ignite the English Civil War; taxes also triggered the American rebellion against colonial rule. It was lack of revenue that forced Louis XVI of France to summon the Estates General in 1789, an act that ushered in the French Revolution.

The critical development in British democracy was probably the 'Glorious Revolution' of 1688–9, in which Britain expelled the Catholic James II and brought the Dutch Protestant William of Orange to the throne. In financial terms, this was like a management buy-in: the Netherlands faced constant pressure from the Catholic Louis XIV of France, and William was eager to take command of the military and financial muscle that Britain could provide. The Dutch king (who reigned jointly with his wife, Mary II) allowed the establishment of the Bank of England, which was granted the right to print banknotes in exchange for a loan to the Crown.

Both the British and Dutch governments proved to be responsible borrowers, and much more reliable than their more autocratic counterparts in France and Spain (the last British default was in 1672, sixteen years before William took the throne). This was hardly surprising: the merchant classes had a significant stake in the governments, and thus owned its debt; they therefore made sure the money was repaid. The author James MacDonald saw this link as crucial, noting that 'It is no coincidence that public borrowing and parliamentary government both originated in Europe.'[2]

If one can accept the idea that those who have to fund the government should have a say in how their money is spent, it is not too big a step to accept that those who have to obey the laws should have a voice in how those laws are decided. And since everybody is bound by the law, the logical implication is that all should have the vote.

Perhaps the first group to argue for this principle were the Levellers, who emerged in the course of the English Civil War. They were not quite true democrats in that they believed in a householder franchise, in which only the head of the household had a vote (so excluding women and servants). But this was still radical stuff for the time.

The English Civil War – during which one king was executed – and the Glorious Revolution – in which another king was overthrown and exiled – made British thinkers and politicians examine the whole basis for government. Not only did they ask who should rule, they also pondered what government was for. The first great modern thinker to opine on these issues was Thomas Hobbes. For him, seventeenth-century life was fragile; 'nasty, brutish and short' was his famous phrase for the state of nature. The average person was at constant risk of having his property, and his life, taken away. He should, therefore, place a high value on security and should be happy to obey a sovereign power that can provide him with protection. On this basis, Hobbes favoured a strong government (preferably a monarchy) that could wield absolute power. The modern state derives part of its legitimacy from this security bargain, particularly where citizens give up liberties (such as the right to privacy) on the understanding this will keep them safe – most notably, of course, on the issue of terrorism. It might seem that Hobbes was merely justifying the absolute rule of a Henry VIII or Louis XIV. But his argument was based more on logic than on the divine right of kings and he did believe that the people were entitled to disobey a sovereign who failed to protect them.

Later in the seventeenth century, John Locke made explicit this idea of a 'social contract' between ruler and ruled, in which each party had rights and duties. In a sense, he transferred the system's emphasis from the ruler to the ruled. It was up to the government to protect the life and liberty of its citizens; those citizens had every right to rebel against a government that took away its liberties. Locke also developed the idea of representative government as the only proper basis for a national administration; significantly, he also made a distinction between the executive (the monarch) and the legislature (Parliament).

Locke's ideas clearly influenced the American revolutionaries. The Declaration of Independence states that the British king had 'a history of repeated injuries and usurpations, all having in direct object the establishment of an absolute Tyranny over these States'. In short, the king had broken the social contract. Indeed, that is pretty clear from another famous passage: 'Governments are instituted among Men, deriving their just powers from the consent of the governed, – That whenever any Form of Government becomes destructive of these ends, it is the Right of the People to alter or to abolish it, and to insti-tute new Government.'[3]

Between 1756 and 1763 the British had fought what became known as the Seven Years War, in which a key aim had been to limit the French role in North America. To the British government, it seemed only reasonable that the colonists should bear some of this cost in the form of excise duties. But to the Americans, these duties were unfair, given that they had no say in their imposition or on how they were spent. Some sort of break between Britain and the colonies was prob-ably inevitable. Many of the original colonists had left Britain because they were religious dissenters and thus had suspicions of British state power. Others saw their wealth as self-made and resisted any taxes imposed by a far-off Parliament. The great distance that separated Britain from America made it difficult for an eighteenth-century government, which had to send orders by ship and receive replies by return, to impose its will; the same distance made it difficult for Britain to maintain a standing army of sufficient size to keep the colonies under control. In other parts of the empire, such as India, the British managed to align themselves with local rulers; this allowed Britain to govern a vast land with little manpower.

Having rejected the rule of one king, the colonists went on to reject the idea of all monarchs and to declare a republic. As already noted in Chapter 1, the founding fathers distinguished a republic from a democracy. James Madison defined a republic 'to be a government which derives all its powers directly or indirectly from the great body of the people, and is administered by persons holding their offices during pleasure, for a limited period, or during good behaviour'. The key phrase here is 'directly or indirectly' which Madison repeats in the same *Federalist* essay,[4] writing that 'It is sufficient for such a government that the persons administering it be appointed, either directly or indirectly, by the people.' The Senate was appointed, not elected, and the president chosen through a system known as the electoral college. There was an echo here of Plato's guardians: Madison believed that wise, elder statesmen (like himself) could prevent the government from slipping into the hands of demagogues.

The founding fathers were also influenced by the work of the French political philosopher of the eighteenth-century Enlightenment Baron de Montesquieu, whose works they quoted more often than any book bar the Bible.[5] Montesquieu admired the British political system for its separation of powers between monarchy, House of Lords and Commons; the Americans adapted this idea into the split between president, Senate and House of Representatives.

The American state developed without an aristocracy, and the rebellion against the British king only increased the colonists' desire to abolish artificial distinctions between classes. As Alexis de Tocqueville, the French political thinker, famously noted when he toured the country during a visit in the 1830s: 'America exhibits in her social state a most extraordinary phenomenon. Men are there seen on a greater equality in point of fortune and intellect or, in other words, more equal in their strength, than in any other country of the world, or in any age of which history has preserved the remembrance.'[6] De

Tocqueville argued that this social equality was bound to be translated into political equality as well.

The founding fathers had to grapple with a particularly thorny problem – the role of a political opposition. As the great American historian Richard Hofstadter explained,[7] the ideal political leader of the age was the disinterested patriot, governing in the national interest. The republic started off with such a figure in the person of George Washington, the Revolutionary War hero. The president would be advised by reasonable men who would agree on reasonable measures. But Washington's new American state also found there were a number of issues on which reasonable men might not agree, from foreign relations – some favoured England, others France – through the treatment of debtors to the relationship between the central government and the individual states. Washington's successor, the prickly John Adams, proved a much more divisive figure, so the consensus quickly disintegrated. The battle between Adams and Thomas Jefferson over foreign policy (the former tending to favour Britain and the latter France) was extremely bitter.

The founding fathers disliked the idea of 'faction', which in the language of the time was interchangeable with the word 'party'. First, it was feared that a party would, by necessity, represent the interests of a narrow class of society and would thus govern in its own interest, and not in the wider cause. Second, the party system in Britain was associated with the great fights of the late seventeenth and early eighteenth centuries, in which first the Whigs engineered the ejection of James II, in favour of William III, and then the Tories supported the Jacobite rebellion of James II's son, the 'Old Pretender'. It was easy to portray an opposition as treasonous; indeed, early American propaganda shows the Federalists (the Adams party) depicted as British stooges, while the Federalists in turn depicted their opposition Republicans (under Thomas Jefferson) as pro-French.

A reluctance to accept the idea of a legitimate opposition is still around today: the Russian government of Vladimir Putin, for example, demonizes many opponents as 'Western agents'. This has been a particular problem in countries that emerged from the shadow of colonial rule; often this struggle was led by an umbrella group, like the African National Congress in South Africa. It was perhaps natural for all such groups to regard opponents as agents of the colonial oppressors. But a consequence of this attitude was the emergence of one-party states.

Although the US founding fathers flirted with oppressive measures in the late 1790s, such as the Alien and Sedition Acts which were designed to muzzle the press, they came to realize that the existence of political parties was essential to a democracy. A loyal opposition – one committed not to the overthrow of the state but to an alternative policy programme – was the best check on government power. A key requirement for healthy democracy is the existence of an opposition party, complete with recognized leaders and policies, that is able to form an alternative government after an election. Giving voters a real choice allows them to dismiss the current administration.

The US steadily became more democratic. By 1824 property qualifications were dropped in most states and adult male suffrage was established. At the end of the American Civil War, the Thirteenth and Fourteenth Amendments to the Constitution emancipated slaves and gave them full civil rights, including the vote. Sadly, the southern white establishment gradually restricted these rights, which were not fully re-established until the 1960s. The election of senators became mandatory in 1913 with ratification of the Seventeenth Amendment, and women received the vote in 1920 under the Nineteenth Amendment.

AMERICA VERSUS FRANCE

While the American democratic model broadened steadily over a period of two hundred years, the aftermath of the French Revolution of 1789 was much more turbulent. French ideas spread rapidly to the rest of Europe but the accompanying violence tarnished the fine rhetoric; in many ways, the revolution was a grim precursor of the horrors of the twentieth century. Although the battle cry of 'liberté, égalité, fraternité' still has an inspirational ring, the revolution consumed itself. In the battle between Jacobins and Girondins, we see a precursor of the fight between Bolsheviks and Mensheviks; the executions and show trials were worthy of Stalin, and the rise of Napoleon Bonaparte seemed to confirm the ancient fears that democracy would decay into tyranny.

What explains the difference between the US and French experiences? The American Revolution was led by a bunch of fundamentally conservative landed gentry. As they showed when setting up their government, they didn't want a country that was run in a dramatically different way from the British system; they just wanted to run the society themselves, rather than have an alien king or Parliament do so. Indeed, they had already set up a mechanism for self-government, in the form of individual states. The American revolutionaries were not radicals when it came to property rights, and there was no question of freeing the slave population on which they depended.

In contrast, the French revolutionaries lived in a state that had been tightly controlled by three groups, or 'estates' – the monarchy, the aristocracy and the Church. There was no tradition of self-government for them to build on. Events were driven as much by the 'mob' in Paris as by the Parliament. All this gave the revolutionaries an incentive to seize the property of the old ruling classes, and for one set of leaders to outbid another in their radicalism. Initially, this gave the revolution a more democratic veneer. The Constitutional committee originally wanted to restrict the franchise to taxpayers. This idea, however, was attacked by Maximilien Robespierre, who said that 'Each individual has the right to a say in the laws by which he is governed and in the choice of the administration which belongs to him. Otherwise it is not true to say that all men are equal in rights, that all men are citizens.'

Like the Americans, the French also decided that representative democracy was the only way forward. 'Democracy is not a state in which the people, continuously assembled, regulates by itself all public affairs, still less one in which a hundred thousand fractions of the people, by isolated, precipitate and contradictory measures, would decide the destiny of the entire society,' said Robespierre. 'Such a government would never exist and if it ever did, all it could do would be to return the people to despotism. Democracy is a state in which the sovereign people, guided by laws which are its own work, does by itself all it can do well, and by delegates all that it could not.'

When democracy turned to anarchy in the wake of the Terror (1793–4), as the leaders turned from executing aristocrats to killing each other, the natural Hobbesian desire for order returned. That gave Napoleon his chance. Indeed, for a while, he did provide order, notably in the field of law: the Napoleonic code is still the basis of French law (and that of many other countries) today. But Napoleon's restless military aggression, while bringing France much initial glory, eventually doomed him to defeat. He could defeat neither Britain at sea nor Russia on land. After Napoleon fell from power in 1815, the great powers of Europe made strenuous (although ultimately unsuccessful) efforts to ensure that nothing similar would ever happen again. Between 1815 and 1870 France itself lurched from monarchy to republic to empire and back to republic again; as the historian Eric Hobsbawm argued, these rapid changes of regime 'were all attempts to maintain a bourgeois society while avoiding the double danger of the Jacobin democratic republic and the old regime'.[8]

THE IMPORTANCE OF FORCE

Why did democracy emerge and survive in the late eighteenth and nineteenth centuries when it had not prospered before? Sometimes it can be easy to get carried away by the philosophical arguments and forget that revolutions are essentially a struggle for power. To the extent that philosophical ideas can be used to justify one side or other of the struggle, they will be adopted. If there is not enough political support for an idea, it may lie dormant for centuries, as was the case with the more radical ideas of the Levellers.

When it comes to translating philosophy into power, the importance of force should not be underestimated. Robert Dahl suggests that the modern development of democracy is linked to the need for lightly armed foot soldiers: a citizen militia.[9] Previous armies were based on cavalry (few could afford a horse) or on mercenaries (at the control of the rich). The development of the musket 'democratised' warfare. 'The invention of fire-arms equalised the villein and noble on the field,' as De Tocqueville put it.[10] As citizen soldiers congregated, they absorbed ideas, some of them (as with the New Model Army in the English Civil War, with a manifesto calling for near-universal suffrage) quite radical. When guns spread to the general population, it became harder for the government to impose its will on an armed populace. (This is the point made by enthusiasts for the Second

Amendment to the US Constitution, which reads: 'A well regulated militia being necessary to the security of a free state, the right of the people to keep and bear arms shall not be infringed.')

Democracy, or the alternative of republicanism, also needs the support of important social groups. It was not just logistics that made it difficult for Britain to hang on to its American colonies; the mother country's rule was opposed by the dominant class of American society. The states were run by their prosperous landowners, and it was they who switched their allegiance from the king. They justified their rebellion in the name of republicanism but had they decided to set up their own monarch instead, the rebellion would probably still have succeeded. Similarly, when one looks at the European democratic movements of the nineteenth century, the initial stages were led by the middle classes. The economic power of these classes was rising, thanks to industry; extension of the franchise represented a recognition of their power by the aristocratic elite. It helped, of course, that the aristocrats feared the ability of the middle class to enlist the poor on their side.

As Napoleon's armies fanned out across Europe, reorganizing the political map as they went, they spread French radical ideas of democracy. Significantly, Napoleon also anticipated European nationalism, helping to found a Kingdom of Italy and abolishing the old Holy Roman Empire. This in turn created the impetus for German nationalism later in the nineteenth century.

NATIONAL DEMOCRACY

This rise of the nation state was the next great development of democracy. It is worth pointing out that, in the early nineteenth century, the world map looked very different from how it looks today. Many people did not live in countries with defined national borders, but in the ancestral lands of one nobleman or another. A dynastic marriage or two, and they might find themselves under the rule of some prince from far away.

Such states as did exist were rudimentary. There was very little welfare spending, and education and health services were in private hands. Most people would live their lives without really coming into contact with, or thinking much about, their national rulers.

Societies were highly hierarchical structures in which hereditary monarchs lived a lavish life in the midst of poverty. This was a far from stable set-up: monarchs were often being deposed by rival members of the same family (or by rival families). Monarchs also had to 'buy off' powerful subjects with grants of land or treasure, a process that often required wars of conquest – and with them the prospect of outright defeat.

The idea that a nation represented a people – a particular community – was only beginning to be formed. Most people lived their lives within the confines of their village or town; travel further afield was time-consuming or arduous. They had little idea of how other peoples behaved or even looked: during the Napoleonic wars, the folk of Hartlepool famously hanged a monkey as a French spy.

The Industrial Revolution helped to spread literacy, leading to the development of an educated middle class. The idea of a national culture started to emerge, based on a common language, or religion, or heritage in the form of folk songs or style of dress.

Nationalism was a unifying cause for those who wished to rebel against the absolute monarchs and assorted princes who held power in much of Europe in the early nineteenth century. In 1848 nationalism helped precipitate the wave of revolutions which spread rapidly across the European continent, rather like the collapse of communism in 1989. Just as the American revolutionaries had found that republicanism was a way to justify their cause, so the European rebels turned to nationalism and representative democracy. Being property owners, however, the middle-class leaders of the revolts were rather keener on liberty and fraternity than on equality.

Kings could survive in this new world but they had to be constitutional monarchs in the British style. The absolute monarchs of the era saw off the 1848 revolts, but the democratic clock was ticking. Indeed, the collapse of the supranational monarchies began in the 1870s with the decay of the old Ottoman Empire and the emergence of Eastern European nations such as Bulgaria and Romania.

In western Europe, the established states moved steadily towards democracy as the century wore on. Voting rights were initially extended only to the middle class, but the franchise was adjusted to reflect the power of the industrial working class. Unlike agricultural workers, industrial workers were grouped together in factories where they could organize, demonstrate and strike. Governments appeased this new force with a combination of strategies, offering social reforms and extending the franchise where necessary. The process was self-reinforcing: the wider the franchise, the greater the pressure for social reform.

Why did the old aristocratic elites extend the franchise when the inevitable result was the erosion of their social and economic status? A paper by Daron Acemoglu and James Robinson, authors of the book *Why Nations Fail*, concluded that 'the elite were forced to extend the franchise because of the threat of revolution . . . extending the franchise acted as a commitment to future redistribution and prevented social unrest'.[11] The British prime minister Earl Grey, speaking before the great Reform Act of 1832, said that 'There is no-one more decided against annual parliaments, universal suffrage and the ballot than am I . . . The principal (aim) of my reform is to prevent the necessity of revolution. I am reforming to preserve, not to overthrow.' Earl Grey was speaking in the aftermath of a second French revolution, which had seen the Bourbon royal family overthrown for a second time – although, as it transpired, the monarchy was maintained under the 'citizen king', Louis-Philippe. In terms of economic evidence, Acemoglu and Robinson find that peak levels of inequality were reached around the times the franchise was extended. Subsequently, inequality fell and taxes rose.

In Britain, the Second Reform Act of 1867 more than doubled the size of the electorate, ensuring that working-class voters formed a majority in urban constituencies. The Act was followed by the first of William Gladstone's four governments, that of 1868–74, which introduced many meritocratic reforms designed to appeal to middle-class voters, such as the introduction of civil service exams. Prime Minister Gladstone also brought in the first national system of elementary education, a major extension of the government's role. Later reforms (in 1893 and 1902) extended the school-leaving age to 12 and created the grammar schools that helped lift the social status of many a working-class child in the first half of the twentieth century.

Meanwhile, in a concession to working-class voters, the legality of trade unions was formally acknowledged in 1871: in 1875 and 1876 a Conservative government led by Benjamin Disraeli legalized picketing and the protection of trade union funds. As Eric Hobsbawm mordantly remarked, the resulting legal system was 'so favourable to trade unionism that periodic attempts have been made ever since to whittle away the freedom they were then granted'.[12] At this stage, the main aims of the working-class movement were work-related, focusing on issues such as working hours, pay and union recognition. These issues did not require formal government structures. It was only later that the unions turned to other issues such as unemployment insurance and pensions, eventually forming the Labour Party in 1900. In response to this electoral threat, the reforming Liberal government of 1906–14 introduced a raft of measures designed to appeal to workers, including pensions and unemployment insurance.

This programme was fiercely resisted by the House of Lords, which caused a constitutional crisis by rejecting the Liberal budget; in the resulting battle, the powers of the Lords were severely reduced by the 1911 Parliament Act. This was part of a turbulent period – later dubbed by George Dangerfield *The Strange Death of Liberal England*[13] – in which Britain was racked by conflict, with the threat of army mutiny over the potential inclusion of Ulster under Irish home rule, strikes by the powerful mining and railway unions, and the Suffragette protests.

In France, universal male suffrage was introduced in 1848, after another revolution had swept away Louis-Philippe. The widened franchise did not last long, as the voters opted for Louis-Napoleon (the nephew of Bonaparte), who declared himself emperor in 1851. But Napoleon III, as he became in December 1852, was careful to legitimize himself by the use of referenda, and in his 'liberal' phase in the 1860s allowed more freedom of the press and Parliamentary supervision of finance. He too legalized trade unions and the right to strike. Napoleon III hoped that rapid economic expansion would earn him support, but his adventurous foreign policy led to disaster and military defeat by Prussia in 1870.

The ensuing Third Republic restored universal male suffrage and also introduced Gladstonian-style reforms. In 1882 seven years of compulsory (and free) education was brought in. Of course, education reforms could be justified in economic terms; the Industrial Revolution required a more highly skilled workforce. But education also fed into the democratization process; a literate workforce could read newspapers and pamphlets, and it could keep a closer eye on the policies that governments were following.

Like France, Switzerland adopted universal male suffrage in 1848 (although the Swiss did not give women the vote until 1971). In Germany, even the ultra-conservative Otto von Bismarck introduced old age pensions and unemployment insurance in the 1880s, which he saw as a way of buying working-class support for his emperor and thereby heading off the threat of revolution.

The German Empire, founded in 1871, had established universal male suffrage, although the Bundestag (lower house of Parliament) could not appoint ministers or discuss foreign policy. It was also balanced by an appointed (and highly conservative) Bundesrat (upper house), while local governments were elected by a system which gave the rich a vote worth many times that of the poor. Nevertheless, a strong social democratic party did emerge (earlier, in fact, than it did in either Britain or France), and Bismarck was alive to the danger it presented. His main concern was foreign policy, where he needed a free hand to keep both Russia and Austria-Hungary happy, in the face of a hostile France.

Reform also occurred in the already-democratic US. In the first decade of the twentieth century the Republican president, Teddy Roosevelt, campaigned against the 'robber barons' in industry and the banks. The issue of the day was 'trusts' – monopolies in fields such as oil and railways that appeared to be exploiting workers and consumers. 'The absence of effective state, and especially national, restraint upon unfair money-getting has tended to create a small class of enormously wealthy and economically powerful men, whose chief object is to hold and increase their power,' he said.[14] Roosevelt's successor, William Howard Taft – another Republican – also engaged in trust-busting. But the two men fell out and split the Republican vote in 1912, allowing a Democrat, Woodrow Wilson, to win a three-way contest. Wilson also pushed through reforms such as restrictions on child labour and a federal income tax; the 1912 election was the peak of what had become known as the Progressive movement.

Worldwide, the democratic movement, along with the rise of nationalism, received a huge boost at the end of the First World War when Wilson made self-determination one of his 'Fourteen Points' for a post-war settlement. The immediate result was the disintegration of Austria-Hungary, a cosmopolitan state which owed its existence to the ancestral holdings of the Habsburg monarchy.

When the US entered the war in 1917, Wilson had declared to Congress:

> we shall fight for the things that we have always carried nearest our hearts – for democracy, for the right of those who submit to authority to have a voice in their own governments, for the rights and liberties of small nations, for a universal dominion of right by such a concert of free people as shall bring peace and safety to all nations and make the world itself at last free.

In his most famous phrase, he declared that 'the world must be made safe for democracy'.

War also accelerated the extension of female suffrage. While eighteenth-century wars had been fought with professional troops, the First World War involved mass conscription, and an expanded female workforce was therefore needed to replace the male workers diverted to the battlefields. Just as it was impossible to deny the vote to people who had sacrificed so much in the trenches, it could hardly be denied to women, who had proved themselves so economically useful.

THE WAVES OF DEMOCRACY

Samuel Huntington, the political scientist, identified three waves of democracy.[15] The first broadly occurred from 1828 to 1926; the second from 1943 to 1962; and the third from 1974 onwards. Between these phases were (slightly overlapping) reverse waves from 1922 to 1942 and 1958 to 1975.

The first wave started in the US in the nineteenth century, when property restrictions on the vote were gradually dropped and more than 50% of adult white males had the franchise by 1828. This pattern soon spread to other Western democracies. This wave started subsiding only in 1920, in the aftermath of the First World War. The newest democracies proved the most fragile: Mr Huntington found that only four out of the 17 countries that adopted democracy after 1910 kept the system through the 1920s and 1930s, whereas only one of the dozen that adopted democracy before 1910 abandoned it.

The closing years and end of the Second World War led to a further surge in democracy, with the defeated powers of West Germany, Italy and Japan leading the way, before another retreat in the 1960s and 1970s, as the newly independent colonies slipped into one-party rule. The third wave began in 1974 with the fall of authoritarian regimes in Portugal and Greece. Just as many were beginning to wonder whether democracy was a phenomenon that prospered only in the West, a number of South American countries returned to their democratic roots after overthrowing their military regimes in the 1980s; so too did parts of Asia. The climax of this process was the great wave of democratization that swept Eastern Europe in 1989.

One can see the pattern in Mr Huntington's data. He found that 45.3% of nations were democratic as of 1922. This had fallen to 19.7% by 1942, just before the start of the second wave, before rebounding to 32.4% by 1962, the end of it. By 1973, just before the start of the third wave, the ratio had dropped again to 24.6%. Mr Huntington found that a past history of democracy made a country more likely to return to the fold. Of the 29 countries that democratized between 1974 and 1990, 23 had previous democratic experience. The third wave had taken the ratio back up to 45.4% by 1990.

As a way of updating Mr Huntington's figures, *The Economist* Intelligence Unit has a democracy index which ranks countries on a spectrum from full democracies to authoritarian regimes. As of 2010, 15% of countries were 'full' and 31.7% 'flawed' democracies. In terms of the world's population, 11.3% lived in full democracies and 37.1% lived in flawed versions. Around a third of the world, by population and country number, lives under authoritarian regimes.

What governed these changes of tides? Two factors were most important: war and economics. Ironically enough, nationalism – which was a driving force behind democracy in the nineteenth century – was behind some of its setbacks in the twentieth. The Versailles Treaty of 1919 may have advanced the cause of democracy in Eastern Europe in the short term, but the idea of self-determination proved a treacherous principle. When new countries emerged from the ruins of the old empires, ethnically diverse populations were mingled within small territories, and there was no way of separating them in a tidy fashion. National boundaries also had to take accord of geography and the natural desire of the war victors to reward their favoured peoples. It was easy for individual nationalities to band together to overthrow a dynastic empire – but less easy for them to get along afterwards.

Post-1918 countries contained many ethnic minorities; some of them were German, a fact ruthlessly exploited by Hitler to demand their inclusion within the Third Reich. Eastern European democracies were snuffed out when the Germans invaded, and attempts to resurrect democratic systems after 1945 were crushed by the Soviet Union. Ironically, the Soviet Union itself was, like the Austro-Hungarian Empire, made up of a ragbag of nationalities: after 1991, it broke into a host of constituent states, between which nasty border disputes remain. Another example of post-communist disarray occurred in Yugoslavia, a state which emerged after 1918 but clearly represented a breach of the principle of self-determination; the ability of nationalist politicians to exploit ethnic rivalries had tragic consequences in the Balkan Wars of the 1990s.

POST-WAR REVERSES

In the wake of the First World War, the economic problems faced by the combatant countries were severe. Governments had used a mix of policies to pay for the cost of conducting the hostilities – high taxes, heavy borrowing and high inflation through money printing. They attempted to return to the gold standard, a system that had kept inflation low throughout the nineteenth century but which required economic policy to be subordinated to the needs of creditors. Fixing the value of money requires other elements of the economy to adjust; at times when the currency was under threat, this meant painful austerity. This was much harder to impose in an era of democracy. After the Russian Revolution of 1917, politicians were not inclined to push their electorates too far.

The risk of imposing austerity policies was amply demonstrated in

Germany in the early 1930s as mass unemployment forced the electorate into the arms of the extremist parties of both the left and right. Meanwhile Italy and Portugal lapsed back into autocracy in the 1920s, while the Spanish democracy was snuffed out in the late 1930s after a bitter civil war.

In the Anglo-Saxon world, politics developed along ideological lines drawn by the economic interests of the different classes. In Britain, the Fourth Reform Act of 1918 which extended the vote to all working-class males (and all women over 30) caused the rapid demise of the Liberal Party. Working-class support moved to the Labour Party, which briefly held office twice between the wars. The second term coincided with the beginning of the Great Depression in 1929 and led to a split in the party, with the Labour leader Ramsay MacDonald leading a Conservative-dominated coalition. A fully reforming government did not emerge until after the Second World War, when the Labour Party had a huge majority: its policies (such as free health care and nationalization of services) were largely accepted by the opposition Conservatives.

In the United States, the 1912 election that brought Woodrow Wilson to power had long-term significance. When Teddy Roosevelt was not chosen as the Republican candidate, he left the party and took many of his Progressive supporters with him. The ideological focus of the Republican Party began to look more like the modern pro-business platform it occupies today, whereas the reform movement focused its attention on the Democrats. It was Teddy Roosevelt's Democrat cousin, Franklin, who introduced the New Deal programme in the 1930s, which included social security (pensions) and the minimum wage.

The New Deal was in essence a new bargain between rulers and ruled. The government would protect workers from the extremes of poverty and provide them with a range of services, from libraries to refuse collection, in return for votes. In the process the government created a vast network of workers dependent on the state for employment – teachers, doctors, transport workers – who were natural supporters of the status quo. Meanwhile, the wealthy paid higher taxes as a way of buying security for their property, a modern version of the old compact against foreign threats.

This bargain was adopted, with a twist, by Western Europe as it emerged from war after 1945. Designed to avoid the social conflict and economic strains that marred the 1930s, this political philosophy was known in Germany and Italy as Christian Democracy: both the Church and the business classes were keen to see off the threat of communism. A welfare state would support workers at a time of unemployment; national pay bargaining would avoid wildcat strikes; close links between banks and corporations would support business; and so on. This statist approach also emerged in France, where political turmoil continued after the war until the re-emergence of General de Gaulle in 1958,[16] whose appeal combined nationalism with economic planning.

Of course, there were plenty of variants on this model, with Sweden being at the most social democratic end of the spectrum and the US at the opposite pole. But by the 1950s, all Western governments held a set of basic assumptions in common: an unrestricted franchise, universal education, the use of fiscal and monetary policy to try to smooth the economic cycle, and the use of unemployment insurance and old age pensions to keep people from poverty. In a sense, all this was a response to communist criticism of capitalism: we can protect the poor, the Western nations argued, while still operating with democracy, free speech and private ownership of property.

AFTER 1945

The 1950s and 1960s were in many ways the 'golden age' for the democracies, with most countries achieving an unprecedented, and sustained, pace of economic growth. The West Germans spoke of the *Wirtschaftswunder*, or economic miracle; the French of *les trente glorieuses*, or 30 glorious years. Unemployment was low for much of the period and politicians thought that they had, with the help of John Maynard Keynes, cracked the problem of economic planning. Millions of people acquired the benefits of modern living for the first time: refrigerators, washing machines, central heating and their first car. And, as we shall discuss later, this was also a time of greater economic equality than had ever been seen before.

For a short while, political focus in the Western democracies seemed to move elsewhere – towards cultural issues. The 1960s is traditionally seen as the era when youth culture started to dominate society. In part, this was due to simple demography: the 'baby boom' generation, born after 1946, was unusually large. Many of these young people went to university, where the congregating effect was similar to that seen in nineteenth-century factories: they shared ideas, demonstrated and, on occasion, 'occupied' their colleges.

What emerged alongside the youth culture in the 1960s and the 1970s was the culture of 'rights' and a focus on groups that democracy had left behind. The most obvious example was the African American population in the US, which had been excluded from the voting booth by Jim Crow provisions, such as the arbitrary application of knowledge tests, and who were forced to use separate and inferior public facilities (drinking fountains, public transport). Significantly, the protesters in the US marched under the banner of the 'civil rights' movement, a label that could easily be adopted by other groups of protesters. Indeed, the late 1960s protests by the Catholics of Northern Ireland also fell under the civil rights label.

Similarly, the movement for gay rights is often dated back to the Stonewall riots of 1969, a protest in New York City against maltreatment by police; the Wounded Knee occupation of 1973 highlighted the plight of Native Americans. At the same time, the feminist movement called for an equal rights amendment to the Constitution; although it passed both houses of Congress in 1972, sufficient states failed to ratify it. The 1960s and 1970s also saw much greater recognition in the West of the plight of people in what was then known as the third, or developing, world. In part, this was triggered by the Vietnam War and the sight of American troops in conflict with Asian peasants. But there was also a growing feeling that the global economic system was rigged against developing countries and that famines, such as those that ravaged Biafra or Ethiopia, were in part the result of Western policy.

Over the long run, civil rights movements have had profound effects on voting patterns. Some of these effects were surprising. Before female enfranchisement, some commentators argued that women would fall under the influence of their husbands, or the Church, and would prove to be a highly conservative force. Initially, this perception was proved correct; evidence from US elections indicates that women were less likely to vote for the Democratic Party until 1972.

Since then, there has been a huge gender gap, with men favouring the Republicans and women the Democrats. In 2008 Barack Obama had a 13-percentage point lead over John McCain among female voters but only a 1-point lead among men. One study[17] relates this to the divorce rate: married women are more likely to be Conservative whereas divorced women are generally worse off, and are thus more likely to favour redistribution. Divorce has become more common over the last 30–40 years, potentially increasing the number of left-leaning women.

Other factors besides economics may be at work. First, while modern women may not always call themselves feminists, they are often interested in feminist issues – reproductive rights, equal pay for equal work, and so on. These issues have generally been adopted by the left but treated with hostility on the right. Indeed, abortion has only become an issue because it was legalized in the UK, US and Western Europe in the 1960s and 1970s. Second, women are now much more likely to go to university than their predecessors. That seems to make them more politically engaged and active: in recent US elections, the highest level of turnout has been seen among women with an advanced degree (over 80% in the 2008 election). And the most-educated people tend to be more left-leaning – although John Kerry lost the 2004 election, he was 11 percentage points ahead among voters with postgraduate degrees.

In Europe, studies indicate that women were more conservative than men in the early 1970s, with a right-wing voting bias varying from 2 percentage points in the Netherlands to 14 in Italy. One factor may have been the role of Christian Democratic (conservative) parties which captured the allegiance of women, who were more regular churchgoers than men. By the 1990s, however, attitudinal surveys[18] suggested that women were generally to the left of men (the exceptions being Finland and Spain).

Rights issues have generally helped the left-leaning parties. In the 2012 election, gay and lesbian voters almost constituted President Obama's entire majority, according to *The New York Times'* 538 model, devised by Nate Silver to analyse the results.[19] He won the gay vote by a whopping 54 percentage points. On the other hand, you could say the Latino vote delivered the election for Obama: he won it by 71% to 29%. But women also voted for Obama by 55% to 44%. It is clearly incongruous to describe these developments as the assertion of minority rights against an unfeeling majority – after all, women are half the population. But rights politics have demonstrated that other issues can matter more than economics. People want their status and concerns to be recognized by the ruling elite.

The development of rights-based politics in the 1960s and 1970s coincided with an era of more general protest. Industrial workers were striking more frequently and with more success; indeed, the coal miners effectively brought down the British Conservative government of Edward Heath in 1974. There was much talk on the television and in the newspapers of Britain being 'ungovernable'. Inflation made the annual pay bargaining process a fraught affair. Around the world, regional groups were demanding their own independence: the Catholics in Northern Ireland, the Basques in Spain and the Palestinians within the Israeli state. Terrorism was used by those groups and by other dissidents such as the Red Brigade in Italy and the Baader-Meinhof gang in West Germany to pursue left-wing political goals.

In the early 1970s, these problems seemed all the more acute because the post-war economic model was breaking down: politicians, it transpired, were not competent at running the economy after all. Some of the grievances that emerged were genuine wrongs that had been ignored for too long. Catholics had been badly treated in Northern Ireland, women were still not treated equally with men (and indeed are still not to this day). As democracies matured, citizens examined their claims to be homes of liberty, fraternity and equality, and found them wanting.

By the 1980s many of these tensions had subsided. It helped that the West had withdrawn from its colonial wars in Vietnam and Algeria (although the Falklands conflict between Britain and Argentina was an odd echo). The political centre of gravity shifted to the right; not just Ronald Reagan in the US and Margaret Thatcher in the UK, but Helmut Kohl in West Germany. As we shall see in the next chapter, there was a change of economic policy that seemed to restore the good times.

CONCLUSION

To sum up, we can see political change in the developed world as a combination of economic forces and four shocks. The economic force was the development of a prosperous middle class, able to challenge the power of the old landowning elites, plus the emergence of the industrial working class, grouped together in factories and thus able to flex their muscles through strikes and demonstrations. First, the franchise was extended to these voters and then, gradually, they used the franchise to influence economic and social policy. This process was hurried along by the four shocks – the two world wars, the Great Depression and the rise of communism – as the governing elites both reacted to these crises and saw the need to head off the threat of revolution.

By the 1980s, there was no serious internal challenge to liberal democracy in the developed world. And the external challenge – communism – was about to collapse. The moment of triumph had arrived.

4

An Economy Becalmed?

We are becoming addicted to monetary and fiscal drugs. We hope they will cure us but they may only be making our problems easier to live with, at least in the short term. Like drugs, however, their persistent use might be associated with unwanted side-effects.

Stephen D. King, *When The Money Runs Out:*
The End of Western Affluence, 2013

Economics is not the only factor affecting political development, but it is the most important one. Of the three waves described by Samuel Huntington in the last chapter, democracy's first expansion followed the start of the Industrial Revolution in the late eighteenth century. Its second great wave of expansion coincided with a period of strong economic growth after the Second World War. The biggest addition of countries in the third great wave came at the start of the 1990s, in the middle of a long economic boom.

Conversely, shifts from democracy to autocracy have been triggered by military defeat or economic collapse, as occurred with both fascism and communism in Germany and Russia. Democracies need prosperity to help them flourish; indeed there is a clear correlation between per capita income and their survival chances. One study of the period 1950–90 found that in countries with annual income per capita of under $1,500 democracies had a life expectancy of eight years; when income per capita was between $1,500 and $3,000 they lasted around 18 years; and democracies in countries with income per capita of over $6,000 were extremely robust.[1]

We have come to expect a higher standard of living every year – and to complain when we do not get it. It is therefore hardly surprising that the debt crisis which began in 2007 is causing democracies to feel the strain. The famous slogan in Bill Clinton's 1992 Presidential campaign, 'It's the economy, stupid', was designed for those campaign operatives who failed to grasp the crucial determinant of the election result.

As noted in the last chapter, it was not until the twentieth century that governments really became responsible for economic management, for making sure nearly everybody had a job and that prices did not increase too rapidly. Indeed, it is now arguably the central problem of government – helping the total resources of the nation to expand and then allocating a large proportion of those resources, apportioned from the total by taxation, in line with its priorities.

Governments try to affect the economy in three broad ways. First, they try to fine-tune the economy through *industrial or social policies*, which give special tax privileges or subsidies to activities that the government would like to encourage, or types of people that the government wants to protect. These will be looked at in the next chapter.

The second way is by *monetary policy*, usually conducted by an arm of the government called the central bank. This aims to support economic growth, without creating inflation, through the level of interest rates and the expansion of the money supply – the amount of money in the form of notes, coinage and commercial bank credit. The latter is by far the biggest element of the money supply; when the banks expand their balance sheets by lending money, they add to the money supply. This new money (an overdraft, a credit card balance) is just as good as a five-pound (or dollar) note for buying goods. The central bank also supports the financial sector by acting as a lender of last resort, with the aim of preventing a temporary liquidity crisis in the banks from dragging down the whole economy.

The third way is by *fiscal policy*, which relates to the balance between the revenues the government receives from taxes and the amount it spends. By running a deficit or (less often) a surplus, governments can attempt to influence the level of activity in the economy. Higher taxes or lower spending cause a slowing of economic activity; lower taxes and higher spending an expansion (at least in the short term).

Broadly speaking, fiscal policy was the government's focus between

1945 and the mid-1970s, while monetary policy has been more important since then. But both ran into problems: the fiscal era ended with stagflation (higher inflation and unemployment) in the mid-1970s while the monetary era led to the debt crisis that started in 2007. While fiscal and monetary stimulus can help economies out of deep recessions, it is more doubtful that they can affect the long-term growth rate; that is related to the education levels of the population, institutional structures (rule of law, property rights, etc.), natural resources, and so on. But both policies are so powerful that they tend to get used for a variety of reasons; politicians want to get themselves re-elected by having the economy boom at polling time and to avoid all recessions (however mild); central banks feel obliged to rescue the financial sector and the stock market. Excessive use of fiscal and monetary policy eventually distorts the economy; for example, the willingness of central banks to cut rates when share prices faltered encouraged the risk-taking of the banking sector. Like park rangers who snuffed out all fires, the effect was to create the dry tinder for a vast blaze – the debt crisis of 2007 and 2008.

Economics is a topic perennially at the centre of public debate. That debate is made more vigorous by the nature of the subject. It is a discipline that works by rules of thumb, such as 'the price of a good or service balances supply and demand'. This is often referred to as the 'law' of supply and demand – that higher prices will lead to reduced demand. But it is not a law. In the case of shares or houses, rising prices tend to mean that more people want to own them.

Thomas Carlyle once dubbed economics the 'dismal science', but it is really more of an art. If it were a science with established rules, there would be little to argue about – we do not debate the law of gravity. But we cannot run controlled experiments to see which economic policy is right for which circumstances – after all, we have millions of people and thousands of variables for which to account. Nobel-winning economists disagree with each other about the right policy mix; whether a government should spend more or less, and on what; whether taxes should be imposed on income, capital or spending, and so on. History has seen some sharp changes of tack in economic policy, and doubtless there will be further big changes in the future.

Thanks to history, we can rule out some extremes. The record of communism shows that it tends to produce stagnation and mediocrity: as the old Soviet joke used to go, 'We pretend to work and they pretend to pay us.' Worse still, the planning power given to a centralized state can lead to megalomaniacal experiments, such as Mao Zedong's Great Leap Forward, which may have led to as many as 45 million deaths.[2] One need but consider the growth record of China in the post-Mao period, when the economy only achieved healthy growth after the economic liberalization policies of Deng Xiaoping were implemented, or contrast the economies of North and South Korea, to demonstrate that communism leads to poor results. Voters have tended to be fairly wise to communism's flaws. Indeed, while communist parties have sometimes received quite respectable shares of the vote in countries such as France and Italy, they have never come to power by democratic means alone.

No modern society operates with completely free markets – even when they say they do. The US, seen as the home of the laissez-faire approach, pays subsidies to support its farmers (and protect them from foreign competition), has thousands of pages of rules to regulate the financial sector, and has a social safety net for unemployed workers. There is plenty of scope for arguing about the right mix between free markets and regulation, between the private and public sectors, and about the level of taxation which offers the best trade-off between fairness and maximizing revenue. Voters should clearly be entitled to decide such matters, or at least to elect (and dismiss) politicians who offer the right or wrong answers to these trade-offs.

But it is one thing to say that voters are entitled to make such decisions, another to believe that they will reach the best possible solutions. 'Democracy is a kind of religion. It too needs faith,' argues the political commentator and former Conservative MP Matthew Parris. In the same breath he cautions that 'Democracy won't work if it's at odds with reality.'[3] The choices of voters cannot be completely unconstrained; they cannot spend (or tax) without limit, for example.

Alas, voters are not always given the right information on which to make their decision. Politicians may be unwilling to confront the public with inconvenient truths. At the 2010 British election, the Labour prime minister, Gordon Brown, was very reluctant to use the word 'cuts', although his chancellor of the exchequer Alasdair Darling had a plan to halve the deficit over five years. The Liberal Democrats, meanwhile, were happy to cast the Conservatives as the skinflints, while the Conservatives themselves were vague about their deficit-cutting timetable.

In the event, the Conservative–Liberal Democrat coalition which was formed after the 2010 election promised to eliminate the UK's structural budget deficit over five years. The Liberal Democrat leader, Nick Clegg, said it was the Greek crisis, which broke in the middle of the campaign, that persuaded him to change his mind in favour of austerity. Perhaps it did, but this appeared to be one of the oldest government tricks in the book: promise something before an election, but change tack afterwards because 'having looked at the books', it was no longer affordable.

A pattern of 'promise now, renege later' can induce voter cynicism. But politicians act this way for a reason: complete honesty may lose elections. Asked to choose between Party A, which promises higher benefits and lower taxes, and Party B, which promises the opposite, politicians assume Party A will win every time. Of course, there are plenty of informed voters and the media can play their part at exposing the more barefaced untruths. Nevertheless, the 2010 British election was a good case in point. Everybody knew the government deficit was huge and had to fall. But all the major parties were reticent about describing how those cuts would be made.

FISCAL POLICY

The current focus on austerity in Britain and continental Europe and the battle over the trillion-dollar deficit in the US, have revived a debate about fiscal policy that dates back to the period between the First and Second world wars. The societies that emerged from the First World War had just witnessed a huge expansion in the size of government and its role in the economy. Men had been plucked from their farms and their factories to fight – as employees of the state. Industry had been redirected into making more armaments, again under state direction. Governments had also regulated private behaviour to an unprecedented extent in order to 'defend the nation'. In Britain, the land of the heavy drinker, pub hours had been shortened to make sure the workers were able to function.

After the war, conservative forces wanted the economy to return to its pre-war state, to 'normalcy', as the 1920 US campaign slogan of the Republican Warren Harding described it. But politicians had to balance that desire with the expectations of the soldiers returning from the trenches – 'homes for heroes' was a slogan in the 1918 British election, promising that the government would increase the level of house-building. In Europe, social democratic parties took office, as a sharp break from the monarchical conservative past of small government. Following the Russian Revolution of 1917, and with the threat of communist revolution looming, pressure was building on Europe's ruling classes to address the expectations of the soldiers and the workers.

Pre-war economic orthodoxy was that governments should balance their budgets, exchange rates should be fixed and currencies linked to gold to prevent inflation. But the war had been financed with borrowed (and printed) money and there had been rapid inflation. International cooperation was affected by the issue of reparations, with the French and British demanding compensation from the Germans (and the Americans demanding that the French and British repay their war debts). The first post-war crisis stemmed directly from the reparations issue; Germany suffered hyperinflation in 1923 as the central bank printed vast amounts of money to keep the government going after the French occupied the Ruhr in a payments dispute.

Economic leadership passed to the Americans, who were enjoying an economic boom and a rising stock market in the 1920s. The Americans temporarily solved the reparations dispute by lending money to Germany in the mid-1920s. For a while, the system was put back together; Britain rejoined the gold standard (which meant restricting the money supply) in 1925 and much of Europe was back on the system by 1927. (The war had seen the abandonment of the gold standard and politicians financed the conflict with borrowed (and printed) money, with the inevitable consequence of rapid inflation.)

But the system broke down in 1929 when an American economic

slowdown caused the supply of credit to Germany to slow up. Banks collapsed, along with consumer and business confidence. The ensuing Great Depression was a huge challenge, both to governments of the day and to prevailing economic theory. Industrial production fell by around 25% in Britain and France, and more than 40% in the US and Germany. Unemployment rose to 25% in the US and more than 30% elsewhere.

Most economists of the day thought the situation would right itself. Wages would fall until business found it attractive to hire workers; prices would fall until consumers were willing and able to buy goods. But as the years passed, this did not happen. Economists still argue about why that was. Some blame monetary policy. Central banks allowed commercial banks to collapse, taking with them the savings of millions and forcing the bankruptcy of many businesses. A related (and to modern eyes, familiar) problem was high levels of debt. The value of debt was fixed but as wages and prices fell, consumers and business found it more difficult to repay their creditors. Some blame government interference in the economy that prevented the excesses of the previous boom from being cleared away; if unemployment benefits had not been available, workers would have accepted lower wages and priced themselves into new jobs.

Before the First World War, when few workers had the vote, that might have been the governmental approach. But in a democracy, voters (or their representatives) could demand action. The experience of the First World War also made government intervention in the economy more acceptable and compelling. If governments could take charge in time of war, surely they could run their economies in a way that avoided depressions and kept most people in a job.

One government that did follow the old orthodoxy was Chancellor Brüning's administration in Germany, which pursued a policy of austerity between 1930 and 1932. In the face of high unemployment, support mounted for the communists and the Nazis; to keep the former out, the old guard of Germany let the latter in.

Elsewhere, governments found the strain of keeping to the gold standard to be too great. Fixing the supply of money forces other elements of the economy to adjust in the face of a shock: prices and wages have to fall. But lower wages and prices make it harder for consumers to service debts. And if workers resist wage cuts, the effect shows up as higher unemployment.

Britain abandoned the gold standard in 1931, the US in 1933, and France was the last major power to leave it, in 1936. Those economies which abandoned gold first recovered first, as the supply of credit was able to grow.[4] A less helpful side effect was the move towards protectionism. The idea was to protect jobs at home by putting high tariffs on goods imported from abroad. Protectionism was embraced widely – even by Britain, which abandoned its long commitment to free trade. Consequently, trade slumped in the early 1930s and those who worked for export industries lost their jobs.

As economies floundered, John Maynard Keynes, the great British economist, developed a revolutionary idea. Fiscal policy could be used to avoid the worst of a depression. He suggested that, contrary to official orthodoxy, it was possible for an economy to get stuck in a rut from which it could not be extricated without a helping hand; the 1930s had shown that a loss of confidence could make consumers reluctant to spend, and business reluctant to hire workers and invest in new plant and equipment. Keynes argued that governments could provide that helping hand and revive the economy by spending money. It almost didn't matter what the government did, even employing workers to bury five-pound notes and dig them up again would be useful. Those workers would spend their wages on goods and services, thereby helping businesses to recover so they could hire more workers in a snowball or 'multiplier' effect.

Keynes's ideas were only patchily adopted before the Second World War,[5] but economists noticed that the process of rearmament – which involved the government spending money – created jobs and revived activity. There was a much greater willingness to adopt Keynes's ideas after the war, not least because of a desire to avoid the mistakes of the 1930s. Keynes himself died in 1946. Whether he would have approved of all that was subsequently done in his name is an interesting question. But politicians drew the lesson that the economy could be driven like a car, with the government stepping on the brake (higher taxes and spending cuts) when growth was too fast and on the accelerator (tax cuts and spending rises) when it was too slow.

In the immediate aftermath of the Second World War politicians seemed to do a pretty good job of this micromanagement. Europe achieved an impressive run of economic growth as it rebuilt its shattered infrastructure, with the help of the far-sighted Marshall Aid plan, devised by the US administration as a way of warding off the threat of communism and of securing markets for American exporters. The US and Western Europe faced relatively little competition in world markets, since Eastern Europe, Russia and China were trapped in communism, and India had an inward-looking approach and a long way to catch up, given how it had remained a largely agrarian economy under British rule. That made it possible for Europe to afford its generous welfare state – the vast array of benefits that were demanded by populations after the depression of the 1930s.

But the later twentieth century saw the emergence of two significant threats to Western economic growth. First, as the Japanese economy picked up steam in the 1960s and 1970s, it made huge inroads into the market share of European (and American) companies. There was as much fear about Japanese economic domination as there is about Chinese domination today. Second, European economies had benefited during the post-war years from a very low cost of energy. In 1955 a barrel of Saudi crude oil cost $1.93; by 1971 the cost had risen to just $2.18, despite inflation elsewhere. This enabled the developed world to switch from coal to oil. In 1950 coal and coke accounted for 83% of Europe's fuel consumption, oil for just 8.5%. By 1970 oil accounted for 60% and coke and coal just 29%. When oil prices accordingly shot up in the 1970s, Europe's economy began to falter, experiencing both high unemployment and inflation, or 'stagflation' as it became known. The continent was beset by strikes, civil unrest and terrorist attacks. The term 'eurosclerosis' first came into being.

The US was also hit by economic problems in the 1970s. Inflation had started to rise in the late 1960s under President Lyndon Johnson, who combined ambitious and expensive social programmes at home with a costly war in Vietnam. Advanced economies were discovering that there were limits to their ability to keep growing. Economic bottlenecks would appear: industries would compete to hire workers or to secure supplies, in the process forcing up wages and prices. Governments, reluctant to let economies slip into recession, injected demand into the economy by cutting taxes or increasing spending: this extra buying power increased the competition for scarce resources and added to inflationary pressures.

Although a Republican president, Richard Nixon essentially continued the economic policies of Johnson, a Democrat. In 1971 Nixon allowed the dollar to float free on the foreign exchange markets – in other words to let the market determine its price. Meanwhile the Arab oil embargo of 1973, which saw crude prices quadruple, caused severe problems in the US as well as Europe.

It was at this point that belief in Keynesianism started to break down. A dogged band of conservatives had held out against it all along, resenting the post-war model of increased government involvement in the economy and the high taxes that had accompanied it. They argued that government intervention distorted the free market. Bureaucrats cannot anticipate what consumers will demand; no civil servant would come up with an iPad. If governments order goods, on the basis of out-of-date and imperfect information, they will end up with surpluses of unwanted goods and shortages of products that people want (as happened under communism). In the private sector, competition means that companies offering bad products go out of business, but that doesn't happen to governments. Furthermore, high taxes destroy incentives; why build a business if the government will take all your gains for itself? The highest British tax rates in the 1970s were 98%, leading many people to head overseas. Conservatives further argued that the effect of fiscal stimulus was illusory – when the government borrowed in the debt markets, it 'crowded out' private capital. Other things being equal, investors would prefer to lend money to a government than risk lending it to a company; as a result, high rates of government borrowing made it more expensive and more difficult for businesses to expand. Furthermore, high deficits today must mean higher taxes tomorrow. Consumers would see through the ruse and adjust their behaviour accordingly – saving, rather than spending, money to prepare for those subsequent tax increases.

The economic problems of the mid-1970s were seen as proof of the revisionists' case, and gave them a willing audience among political leaders. One such was Jim Callaghan, the British Labour prime minister who (in a speech written by his son-in-law, the economist Peter Jay) told a party conference in 1976:

> We used to think that you could spend your way out of a recession and increase employment by cutting taxes and boosting government spending. I tell you in all candour that that option no longer exists, and in so far as it ever did exist, it only worked on each occasion since the war by injecting a bigger dose of inflation into the economy, followed by a higher level of unemployment as the next step.

A change in fiscal policy turned out to be inevitable in Britain's case; in the face of a soaring deficit, high inflation and a fall in the pound, the country was forced to turn to the International Monetary Fund for a loan that year. An IMF team arrived in London and oversaw attempts to reduce the budget deficit.

In America too the tide was turning against higher government spending, and the taxes needed to pay for it. The trigger came in California, the state that has often been a trendsetter. A key part of local finance in the US is the property tax, based on home values. Between 1972 and 1977 house prices in southern California more than doubled, with taxes rising in line.[6] A local property lobbyist, Howard Jarvis, led a rebellion against the tax increase. He used the state's referendum process to launch an initiative, called Proposition 13, asking voters to approve a cut in the property tax of more than half, and to cap subsequent annual increases to 2%. It also prevented the state legislature from compensating with other taxes by requiring a two-thirds majority for tax increases. The proposition passed by two to one.

The effect was to slash the budgets of the local bodies, particularly school districts that relied on the property tax. But the state of California, which had other revenues such as income taxes, was able to bail them out; ever since, the state has been the main supplier of local (city and county) revenues. So instead of taxes being raised and spent locally, they are now decided at a higher level. Local government has become less democratic, all as the result of a popular initiative.

By the end of the 1970s it was starting to seem as if fiscal policy was a busted flush. Endless deficits had led to bigger government – but bigger government had not led in turn to higher growth. This left politicians with the need to find a mechanism for managing the economy. So they turned their attention to monetary policy.

THE MONEY POWER

The developed world feels as if it is in deep crisis today; the same was true in the 1970s. Then, as now, power seemed to be shifting to another region: today it is China, but 40 years ago it was to Japan and the oil producers of the Middle East. The 1973–4 recession, triggered by an oil shock as the Opec producers quadrupled prices in protest at Western support for Israel, was followed by the recession of the early 1980s, associated with another oil price spike that followed the fall of the shah of Iran in 1979.

Worse still, these downturns were accompanied not by falling prices, as theory suggested they should be, but fast-rising ones. If workers lose jobs, they should not be able to afford to pay higher prices; if businesses have spare capacity such as idle factories or stockpiles of unwanted goods, they should cut prices to attract sales. The first instinct of Western governments was to try to legislate the problem away by imposing controls, as they had done during the war years: businesses would be forbidden from increasing their prices by more than a set amount and the wage increases of workers would be capped. But these controls caused immense resentment among trade unionists and fuelled a wave of strikes across Europe in the 1970s. The controls were also a blunt instrument. Governments could not control prices set on international markets – oil being an obvious example. If oil prices rise, then the costs of business go up. And if businesses cannot pass those costs on to customers, some companies will have to lay off workers or even go bankrupt.

In the face of this mess, economics needed a new guru: they found one in Milton Friedman. Friedman revived an old idea, one that had existed ever since Spain's silver and gold discoveries in the sixteenth century had led to rising prices. Inflation is the result of too much money chasing too few goods. Or, as Mr Friedman put it: 'Inflation is always and everywhere a monetary phenomenon.'

In 1971 the last link between the dollar and gold was abolished and the system of fixed exchange rates broke down. The world was operating for the first time in its history with a system of 'fiat' money – in other words, money was merely what the government said it should be. Previous instances of fiat money systems had deteriorated rapidly into hyperinflation; now, the same thing seemed to be happening again. Free of the need to maintain their exchange rate pegs, governments dashed for growth; running budget deficits and allowing their banks to lend more money. Prices and income policies were a waste of time, in Friedman's view. Governments should leave control of inflation to the central bank, which would target a level of money supply growth. In a sense this 'monetary target' would replace gold as the anchor of the monetary system.

Friedman's theories would make central banks important again. Between the wars, they had been powerful institutions: as guardians of the currency, and of the nation's gold reserves, they had dictated to governments. In 1931 the Bank of England told the then Labour government that it must cut public spending to retain market confidence in sterling. In the resulting furore, the government fell and was replaced by a coalition, an episode that went down in Labour folk history as the 'bankers' ramp'. Fifteen years later Labour had its revenge when it nationalized the Bank of England.

In contrast to the interwar years, after 1945 many central banks operated as an arm of government policy (Germany's Bundesbank being a notable exception). Even Arthur Burns, head of the nominally independent US Federal Reserve, fell under the sway of President Nixon. Politicians tended to want lower interest rates rather than higher ones, particularly in the run-up to an election, since this boosts the economy (and makes voters happier). The cumulative effect was that monetary policy became too loose; interest rates were too low to reward thrift and to deter borrowers. The result was rapid expansion of lending (and thus the money supply) and high inflation.

The big shift in monetary policy came when Paul Volcker was appointed chairman of the Fed in 1979. He was far from a doctrinaire monetarist and he was often criticized by Friedman. But he did prove robustly independent of political control, pushing up interest rates to levels that had never been seen before, sending the economy into recession and sabotaging the re-election efforts of Jimmy Carter in 1980.

But the policy worked, in the sense of bringing down inflation. Oddly enough, the formal element of monetarism – setting a precise and stable target for money supply growth – proved pretty unworkable. Money comes in various forms, from the small change in your pocket to the savings in an American's money market fund. As a result, it proved very hard to define which measures a central bank should target; restrict one form of money (say credit card loans) and banks found a way to create money elsewhere. Indeed, the economist Charles Goodhart suggested a law that any economic indicator such as the money supply would misbehave as soon as it was targeted.

It seems probable that the key factor in Volcker's success in keeping down inflation was credibility. If voters could be persuaded that price rises were temporary (for example, a sudden spike in oil prices because of a Middle East conflict), then they would not demand higher wages. But since politicians always have an eye on the next election, they had very little anti-inflationary credibility. In contrast, workers and investors believed that Volcker, a technocrat with no obvious short-term political axe to grind, would stick to his task. Similarly, in Germany, the independent Bundesbank showed that it was able to deliver the strongest currency (and modest inflation) in the EU.

The long-term solution was thus to make central banks formally independent, since the bankers would be free of political pressures. New Zealand was the first to make the move in 1989, giving its central bank legal independence and an inflation target. In Britain, after the pound's exit from the Exchange Rate Mechanism in 1992, an element of transparency was introduced into the rate-setting process, with the publication of the minutes of the meetings between the chancellor of the exchequer (first Norman Lamont and then Ken Clarke) and the governor, Eddie George. In 1997 the new Labour government went much further, giving the Bank of England the independence to set rates, subject to an inflation target. The system, under which nine members of a monetary policy committee vote each month, survives to this day.

For much of the 1980s and 1990s, economic policy appeared to deliver astonishing success. Not only was inflation low but periods of economic growth lasted much longer than before, and the recessions were shallower and shorter. The era was dubbed the 'great moderation'. The Western democracies seemed to have cracked the secret of economic management once again. Alan Greenspan, the chairman of the Federal Reserve from 1987 to 2006, was given a lot of credit for this: in 2000, Republican Senator John McCain joked that, when Greenspan died, he should be propped up in a chair and allowed to continue in office.

But in fact other factors were at work beside central bank brilliance. The power of the trade unions, so influential in keeping wages high in the 1970s, was broken in a series of legal reforms, such as the outlawing of secondary picketing, and by the decline of manufacturing industry in the early 1980s. The entry of China, and eventually Eastern Europe, into the capitalist world added millions of workers to the global labour pool, exerting downward pressure on both wages and prices. The Opec nations, which had controlled the oil price in the 1970s, over-reached themselves; new sources of crude oil appeared and the price fell by around three-quarters in real terms, between the late 1970s and the late 1990s.

Demographically, the developed world benefited as the baby-boomer generation (those born between 1946 and 1964) joined the workforce; women were also working in far greater numbers than before. The emergence of the personal computer in the mid-1970s and the Internet in the mid-1990s boosted productivity – companies were now able to track their sales and did not need to tie up their capital in unsold goods; offices lost their typing pools; the development of the mobile phone in the 1980s made communication far more rapid. In the EU, the single market made it easier for companies to sell goods across the continent.

During the 1980s and 1990s Western governments were only too happy with the job that their central banks were doing. As inflation fell, so did the cost of government borrowing. As economies grew, so did tax revenues. There were plenty of eager buyers of Western government bonds. The crises of the 1970s seemed a distant memory.

THE DEBT MOUNTAIN

If the financial markets had traded a security linked to their confidence in the brilliance of central bankers,[7] it would surely have peaked in 2000. Bill Clinton's presidency ended with the US government in surplus, with inflation and bond yields low, and with the American stock market close to an all-time high. The Internet seemed to promise a whole new era of economic advance, along with a way for twenty-somethings with a bright idea to turn themselves into millionaires. But underneath this veneer of prosperity, there were some disturbing developments. Governments were not the only bodies that found it easier to borrow. There was a huge build-up of debt, among consumers and companies and most notably in the finance sector.

The contemporary dominance of finance really dates from the early 1980s. It was at this point that the relative wages of the sector took off and every other bright young graduate wanted to work for an investment bank. Banks make money by lending; in the 'great moderation', recessions were less common and borrowers were less likely to default. Banks make money by trading assets; asset prices were rising. Banks make money by advising on deals like takeovers and stock-market flotations; such markets were very active.

Crucially, profitable banks can earn higher returns, particularly for their staff, if they expand their balance sheets. If you can borrow at 5% and earn a return on that money of 10%, it makes sense to borrow as much as you can, provided you are sure those excess returns are reliable. Risk-taking paid off and banks were increasingly led by more aggressive types, such as Jimmy Cayne at Bear Stearns and Dick Fuld at Lehman Brothers, who encouraged a trading culture with eventually disastrous results as their banks collapsed in 2008.

Central banks acted as the enablers of this process. When the stock market faltered, as it did spectacularly in October 1987, central banks cut interest rates and announced their willingness to stand behind the financial system. That led to the belief in the 'Greenspan put' – the idea that central banks were underwriting the market. This belief helped fuel a whole series of bubbles in asset prices, from emerging markets in the early 1990s, through Internet stocks in the late 1990s, to houses in the last decade.

As the economist Hyman Minsky pointed out in 1992,[8] these bubbles can be self-perpetuating. Banks lend money to people to buy assets. This in turn causes asset prices to rise, making borrowers more enthusiastic and lenders feel more secure. As this process develops, it becomes more and more speculative, which the US housing market demonstrated – for example, the practice of 'condo flipping', with people buying apartments and selling them again before they were even built. And then there were 'liar loans' – people who were extended credit to buy houses although they failed to meet the lending criteria.

Unless lending is restricted in some way by the authorities, this feedback loop may be inevitable. Easy credit means that asset prices rise much faster than people's incomes. As a consequence, lending criteria must be relaxed to ensure a willing pool of buyers. And a willing pool of buyers is needed to keep prices moving higher. It all resembles a pyramid-selling scheme. Eventually, however, the 'Minsky moment' is reached when confidence evaporates or no more buyers can be found. At that point, the whole process goes into reverse: investors are less willing to buy and banks are less willing to lend. Prices fall very sharply as distressed sellers offload their unwanted assets.

The underlying philosophy of central banks, as enunciated by Alan Greenspan, was that market prices were the best guide to the true value of an asset, that any action used to try to burst bubbles – such as raising interest rates – would harm the rest of the economy, and that the best thing to do was to take action only when the bubble had finally burst. Mr Greenspan also believed that a free market was the best safeguard against excessive risk-taking: it was in the interests of creditors and shareholders to keep a close eye on the banks.

His judgement was spectacularly wrong. As it turned out, the incentives were all in favour of risk-taking. A successful trader or bank executive would become extremely rich if his gambles paid off; if they failed, he would (at worst) lose his job. The temptation was to do business that was profitable in the short term – such as providing loans to homebuyers with poor credit records – and let the long term take care of itself. Shareholders and creditors did not realize the risks that the banks were taking, some of which were hidden off their balance sheets.

In 2007 and 2008, as house prices fell, panic spread through the system. US mortgages had been packaged and repackaged into various securities and sold throughout the world. Everybody had assumed that house prices could only go up; they had not bothered to look too closely at the assets they were buying. When homeowners started to default, the prices of mortgage-related securities collapsed. Many banks had extended their balance sheets so far that even small write-downs threatened their solvency. And nobody was sure which banks were most exposed. The prudent course for any individual bank seemed, therefore, to be to avoid lending to any other banks. In aggregate the effect was to make it difficult for all banks to borrow money. Central banks stepped in to avoid the total collapse of the finance industry, and a consequent economic meltdown.

THE RETURN OF KEYNES AND THE POWER OF CENTRAL BANKS

As the authorities quickly realized, this proved to be the worst economic crisis since the 1930s. The banks are at the heart of our economy. Businesses suddenly found it difficult to get credit and world trade collapsed. US homeowners defaulted on their loans as house prices fell; the surfeit of empty properties caused prices to fall further. Construction collapsed as no more houses needed to be built. Stock markets crashed, adding to the air of panic.

In the wake of the crisis, governments returned to the policies of Keynes once more. Their deficits widened as tax revenues plunged and they added to the effect by trying to stimulate their economies with a variety of tax cuts and spending increases. One of the biggest stimulus packages was pushed through by China: it proved highly successful.

Despite their mistakes during the boom, central banks became, if anything, even more powerful in the wake of the crisis. For a start they had to play their role as 'lenders of last resort' to the financial system.[9] If no one played such a role, there remained the risk that problems at one bank could spread to the others. (When the US suffered a bank panic in 1907, the wealthy banker J. P. Morgan had to assume the role of lender of last resort on his own. It was, in part, as a response to this problem that the US established the Federal Reserve in 1913.)

As well as lending money to the commercial banks, central banks around the world slashed interest rates. The idea was to ease the strain on borrowers. In the case of the Bank of England, rates fell to 0.5%, below the 2% level for the first time since the Bank was established in 1694. And when near-zero rates proved insufficient, the banks took a further step called quantitative easing (QE). This involves the creation of new money, much of which was used to buy government bonds. (Note that the Bank doesn't actually have to print new money. It can create money with a click of a computer mouse. When it buys bonds, it simply credits the account of the seller.)

Remember that money is as much the creation of the commercial banks as it is of the state. If the banks stop lending, the money supply will not grow; if they demand repayment of their loans, the money supply will fall. The result will be a decline in prices and incomes, making it harder for consumers and businesses to buy goods and services and impossible for borrowers to service their debts.

The idea behind QE was to force down long-term yields on government bonds and to encourage investors to buy riskier assets such as shares and government bonds. If companies find it easier to raise money, they will build more factories and employ more workers. This has been a controversial policy. In September 2011 Republican leaders wrote to Ben Bernanke, head of the Federal Reserve, arguing against QE and stating:

> We have serious concerns that further intervention by the Federal Reserve could exacerbate current problems or further harm the U.S. economy. Such steps may erode the already weakened U.S. dollar or promote more borrowing by overleveraged consumers. To date, we have seen no evidence that further monetary stimulus will create jobs or provide a sustainable path towards economic recovery.[10]

Rick Perry, one of the candidates for the Republican presidential nomination, called the Fed's actions 'almost treasonous'; Mitt Romney, the eventual nominee, said that as president he would not reappoint Mr Bernanke when his term expired.

No doubt part of the reason for the Republicans' views was a fear that Federal action, by stimulating the economy, would help the re-election programme of President Obama. But they also had a philosophical worry. There is a long and ignoble tradition of bankrupt governments manufacturing money to fund their spending – stretching as far back as the Roman Empire. From AD 70 to 270, emperors, short of silver to pay their troops, melted down the coins and adulterated them with copper and lead. The silver content of Roman coins fell from 100% to 4% over two centuries. More recent examples include the Confederate government in the American Civil War, which printed money to pay its bills and its troops, and the German government during the Weimar Republic. The result in each case was hyperinflation: eventually the money becomes worthless.

Could the same happen this time around? The policy could be taken too far, but at the time of writing there has been no sign of rapid consumer inflation. As already noted, central banks are not the only source of money creation: normally the commercial banks play the largest role. And the banks are trying to retrench, so money creation in the form of QE may simply be offsetting money destruction (less lending) by the commercial banks.

There are plenty of risks, however. Monetary policy could be like ketchup: you can shake and shake the bottle with nothing happening for ages, and then it all goes splat. Another problem is that the central banks are supposed, in theory, to get rid of all these bonds, either by selling them or by not reinvesting when the bonds mature. (In practice, there is not much difference between the two approaches; the private sector will have to buy a lot more bonds.)

Take the Bank of England, for example, which as of late 2012 owned £375 billion of government bonds, about a third of the market. It could plan to run that pile down over five years. That means finding new buyers to the tune of £75 billion a year. But that is only part of the problem. The Bank has bought the equivalent of almost three years of bond issuance, or three years' worth of deficits. When the policy is reversed, the private sector will have to absorb the £375 billion of existing debt plus whatever new debt is issued over that five-year period. With so many bonds to buy, investors will demand a higher return; the effect could drive up the cost of government borrowing sharply. But will the economy (or government finances) be strong enough to absorb the strain?

The option of inflating away your debts, or devaluing them, is always open to a government that can borrow in its own currency. In real terms, such a strategy represents a partial default: creditors will be unable to purchase the same amount of goods when their capital is repaid. But governments may not be able to get away with it for ever. As their strategy becomes clear, smart creditors will refuse to lend at all – or will charge a much higher interest rate to compensate them for the inflation risk.

A GAME OF OLD MAID

One way of thinking about the debt crisis is like the card game of Old Maid, in which the object is to offload the Queen of Spades on to another player. When US homeowners could not pay their debts, the bad debts landed on the banks. And when the banks could not pay their debts, they were rescued by the government. But what happens when a government cannot pay?

Government debt is often described as risk-free, but as Carmen Reinhart and Kenneth Rogoff showed in their excellent book, *This Time is Different*,[11] historians would regard the notion as very odd. Monarchs have been defaulting on their debt since ancient times and modern states have done the same: Latin America had waves of default in the 1890s, 1930s and 1980s, with Argentina having another go in 2002. It is very difficult for a foreign lender to safeguard its rights in such situations; domestic courts are unlikely to rule against their own governments and international courts cannot enforce their rulings. But in the aftermath of such defaults, creditors will usually be unwilling to lend more money – or at the very least, will only lend money at a higher rate of interest.

The problem is particularly acute if a government has borrowed in another nation's currency. This has been quite obvious in the euro zone, where small nations like Greece have been denied the options of higher inflation (or devaluing their currency) as a way of reducing their debt burdens. Their governments cannot create euros at will, just as those developing nations that have borrowed in dollars cannot suddenly print greenbacks. Such countries have to turn to official lenders – other governments and the International Monetary Fund. But those bodies set conditions for their loans – they demand that governments reduce their budget deficits and embrace reforms. This will involve making cuts to public services and increasing taxes. Such austerity is unpopular.

If a government rejects the conditions of bodies like the IMF and cannot borrow from the markets, it will have to default on its debts. But having done that, how will the government finance its existing spending? In the absence of private sector lending, it will have to balance its books immediately – in other words, enact the very austerity measures it is attempting to resist. Indeed, the pain may be even worse. Official creditors such as the IMF usually demand that the country moves towards a balanced budget over several years; in the case of default, the adjustment happens immediately.

Even when countries have borrowed in their own currency, creditors will demand higher interest rates from countries with a high existing level of debt, or with a very high budget deficit. The reason is simple prudence. Let us say a mutual fund has £100 million that it wants to invest in government bonds. It will not want to put all, or even most, of that fund in the bonds issued by a single government. It will want to spread its risk. A highly indebted government will have to offer higher interest rates to tempt investors to keep buying its bonds; in other words, the cost of borrowing will rise.

The beauty of QE, as far as governments are concerned, is that central banks have almost unlimited ability to buy bonds and their purchases keep down the cost of borrowing. But this of course makes the option almost too tempting. As the investment strategist Dylan Grice argues, why would a government run the political risk of raising $1 billion from its taxpayers when it can persuade a friendly central bank to create the money instead? In theory, this seems like a cost-free $1 billion, but the cost must show up somewhere. For example, if it spends the $1 billion on building an airport, the company that builds the airport (and its workers) will have more money; they will spend the money or use it to buy houses, driving up prices for everyone else. In effect, Grice believes, money creation is an underhand way of re-distributing wealth.

It is worth pausing to reflect on just how much central banks have done in the last five years. With the best of intentions, they have pur-sued a radical and as yet unproven monetary policy. By cutting interest rates so dramatically, they have penalized savers and rewarded bor-rowers. This policy has increased the burden on pensioners and pension funds: it now takes a much larger capital sum to buy a given retire-ment income. All this has been done without any real democratic mandate. Yes, governments could instruct their central bank to change policy or fire the central bank governor. But think about it. What gov-ernment would not want a central bank to be a willing buyer of its debt? Voters cannot oust their central bank governors; nor does mon-etary policy feature much in election campaigns. Even if the policy were the best thing for the economy in the long run, this development should give democrats pause.

THE ULTIMATE CONSTRAINT

Voters in the developed world may have been fed the idea that there is no real limit to their nation's spending power. They may feel that extra money can be found by taxing the rich, cutting foreign aid, or whatever. They may believe that their governments can and should create jobs for those who need them.

Wealth is generated by all parts of society, public sector as well as private. In a modern economy, a nation's most critical resource is probably its human capital: the ingenuity and intellect of its citizens. Teachers are creating the human capital of the future. Doctors and nurses enable that human capital to stay healthy; policemen and sol-diers protect that capital. Yet no nation is self-sufficient. Countries must import goods from elsewhere – food, oil, metals or goods that are simply made more effectively or cheaply overseas (consumer elec-tronics, for example). How does a nation afford these imports? By exporting goods and services of its own. And those exports come, almost exclusively, from the private sector.

However, in Europe more than the United States, profit is sometimes regarded as a dirty word. Businessmen are rarely portrayed on television, in the cinema or in novels in a positive light. Part of the reason for this negative attitude to business may be down to education. A study of French high-school economics textbooks by the Institute of Economic and Fiscal Research found that, out of 400 pages, only a dozen were devoted to companies, and none to entrepreneurs.[12]

If our producers are inefficient, or overtaxed, or over-regulated, they will not be able to sell as much – and in the long run that means consumers will be able to buy less, as the history of the Soviet Union amply demonstrated. One does not need to believe in the elitist philosophy of Ayn Rand[13] to understand that businesses need to be valued by their society. It is easy to develop an anti-materialist view of the world; it is harder to manage without all the goods that world provides.

If a country does not export enough, it ends up with a trade deficit. When countries run persistent trade deficits – as has been the case in America, Britain and parts of southern Europe for at least 25 years now – they end up borrowing more and more money from overseas. These debts need not be in the form of government bonds. Banks and companies could also be borrowing from abroad. The challenge for such nations is to retain the confidence of those international investors, so they keep rolling over their loans and are willing to extend further credit if the deficit continues. There is a point at which foreigners do not want to own any more of another country's bonds – which after all are just pieces of paper in a currency the foreigners cannot control. If the debtor is determined to resist, it is very hard for a foreign creditor to enforce its claims in the debtor country's courts.

For long periods, these constraints may not seem to apply. In early 2013 the US was still able to borrow at less than 2% on its 10-year bonds, even though its government debt was almost $16 trillion. America is also the world's largest economy, a democracy with a strong legal system and a long record of repaying its debts. Any investor who buys its Treasury bonds knows that they will be able to sell them at a moment's notice (in the jargon, the market is highly liquid). In addition, investors who decided to boycott American debt would have to buy something else instead. But Europe is wracked by problems, Britain has a huge debt problem, and China restricts the ability of foreigners to invest. America looks the least bad option. Even so, one has to imagine that there is some point at which America might exhaust the appetite of its creditors.

Is it right to assume that a government can always raise more taxes, or print more money, to meet its debts? There is a limit to the amount of tax a government can raise from an economy, although it is impossible to know in advance what that limit will be.[14] At some stage, taxes will be high enough to destroy all enterprise; at some stage, citizens will take themselves (or their capital) elsewhere. And, as we have seen in Weimar Germany or Zimbabwe, there is a limit to the amount of money a government can create without that money ceasing to be acceptable as currency.

It is at this stage that Mr Parris's dictum that democracy must cope with reality holds true. Economists don't like it when writers or politicians compare a nation with a household: they sneered at Margaret Thatcher's comparison between fiscal policy and a housewife balancing her budget. But analogies are still useful, so let us compare a nation with a loss-making business. Would it help such a business if all the managers and employees voted that sales should increase, or voted that the local bank should lend them money? Clearly not. A simple way of describing the problem is that voters cannot vote themselves instant prosperity. They can only do so over the long run, if they create a society with certain basic conditions: the rule of law, property rights and a functioning free market.

When the underlying growth of an economy is strong, it almost doesn't matter what voters, or their representatives, decide: most economic models will work. Few would argue that the Chinese model is perfect, given that it includes lots of state planning, banks that make dubious loans based on political criteria, and an over-emphasis on investment rather than consumption. But the Chinese economy was in such a poor state when reform started in 1979, and the productivity gains from moving peasants from inefficient agriculture into industry are so huge, that the country grows at 8–10% a year regardless.

The developed world does not have the same motors of growth as China or much of Asia. Western Europe's workforce had shifted out of agriculture by the 1970s. Economic growth comes from three sources – more capital, more workers and 'productivity' – making that capital and those workers more efficient. More capital is the result of accumulated savings. China has a high savings rate and is building new roads, power plants and factories. In the West, by comparison, we haven't saved a lot and it is hard to see where a wave of new investment will come from. Europe's demography is also deteriorating. The baby boomers are retiring and there are not enough children to replace them in the workforce. By 2035 the working-age populations of Germany, Finland, Austria and Italy will all have fallen by more than 10 percentage points as a proportion of the total.[15]

All the burden of economic growth is thus falling on productivity. But even here the trend has been deteriorating. In the 1970s European productivity gains averaged 2.5% a year, a faster rate than the US. In the first decade of the twenty-first century, the gains had slowed to a little more than 1% a year.[16] Now, it may well be that technology will come to the rescue. Japan, for example, has had a dismal overall growth record over the last 20 years, but its technological expertise has helped it perform well in growth per capita. The trouble is that this growth has not been sufficient to dent Japan's debt mountain. Without rapid growth, it is much more difficult to erode debt.

Indeed, taking on debt is a sign of confidence – on the part of both the lender and the borrower – that the latter's income will grow. Which of us would want to take on a lot of debt if we knew we were facing a wage cut, or unemployment or retirement? Would a bank want to lend its money in such circumstances?

It is very hard to say what the maximum level of debt in an economy should be. But we can appreciate there must be some level which is too high, and that Iceland and Ireland probably surpassed it in the early 2000s; their banks became so big that, when they failed, the government was not big enough to save them. We can also say that it doesn't matter how the debt is divided up – whether it is the governments, the banks or the consumers who are the borrowers. The recent crisis showed that, when push comes to shove, it will all end up on the government's books.

The 1945–74 economic model was built on the use of fiscal policy to maintain growth. The 1982–2007 economic model was built on monetary policy and debt-fuelled growth. The central banks may have staved off complete disaster since 2007 by taking monetary policy in new directions. But that monetary policy is only supposed to be a temporary expedient until growth returns. What happens if it does not and governments run out of ways to reward the electorate? How, in short, does democracy combine with austerity?

As Stephen King notes in his book *When the Money Runs Out*,[17] growth in the developed world during the first decade of the twenty-first century was just 1.5%, the weakest in any period since the Second World War. 'Without reasonable growth, we cannot meet the entitlements we created for ourselves during the years of plenty,' he notes, adding that 'Put simply, our societies are not geared for a world of very low growth. Our attachment to the enlightenment idea of ongoing progress – a reflection of persistent post-war economic success – has left us with little knowledge or understanding of worlds in which rising prosperity is no longer guaranteed.'

An academic paper[18] that looked at the history of Europe over the last century found that austerity led to more political unrest. The authors came up with a neat way of assessing the problem: they counted the numbers of demonstrations, riots, strikes and attempted assassinations in each country in every year. This score, which they dubbed CHAOS, was then compared with the change in government expenditure as a proportion of GDP. The academics found that, in years when expenditure was increasing, the average CHAOS score was 1.4 events per year. But when expenditure cuts were more than 1% of GDP, the CHAOS score jumped to 1.8, and if cuts reached 5% of GDP, the average number of events was 3.

This effect is hardly surprising. Most government spending is used to pay wages or benefits to citizens. If spending falls, then significant numbers of people will lose their jobs, have lower wages or receive reduced benefits. They will naturally be aggrieved. Worse still, government spending is most likely to be cut when the economy is in, or close to, recession, since that is when large deficits tend to occur. At such times, it will be extremely difficult for workers to find new jobs. In addition, years of working on the public payroll, or indeed being on benefits, may have left people ill-suited to alternative employment. An employer at, say, an insurance company or a software developer may not take the risk on a worker who has spent 30 years as a nurse or a teacher.

Workers may have planned their lives on the basis of, say, retiring from teaching at 60, or on getting by on disability benefit because of a chronic condition. They will resent having to change their plans. Indeed, in the US, these social benefits are known as entitlements precisely because people feel they have earned them by making contributions.[19]

For all these reasons, we are likely to see more strikes and demonstrations when benefits are cut (as in Greece) and, at the extreme, riots and assassinations. Of course, this does not mean governments should never impose austerity. But it does indicate why the current crisis could be a threat to the democratic system.

That is because the mainstream parties, for all their faults, are usually 'responsible', believing that countries should repay their debts, that market discipline is important, and that very high inflation is economically damaging. They will react to a crisis by imposing austerity, slowly at first, but more rapidly if market confidence deteriorates. The centre-left will behave in a similar fashion to the centre-right. The public, however, may become sick of the lot of them.

5

The Dead Weights of Democracy

*The revenue creates pensioners, and the pensioners urge for
more revenue. The people grow less steady, spirited and virtuous, the seekers more numerous and corrupt, and every day
increases the circles of their dependants and expectants.*

John Adams, second US President,
quoted in *The Idea of a Party System* (1970)
by Richard Hofstadter

The fiscal and monetary policies described in the last chapter are quite
blunt tools for economic management. They affect the overall level of
demand in the economy. But modern governments want to do much
more than this: they want to discourage some activities and encourage
others, while helping some people and paying for this help by charging
others. The effect of this kind of intervention is to make the government
by far the most powerful agent in the economy. And such intervention
has inevitable consequences. Businesses, special interests and workers'
groups all lobby the government because, as the notorious American
bank robber Willie Sutton said of banks, 'that's where the money is'.
Autocracies suffer from the power of special interests as well. But
democracies have failed to curb their power. And now that economies
are struggling to grow, special interests may obstruct much-needed
economic reform.

After the Second World War, governments promised citizens generous welfare benefits, which they paid for with high taxes. But the high
tax regime was dismantled in the 1980s, partly through a conscious
political decision and in part because high taxes are harder to sustain
in a globalized world in which capital and skilled labour are very

mobile. For a while, in the late 1990s, the circle seemed to be squared because the technology boom temporarily boosted tax revenues.

The gap in public finances re-emerged in the current millennium and was covered by government borrowing. But in the wake of the financial crisis deficits exploded, leaving governments, in the absence of a strong rebound in growth, with the tricky choice of cutting spending or raising taxes in a competitive world. These decisions were made all the more difficult by a tax code, benefits system and raft of business subsidies that had distorted the economy – the result of years of lobbying by special interest groups. It seems unlikely that governments can afford social safety nets for the poor, middle-class benefits and tax breaks for special interests, without imposing impractically high tax rates – something will have to give.

THE LOBBY

How has the economy become so distorted? As the informer Deep Throat told the reporters in the film *All the President's Men*, the motto is 'Follow the Money.' There is a big incentive for a lobby group such as farmers or steel producers to get a subsidy, or special tax break, from the government. Each of its members will get a sizeable benefit. The cost, though, will be spread among millions of taxpayers, so to them it will appear quite small. Since there are costs involved in forming an organization, it will be worthwhile for small groups to form a lobby, but not for large groups to do so.

The social scientist Mancur Olson proposed a rule to describe this principle: 'The larger the number of individuals or firms that would benefit from a collective good, the smaller the share of the gains from action in the group interest that will accrue to the individual or firm that undertakes the action.'[1] It is easy to find clubs of goods producers or service providers (the British Bankers' Association, for example), but most taxpayers will not join a taxpayers' association, while the unemployed do not band together to form a jobless pressure group.

In part, this is a question of effort. A lobby group may require its members to pay subscriptions, to attend meetings, contact their elected representatives or demonstrate. This is particularly the case for consumer groups who end up paying for a subsidy. Say that a cartel of two bread producers receives a tax break of £120 million a year; that is worth £60 million apiece. But the cost to 60 million Britons is just £2 a year, or 4p a week. Who will get off from the sofa to campaign for that? The collective cost to society of all these subsidies might be great; taxes would be higher than they would otherwise be and resources are diverted away from businesses that do not need a subsidy.

It is an example of a 'free rider' problem. Suppose you live, along with four other households, at the end of a dirt track that would cost £10,000 to pave over. If you undertake the work, all the others will benefit without paying. In the absence of universal agreement, no one stumps up the cash and the road stays unpaved. Similarly, individual consumers or taxpayers might feel it is not worth lobbying against subsidies or tax breaks for others. But if most people applied that reasoning, very little consumer lobbying would be done.

Mr Olson proposes that special interest groups reduce the efficiency and aggregate income of the societies in which they operate and make political life more divisive. In addition, they slow down a society's capacity to adopt new technologies and to reallocate resources, thereby reducing the potential for economic growth. Finally, their actions lead to more regulation and bigger government.

This is quite a charge sheet. Mr Olson was writing in the wake of the 1970s, a period in which the glorious post-war growth record of the developed world had appeared to stutter. His book came out in 1982, a year which would later be seen as the start of the 'great moderation', a long period of steady growth and low inflation, as the personal computer ushered in a new period of technological change, and as the Thatcher/Reagan efforts to reduce the size of the state were getting under way.

Nevertheless, a decade later the columnist Jonathan Rauch was still able to describe a process known as demosclerosis,[2] in which government programmes create new constituencies (workers on the government payroll, recipients of government benefits) which in turn create lobbies to ensure they stay in place. Using similar logic to Mr Olson, Rauch declared that what united these bodies was the remorseless pursuit of their self-interest: 'The calculus of distributive warfare implies that interest group activity can, in principle, drive a society to complete destitution and then keep right on going.'

How does this disastrous process work? Economies develop through what Joseph Schumpeter described as 'creative destruction', in which old methods of work are replaced by new, more efficient, systems. In macroeconomic terms, this means that capital and labour are freed from the old inefficient tasks and transferred to the new operations. In human terms, however, this means that businesses go bust and workers lose their jobs. This causes hardship and unhappiness and is naturally resisted and resented.

But it has to happen. Suppose that in 1900 horse-and-cart manufacturers had insisted on a high tax on the new-fangled motor car, or that domestic servants had unionized and declared that it was impossible for them to be made redundant. Would we still be riding in buggies and employing footmen? Of course not. Eventually our societies would have been so poor that we could afford to keep neither horses nor footmen. Even slowing the process of change would have retarded the growth of new businesses and reduced national wealth.

Producers may not be able to prevent new products from being invented or developed, but they may be able to maintain their competitive position by persuading governments to give them subsidies. A classic example relates to wool, which the US Army decreed was vitally important for military uniforms. A subsidy for wool and mohair – the yarn made from the coat of an Angora goat – was duly granted in 1954. While wool was dropped from the Pentagon's requirements in 1960 in favour of lighter materials, the subsidy stayed in place. By 1992 it was costing $191 million a year and although it was repealed in 1995, the US still kept duties on wool imports in place.[3]

The American electoral system also seems to help subsidies to flourish. The first date in the calendar for the Presidential elections is the Iowa caucuses, a series of town hall meetings in which voters express their opinion directly (most states hold primaries in which electors simply fill in a ballot sheet). These were generally seen as unimportant until 1976, when Jimmy Carter's success in the state helped propel him to the Presidency. Iowa is a rural state with a small population of 3 million (less than half that of New York City), but Presidential candidates who fail to make the grade in the caucuses are often forced to drop out of the race. Unsurprisingly, this encourages candidates to pander to the caucuses, which in Iowa involves pursuing policies that encourage the production of ethanol, a corn-based fuel. The US could import ethanol from Brazil, where it can be produced more cheaply – but that would not suit American farmers.

The ethanol subsidy was phased out in 2011, which might seem an encouraging sign that the power of the lobby can be defeated. But as so often happens, the ethanol industry found a new way to get government support. As the conservative thinktank the American Enterprise Institute (AEI) noted, Congress had already passed the renewable fuel standard (RFS), which mandates that 37% of the corn crop be converted to fuel and blended with gasoline. The AEI's Aaron Smith remarked that 'Removing the tax credit but keeping the RFS is like scraping a little frosting from the ethanol-boondoggle cake.'[4] In other words, Iowa farners were still getting a lot of help from the government.

Another crucial state is Florida, which helped decide the closely fought 2000 Presidential election. George W. Bush won the state by just over 500 votes, after a tortuous process involving the interpretation of 'hanging chads' and the intervention of the Supreme Court. In a state that marginal, an industry lobby has a lot of power since candidates will be desperate to win their favour (and their funding). That has been good news for Florida sugar farmers, who have long enjoyed a subsidy. As the Cato Institute, another right-wing thinktank, argued in 2012,[5] the cost to consumers of government sugar policies was $1.9 billion a year. Around 42% of all sugar subsidies went to just 1% of sugar growers. In June 2012 an attempt to phase out the subsidy failed in the Senate by 50 votes to 46. One of those voting with the sugar farmers was Marco Rubio, a rising Republican star and Tea Party favourite. Contrary to the Tea Party's anti-government-spending stance, Rubio found that this was one spending item he did not want to eliminate.

Subsidies and special breaks are not always confined to producer groups. The mortgage interest subsidy is one of the most expensive tax breaks in the American system, worth more than $100 billion a year and double the budget of the housing department.[6] It was put in place to encourage home ownership. But it doesn't make much sense in economic terms. For a start, it favours owning, compared with renting. Yet people who rent homes find it easy to move more quickly than those who own houses; in this way, they are a more flexible labour force. Second, the mortgage deduction is a much bigger benefit for wealthy homeowners than for poor ones, and is thus a regressive part of the tax system. To the extent that the subsidy makes it easier for homeowners to afford a bigger mortgage, house prices are pushed up, making it harder for young people to buy their first home.

But once a mortgage deduction is in place, it is hard to get rid of it.[7] Immediate abolition would cause a sharp increase in the costs of homeowners, some of whom might not be able to afford them. House prices would probably fall, causing some people to fall into negative equity (owing more than the value of their home). All this creates a powerful lobby behind the tax break, since along with home-owners, banks, real estate agents and house-builders will all argue for its retention.

It is not just groups seeking subsidies that need to lobby government. If group A lobbies to change the law, then group B may need to lobby to resist the move. Such polarization over an issue simply causes industry bodies to proliferate. Mr Rauch noted that membership of the American Association of Association Executives rose sixfold between 1970 and 1990. As of late 2012, the group claimed it represented 21,000 executives and industry partners from 10,000 organizations.[8]

Is the Tea Party movement a pressure group for the taxpaying majority, and thus a refutation of Olson's rule that those who bear the cost of subsidies do not band together? This campaign for smaller government sprang up in response to the bailout efforts that followed the financial crisis of 2007 and 2008. However, it is not clear whether Tea Party members are against government spending per se, or whether they are against two bits of legislation in particular: the bank bailout and President Obama's health care plan which made it compulsory to buy health insurance. Many of the group's supporters are benefit recipients; one placard at a Tea Party demonstration famously read 'Government hands off our Medicare'.[9] And one of the support groups for the Tea Party, the Americans for Prosperity Foundation, is funded by the billionaire Koch brothers, who vehemently oppose environmental regulations because of the costs they impose on their businesses.[10] In other words, the Tea Party draws part of its funding from a special interest group.

These days, global companies don't only have the option of lobbying to keep their tax bills down: they can also take advantage of the different regimes (and tax rates) that apply in different countries. One standard tactic used by hedge-fund managers is to site the holding company in a location where no tax is charged, such as the Cayman Islands in the western Caribbean. Another approach is to exploit the fact that different subsidiaries of companies transact with each other, and have the operation in a low-tax country charge a high price for a service provided to a business in a high-tax country. The result is that the operation in the low-tax country records a profit and the operation in the high-tax country records a loss. The overall tax bill of the company is therefore reduced.

This system of transfer pricing is controversial. In 2012 Starbucks, Amazon and Google were criticized by the UK Parliament for the low taxes they paid despite their apparently successful operations in Britain. Starbucks paid just £8.6 million in tax between 1998 and 2012, despite running up £3 billion in sales and having a 31% share of the coffee shop market; the key factor was a 6% royalty paid by the UK operation to its Netherlands unit.[11] Starbucks buckled under the glare of publicity and agreed to pay the UK government £20 million in taxes. But the tactics it had been using were perfectly legal and are widespread in a world where countries compete to attract corporate investment.

Countries cannot afford to get too aggressive towards the corporate sector, for they need companies to employ workers. Corporations contribute tax revenue of 2–4% of GDP in most countries;[12] Ireland, with its very low tax rate, raises more as a proportion of GDP than France, with its very high rate. It is also worth remembering that taxes on profits may simply be passed on to customers in the form of higher prices, or to workers in the form of lower wages.

Some might feel the only way to reduce the lobbying power of business is to bring more of it under public control. But this would not avoid the problem of special interests. The record of nationalized industries in Western Europe is not particularly encouraging. When the Labour Party took industries such as coal mining and steel into public ownership after the Second World War, the idea was to manage those industries for 'the people' rather than for private profit. But what did it mean by 'the people'? Customers? Their priority might be a cheap and reliable source of coal or steel. And that might require more efficient production: replacing workers with machinery, for example. But the Labour Party, with its close ties to the trade unions, hardly found that an attractive proposition. One reason why the coal and steel industries had been nationalized in the first place was that both had been the subject of bitter disputes between workers and owners over pressures to increase mechanization, which would have resulted in cuts to the workforce.

Someone had to manage the nationalized industries, of course. Inevitably, the answer was civil servants – 'bureaucrats' is the more pejorative term – who were not by nature inclined to be entrepreneurial. Their natural priority was to avoid troublesome strikes and keep the coal and steel flowing. They did not have to worry about domestic competition (international competition was another matter, but it took time to appear). And their judgements were subject to government approval. New steel plants should be opened, not at the best site possible, but in the regions where unemployment was highest. Investment plans were subject to change, in any case: governments were quick to cut capital spending when they faced budgetary difficulties, leading to a general decline in their efficiency and leaving nationalized industries vulnerable to foreign competition.

Like the examples we have seen elsewhere in the book, the nationalized industries were a classic case of 'insider capture', where a business is run on behalf of its employees rather than its customers. This can happen in the private sector too; it helps explain the massive rise in executive pay detailed in Chapter 10. But the difference between the public and private sectors is competition and consumer choice. We have all had terrible service in shops and restaurants and vowed never to go back again: such businesses risk bankruptcy if they do not offer a better service. But a nationalized industry can almost ignore its customers as it does not have to fear going out of business. Before British Telecom was privatized, for example, customers had to wait three months for a telephone line to be installed.[13]

THE WELFARE STATE

Much of a government's budget is spent on what are called 'transfer payments' – money taken from one group of voters and given to another. The trouble with these payments is that voters become accustomed to them, and resent it when they are taken away. And taxpayers resent paying just as much. That creates a natural temptation for governments to finance the payments with borrowed money.

Many people are unaware of where government money goes. Around a third of all UK spending goes on welfare and pensions, and almost another third on health and education. Defence and interest payments make up almost another tenth.[14] In the US, around 45% of the budget goes on pensions, health and welfare, and another 30% or so goes on education and defence.[15] In the US, even defence spending is hard to reduce because towns that have a military base tend to rely on the spending it generates.

'Growing transfer programmes financed by increasing public debt has proven to be a powerful combination,' argues Christopher DeMuth of the Hudson Policy Institute.[16] This combination, he continues, 'has undermined democratic accountability, making our political representatives at once more beholden to interest groups and less responsible for making judgements for the public at large on competing claims for public resources'.

At first sight, the rise of the modern welfare state seems to exemplify one of the early fears of the ruling elite about democracy: that the poor majority would vote to tax away the property of the wealthy. Writing in the 1830s, de Tocqueville thought he could detect this tendency in the fledgling American state:

> As the great majority of those who create the laws are possessed of no property upon which taxes can be imposed, all the money which is spent for the community appears to be spent for their advantage. The government of the democracy is the only one under which the power which lays on taxes escapes the payment of them.[17]

Oddly enough Sweden, often seen as the exemplar of the social democratic model, has shown the limits of this process. At its peak, after a swathe of social programmes were introduced in the 1970s and 1980s, Swedish government spending was 67.2% of GDP. But this growth in spending was accompanied by a decline in the country's economic performance; over the same two decades, Sweden fell from having the fourth highest GDP per capita in the world to seventeenth. A financial crisis in the early 1990s brought in a centre-right government, which pushed through a programme of reforms, and the process was repeated after 2006.

Even under the Social Democrats, Sweden had made great efforts to keep its budget under control: it ran surpluses between 2004 and 2008 and now has a debt-to-GDP ratio of around 30%.[18] Mr DeMuth points out that the country has managed to combine high social spending financed by high taxes, without an ever-rising debt burden. Government spending is still very high by American standards, at 51% of GDP. But Sweden has demonstrated that while government intervention can go too far, and that a nation can prosper if such intervention is scaled back, it is still possible to prosper while providing a social safety net. By late 2012, Sweden had a balanced budget, a current account surplus, low inflation and interest rates, and an unemployment rate of 7.2%, well below the European average.

Other European social democracies such as France or Italy illustrate how the public sector focuses power on itself: it employs a large number of workers, who naturally support politicians that promise to maintain public sector employment and public sector pay. Trade unions tend to have higher membership levels in the public sector and help fund political parties that protect the jobs of their members. By their nature, of course, many public services are monopolies; there is no market pressure to make businesses more efficient.

Governments also make promises to its citizens in the form of future benefits, which will eventually result in a huge budget cost. A classic example is pensions. One can promise a 25-year-old fireman, policeman or doctor a generous pension at the age of 55. But unless you account for this promise very carefully and honestly, the full cost will not start to show up for 30 years – by which time, the problem will have been inherited by another set of politicians. Unsurprisingly, politicians have not accounted for this cost properly. Meanwhile the price of providing pensions has risen very substantially as a result of improved longevity;

the average OECD[19] citizen is living four to five years longer than he or she did in 1970, an improvement that has been taken entirely in the form of longer retirement. Many public sector workers have been able to take their pension well before the state retirement age.

Pensions are paid for in two ways: from general taxation (so-called pay-as-you-go systems), and from an accumulated investment fund. In both cases they are a claim on future workers. In a pay-as-you-go scheme, the pensions are paid from future taxes. An investment fund, by contrast, acquires company shares, bonds and property: all of these will only have value in future if companies are able to pay dividends, interest and rent – and that, in turn, depends on the efforts of future workers.

The maths of pensions is complex, as it depends on a number of variables: the number of retirees relative to the number of workers; their life expectancy post-retirement; the level of pension relative to earnings; and the extent of any additional benefits such as inflation-linking or a spouse's allowance. For funded schemes, additional factors apply, such as the rate of investment return and the level of interest rates, since the pension pot is converted into an income on retirement. As anyone who has a private pension will know, the maths have deteriorated drastically since 2000. Investment returns have been poor while interest rates have dropped sharply: a given pension pot buys a much lower level of income. Meanwhile, most of us are living longer.

All this has made traditional company pension schemes – in which retirees' income is linked to their final salary – much more expensive to provide. As a result, many companies have dropped such schemes, and now only offer schemes where no level of income is promised. As far as employees are concerned, such schemes are pot luck; if fund returns are low during their working life, pensions will be low as well.

Some public sector pensions use funded schemes and so face exactly the same cost pressures as private schemes. But few public sector pensions have switched to this cheaper option. In the US, that is because the accounting rules do not force them to reveal the true cost; they can simply assume that future returns will be high. The real deficit on US state and local schemes may be as much as $4 trillion.

Pay-as-you-go schemes face a different problem. Often, such schemes are not run on an actuarial basis; what people pay in is not equal to what they get out. This is often misunderstood by workers, who believe their contributions are equivalent to the full value of their benefits. It costs around 25–30% of wages to provide a traditional final salary pension; employees tend to contribute only a small proportion of that amount.

When such schemes began, there were many more workers than pensioners: it was easy to pay benefits out of current contributions. But gradually the baby boomers are retiring and there are not enough workers to replace them: by 2050, there will only be around 1.5 French and German workers for every pensioner. Either benefits will have to be cut or taxes will have to shoot up – or, most likely, we will have to retire later.

THE BENEFIT BILL

A more insidious danger of the European social democratic model is the misallocation of resources. Ever since the Industrial Revolution, the economy has been marked by long-term shifts of workers and resources from one industry to another – initially from agricultural to the cottage textile industry, then from home-working to factories, and then in the twentieth century into huge new industries like car production or power provision. At each stage, workers have had to be reassigned to new roles; if they had not, we would all still be tilling the fields, or we would be housemaids and footmen at Downton Abbey.

Many public sector jobs are and always will be essential – doctors, teachers, policemen among them. But in other cases, jobs will become outdated or could be replaced by technology, just as we no longer wait to deal with a bank teller every Friday but get our cash from a machine. If, however, public sector workers have more job security and better pensions than private sector workers, they will be reluctant to leave their posts; if they have stronger unions, it will be harder to force them out.

Another classic deadweight effect arises from rules designed to protect employees from being fired. Again, these are introduced with the best intentions: some employers have been known arbitrarily to fire their staff. But a firm that cannot reduce its workforce becomes inflexible, finding it difficult to shift resources from unproductive to productive areas. It becomes reluctant to hire new and – especially – young staff, knowing that each hiring decision may involve a decades-long commitment. As a result, the economy becomes separated into groups: insiders secure in their jobs, and outsiders mired in joblessness. Again, this is a waste of an economy's most precious resource – labour. Another waste of labour can arise if social benefits become too generous. There will be less incentive to take low-paying jobs. This does not mean that everyone who receives a benefit is work-shy. It just means that, at the margin, someone who might work will choose not to; society will lose the output that citizen might have produced.

This raises some issues. Take Britain, where the number of workers claiming incapacity benefit (because they are too sick to work) has risen from around 400,000 in the 1970s to 2.6 million by late 2011. However, a separate survey of households asking residents to assess their own health has shown no signs of a big change in long-term sickness rates; the proportion of men with such a condition actually fell from 17.4% to 15.5% over the period 1980 to 2006, whereas the proportion of women increased only from 16.1% to 16.7%.[20]

Incapacity claimants are highly concentrated in the old industrial areas of northern England, Scotland and Wales, where lots of jobs were lost in the early 1980s. Of course, many of those workers will have been involved in heavy manual labour such as mining and steel production, and will naturally suffer more physical problems than office workers. But survey data show that around 40% of claims are for mental problems such as stress – more than twice as many as for musculoskeletal issues.[21] Being out of a job is likely to lead to more stress and depression, and make people feel even less willing to take work. Even among those claimants surveyed who would like a job, three-quarters believed employers would be unwilling to take a risk on them, given their health. And they may be right in that assumption. A long period out of work makes it harder to get hired. Whatever the explanation, some 2 million people seem permanently shut out of the labour market. The British coalition government, elected in 2010, is trying to reduce the numbers of those claiming incapacity benefit by getting them back to work. However, it is attempting to do so during a recession when even exceptionally eager workers find it difficult to get jobs. And inevitably the process will create many hard cases of genuinely incapacitated people who will be made much worse off.

Then there is the problem of universal benefits. All British pensioners get a winter fuel allowance, free bus travel and a free TV licence, even though they may be retired investment bankers.[22] The coalition government is cutting back on one area – child benefit paid to the wealthy. It seems sensible and cheaper to limit such handouts to the poor. Collecting revenue from a woman in the form of income tax, and then giving it back to her in the form of child benefit inevitably involves bureaucracy and inefficiency. The policy has survived in part because it was thought that middle-class voters would only support the welfare state if they thought they were also receiving benefits. In addition, means-testing complicates the system and can create huge marginal tax rates – for those on low wages, a small increase in pay will lead to a big loss in effective income. But as governments struggle to balance their budgets, tough decisions are having to be made.

THE RISE, PAUSE AND RISE AGAIN OF PUBLIC SPENDING

The state is a lot bigger than it was before societies became democratic. An academic study by Toke Aidt and Peter Jensen[23] found that before 1880 government spending in 10 leading countries[24] surveyed by the academics averaged just 6.8% of GDP; between 1880 and 1914 it averaged 7.7% of GDP; between 1920 and 1938, as the franchise widened substantially, it reached 14.1% of GDP. The longer-term chart (Fig. 5.1) shows that government spending continued to grow very rapidly until around 1980.

A further study[25] found that an extension of the franchise led to increased government spending in general and on infrastructure in particular. Urbanization clearly plays a key effect here, both by concentrating the population in places where they can easily organize (and demonstrate) and in requiring greater levels of infrastructure to make cities habitable. This extra spending required higher taxes, which were initially imposed during times of war. Britain first introduced an income tax in 1799 during the Napoleonic wars, and the

Figure 5.1 The rise of government spending

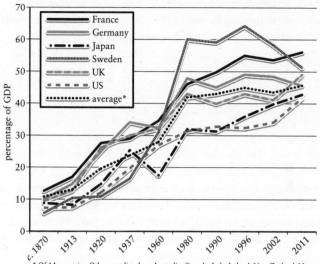

* Of 14 countries. Others not listed are Australia, Canada, Italy, Ireland, New Zealand, Norway and Switzerland.
Source: Vito Tanzi, 'The Economic Role of the State in the 21st Century' *Cato Journal*, 2005; figures for 2011 from OECD

First World War saw taxes rise sharply in combatant nations. It is harder for the rich to resist the appeal of 'we are all in this together' during wartime. For a start, they lack the ability to take their wealth elsewhere in such circumstances; in addition, military defeat might lead to the loss of all of their assets.

In the view of Douglas Carswell, a British Conservative MP, 'it was the invention of disproportionate taxation – which had to mean a tax on income – that made the growth of big government possible . . . far more significant than the extra revenue it generated, a graduated income tax has enabled the cost of more government to be raised without provoking a backlash'.[26] Mr Carswell is certainly right that a big shift in taxation did occur over the course of the twentieth century, as the burden of revenue-raising moved from taxes on consumption (such as tariffs and duties on goods like alcohol) to taxes on income. The Aidt/Jensen study found that 'the share of direct taxes (including the personal income tax) is positively affected by the franchise extension' and that 'the gradual relaxation of income and wealth restrictions on the right to vote contributed to growth in total government spending and taxation'.

Aidt and Jensen argue that a shift towards income taxes was, in part, driven by a reduction in the cost of collection:

> Improvements in the institutional capacity to collect taxes were brought about by a mixture of institutional reforms, the spread of elementary education, adaptation of modern record keeping, and economic and social progress in general. This reduced the transaction cost of collecting more complex taxes, such as the personal income tax, that required taxpayers to keep detailed records and the tax authorities to audit self-assessed tax returns.

In contrast, Mr Carswell believes that government has grown despite democracy, not because of it. He points to the fact that America achieved universal male suffrage in the 1820s and 1830s, but did not see a huge rise in government expenditure until a century later. What he fails to mention is that the popularly elected House of Representatives was balanced by a Senate which was not democratically elected until 1913. And the move to an elected Senate coincided with the election of the progressive Democrat Woodrow Wilson, the installation of the federal income tax and the creation of the Federal Reserve.

Nevertheless, the broader issue is whether the sheer size of the public sector acts as a deadweight on economic growth. This argument was made in the 1970s and early 1980s, on the last occasion when the developed world faced an economic crisis. Ronald Reagan's famous quip 'The nine most terrifying words in the English language are "I'm from the government and I'm here to help"' was so telling because it had the ring of truth. People were interacting with governments in a way that would have been unimaginable in the nineteenth century; to the extent that services were poorly provided, it was tempting to assume that the public sector was the root problem.

In the 1970s right-wing academics provided the theoretical justification for Reagan's instinct. First, as already mentioned, public service provision is often not subject to competition – there is no incentive to improve a service because customers have nowhere else to go – and a bureaucratic inertia sets in: things are done because they have always been done that way. Second, staff are motivated by a public service ethos rather than by profit. This may be all well and good, but it does mean there is little incentive to make provision more efficient. Rather than deliver the best service with the fewest people (releasing surplus workers for more productive work elsewhere), public providers become overmanned. British Telecom employed some 238,000 workers when it was state-owned; by 1999 employment had fallen to 125,000. But a whole bunch of rival mobile telecom companies had emerged; in short, labour was reassigned and the service improved.

Third, as the Austrian political theorist and economist Friedrich Hayek argued, state management of the economy requires planning. And planning is immensely difficult. The economy is too complex for any one body to determine how it will develop, what services will become redundant, what new services will be needed, and so on. That is where the market provides a useful service. Individual businesses test their products against consumer demand. If these products fail, the companies fold quickly; if they succeed, they expand. Market prices provide a fantastic signal as to which products are desired and which rejected; typewriters and fax machines are replaced by desktop computers, which in turn are replaced by laptops, which in turn give way to tablets and smartphones.

Both Reagan and Thatcher sold themselves as populist, anti-establishment figures, and their message proved highly successful. In the 1970s the establishment was broadly social democratic; Reagan and Thatcher successfully shifted politics to the right. Even after both had left office, and the likes of Clinton and Blair had replaced them, there was no sharp reversal of policy. But it is worth noting that the social protection programmes introduced in the mid-twentieth century did not disappear. The state did not shrink massively. Public sector spending was higher in real terms when Mrs Thatcher left office in 1990 than when she became prime minister in 1979.

But things changed again in the wake of the 2007–8 financial crisis. Governments adopted classic Keynesian stimulus plans in an attempt to revive their economies, while unemployment rose and pushed up benefit spending. By 2011 the average spending rate across the 14 economies in Figure 5.1 was 45.7%; France was now the outlier at 56.1%.

Isn't higher government spending a sign of a more civilized and caring society? Not according to Vito Tanzi, a former director of the fiscal affairs department of the IMF.[27] He points out that there is no correlation between public spending as a proportion of GDP and the UN's human development index, which looks at measures such as life expectancy and educational attainment. 'Much public spending benefits the middle classes broadly defined,' argues Mr Tanzi. 'At the same time, much of the burden imposed by the government in the form of taxes falls on the middle classes. Putting it differently, the government taxes the middle classes with one hand and subsidizes them with another.'[28] In the process of this 'fiscal churning', the government creates a lot of distortions and perverse incentives that adversely affect the economy. People invest heavily in property because it is tax-advantaged; companies raise debt instead of equity because interest costs are tax-deductible and dividends are not.

This is all part of a political game in which conservatives are often just as guilty as social democrats. A classic example was the prescription drug benefit added to Medicare by George W. Bush in 2003. As Bruce Bartlett, a former Treasury department economist, described it:

> According to the 2003 Medicare trustees report, spending for Medicare was projected to rise much more rapidly than the payroll tax as the baby boomers retired. Consequently, the rational thing for Congress to do would have been to find ways of cutting its costs. Instead, Republicans voted to vastly increase them – and the federal deficit – by $395 billion between 2004 and 2013.[29]

Dissident Republicans were leant on to vote for the bill. Six years later, as Bartlett points out, Republicans almost unanimously opposed President Obama's health care bill, in part because of its effect on the national debt.

CHALLENGE TO THE WESTERN MODEL

Democracies appear to have been phenomenally successful in economic terms, relative to the competition. Both communism and right-wing authoritarianism seem to crush the creativity needed to produce new products and services and the entrepreneurial initiative needed to bring them to market.

There seems to be a strong correlation between income per head and democracy – although whether that is because economic prosperity ushers in democracy or because democracy brings prosperity is harder to tell. Britain's Industrial Revolution occurred well before adult suffrage; Germany overtook Britain as a manufacturing power while ruled by the Kaisers; and since the Second World War, Asian countries like South Korea and Taiwan have seen some of their strongest economic gains occur under semi-authoritarian rule.

Now the developed democracies are facing the challenge of an alternative model in the form of China. The People's Republic has managed two decades of consistently rapid growth, without loosening the party's tight grip on political power: while Eastern European governments crumbled in 1989, the Chinese crushed student protesters in Tiananmen Square. Modern technology has occasionally challenged but not severely disrupted the party's control; dissident websites are shut down or made inaccessible. Ironically for a communist country, China is dismissive of the Western social security model: when US debt was downgraded in August 2011, the Xinhua news agency said America should reduce its 'bloated welfare costs'.[30]

China has also managed to grow without being dominated by the markets or the financial sector. The Chinese currency, the renminbi, is managed carefully so that it does not rise too fast and suck in foreign capital too quickly. The Chinese authorities have learned the lessons of the Asian crisis of the late 1990s, when hot money (capital that can be withdrawn quickly, such as bank deposits) suddenly exited the likes of Thailand and Indonesia. Other countries in the developing world are also keen to attract Chinese investment, particularly if their governments are authoritarian: there will be no awkward questions about human rights.

The Chinese economy may become larger than the US in the next couple of decades, although this reflects its much bigger population. On an individual basis, the higher productivity of American workers means they will remain much better off than their Chinese counterparts, and also explains why America will remain a powerful manufacturing nation, even though Chinese wages are so much lower.

This higher productivity is explained in part by the fact that Americans are better educated; and in part by the fact that they have access to better capital (in the sense of better machines).

Just because the Chinese are becoming relatively more prosperous does not mean citizens of the Western world will become poorer in absolute terms – indeed, quite the reverse. Britain was overtaken by the American economy in the late nineteenth century and lags a long way behind it today. Yet the standard of living of a modern Briton is much higher than that of his 1890 counterpart, thanks to the income the UK gets from selling goods and services to America and the products it gets in return.

Nevertheless, political power tends to follow economic power. Just before the fall of the Berlin Wall in 1989, the Yale history professor Paul Kennedy argued convincingly that there was 'a very significant correlation over the longer term between productive and revenue-raising capacities on the one hand and military strength on the other'.[31] Richer countries can afford bigger armies and better military technology. But if the country overstretches itself militarily, then the costs of maintaining its forces will drag on its economy, eventually eroding its military advantage.

Mr Kennedy's book appeared at a time when Americans were briefly worried about national decline, and in particular by the economic challenge from Japan. There was talk of 'imperial overstretch' and comparisons were made with the fall of the Roman Empire. But the country to which Mr Kennedy's lessons really applied was the Soviet Union, whose poor economic performance in the 1970s and 1980s undermined the confidence of the Russian leadership, and allowed the astonishingly rapid collapse of its empire in the late 1980s and early 1990s. That development, combined with the bursting of the Japanese financial bubble, made fears of an American decline look premature: within a decade, there was talk of a unipolar world in which America could act virtually as it liked.

But Mr Kennedy made it clear that there was a considerable lag between the trajectory of a country's economic strength and its military power, both on the way up and the way down. In the closing sections of his argument, he worries about the US national debt (a mere $1.4 trillion in 1988; it was more than $16 trillion as of late

2012): 'The only other example of a great power so increasing its indebtedness in peacetime is France in the 1780s, where the fiscal crisis contributed to the domestic political crisis,' he writes. The signs of imperial overstretch look greater now than they did in 1988, given the military adventures in Iraq and Afghanistan, the 'war on terror', and the US use of drones to eliminate enemies in small countries like Yemen, as well as the challenge from the growing naval power of China. All these military commitments have to be squared with a long-running domestic political battle over the country's fiscal commitments, especially on entitlements such as pensions and health care.

A different thesis arises from the book *Why Nations Fail* by Daron Acemoglu and James Robinson,[32] which contrasts the likes of North and South Korea, and Mexico and the US, to show convincingly that the quality of a country's institutions is key to its economic development. Acemoglu and Robinson contrast 'extractive' and 'inclusive' elites, the former being the likes of kleptocratic dictators such as Joseph Mobutu of Zaire or the old Russian aristocracy. Such elites seize control of a country's natural resources – whether land, minerals or energy – and use them to enrich themselves and buy off opposition to their power. The result is that other industries find it hard to develop and the economy becomes too dependent on one sector – and thus vulnerable to a collapse of commodity prices.

In contrast, countries with inclusive elites find it easier to develop a broad range of businesses. Nineteenth-century Britain was not a full democracy, but it did allow inventors and entrepreneurs to protect their property rights in court, rather than have them seized by the ruling aristocracy. That was one reason why a cloudy island on the edge of Europe was in the vanguard of the Industrial Revolution.

But the last 30 years may illustrate that an 'extractive elite' can appear in many guises. In Greece, power has alternated between two main parties since the restoration of democracy in 1974: Pasok on the left and New Democracy on the right. Each has pursued a policy of 'clientilism', rewarding its supporters with jobs, benefits and subsidies while in office. At the same time, the Greek government has had little success in collecting taxes; the country is notorious for using cash payments.[33] Over time, this led to the build-up of the high levels of government debt that have caused such a problem in recent years.

Another form of extractive elite is the financial sector. As is argued elsewhere in this book, a whole range of policies over the last 30 years has allowed the financial sector to grow substantially around the world. Its wealth gave it access to the ears of politicians and its size obliged the same politicians to expend vast effort in rescuing it in 2007 and 2008. Indeed, the financial sector may be the classic example of the lobby group Mancur Olson described. And as we shall see in Chapter 10, the sector has played a big part in another development – the rise in inequality.

So to sum up the last two chapters, governments and central banks have meddled in the economy in many ways over the last 70 years, changing tax and benefit rates, altering interest rates and subsidizing favoured activities. All this has been designed to boost the long-term growth rate and to avoid recessions. But some of this may have been an illusion; the economy might well have grown without government intervention (thanks to population growth and technological change) and sometimes it might have grown faster if the meddling had not occured. But citizens have come to expect politicians to produce growth, like a rabbit out of a magician's hat. Now that the economy is struggling to grow at all, it is the politicians who will take the blame.

6

Going to Extremes

The rise of populist extremism is one of the most pressing challenges facing European democracies.

Chatham House report, September 2011

The economic problems described in the last two chapters have led to disillusionment with mainstream politicians, something which has created an opportunity for fringe parties of the right and left. When conventional politics appears to fail, voters naturally start to consider the unconventional. This was demonstrated most dramatically in Italy in February 2013, when the Five Star protest movement led by the comedian Beppe Grillo received 25.6% of the vote, placing it second in the poll for the lower house of Parliament.

The echoes of the 1930s, when the Great Depression prompted mass support for communist and fascist parties, are worrying. The Nazi Party received only 3% of the vote in the German elections of December 1924 and 2.6% in 1928. But the collapse of the global economy in 1929 and 1930 catapulted their vote to 18.3% in the September 1930 poll. It also made the Nazis the largest right-wing party in Germany. With the Communist Party steadily increasing its share of the vote (13.1% in 1930, 16.9% in November 1932), conservative forces turned to Hitler as the best hope for staving off revolution.

The comparison between then and now is not as fanciful as it might seem. In the French general election of 2012, for example, the National Front's vote was akin to the Nazis' 1930 vote share, and France's mainstream right-wing forces are in disarray after the defeat of Nicolas Sarkozy in the Presidential election. It is not difficult to imagine the National Front becoming the leading party of the French right.

Once parties move from the fringe to the mainstream, they may develop a veneer of respectability. That will attract voters who might otherwise have shunned them, or who previously regarded a vote for such parties as a wasted one. Such parties also become plausible members of governments: extreme right-wing groups have recently been in coalitions in Austria and the Netherlands.

Europe resembles early 1930s Germany in another way too: the established parties seem to offer only a diet of austerity as the price for keeping the euro together (or, in Britain, for keeping the markets happy). Even the socialist French president, François Hollande, elected in 2012 on an anti-austerity platform, plans to balance his government's budget by 2017, one year before the British pro-austerity coalition plans to do so. Back in 1930, the fierce austerity policies of Chancellor Brüning caused German unemployment to soar and hastened Hitler's rise.

So it seems that we have the preconditions for a further surge in extremist support, particularly in Europe. As Chapter 9 will explain, the creation of the euro, well-intentioned as it might have been, has prompted the worst crisis in the EU's history. The euro was thrust upon voters by the continent's political elites. While it may have brought some benefits in the early years of its existence, euro membership now seems to be demanding a very high price from its citizens.

João Carlos Espada, director of the Institute for Political Studies at the Catholic University of Portugal, argues that the European response to the crisis sent a consistent message to voters:[1] 'The euro was beyond dispute, demanded balanced budgets, and decisively removed crucial national questions (such as what currency to use or how to design fiscal policy) from the hands of national parliaments and mainstream parties.' The feeling that decision-making has been taken out of the hands of voters has caused resentment right across Europe. In Cyprus in 2013 a €10 billion bailout from the EU was greeted with mass protests because of the price demanded: a levy on bank depositors. Posters appeared comparing the German chancellor Angela Merkel with Hitler.[2]

Resentment may grow even more as Europe pursues further integration. As part of the so-called two-pack process, countries will have to submit their draft budgets for the following year to the European

Commission and the Eurogroup of other governments. As the Commission briefing note remarks, 'If the Commission assesses that the draft budgetary plan shows serious non-compliance' it 'can require a revised draft budgetary plan'.[3] In other words, countries will find their budgets subject to pre-approval and potential veto in Brussels, a historically huge loss of national sovereignty.

The dithering response of the EU to the crisis has also given the impression of impotence and incompetence. 'The lack of authoritative democratic political institutions at the regional level has robbed the EU of the ability to respond forcefully to the crisis, thereby fanning the flames of nationalism and extremism and creating a backlash against the European project itself,' said Sheri Berman, professor of political science at Columbia University's Barnard College.[4] European solidarity has been replaced by the return of national sterotypes – the Germans speak of feckless Greeks, the Greeks of bullying, arrogant Germans.

Support has risen for extremist parties of the left as well as the right. In the 2012 French Presidential election, Jean-Luc Mélenchon, the candidate of the Left Front, proposed a maximum wage, tariffs on goods that did not meet social and environmental norms, and a retirement age of 60. He received 11.1% in the first polling round, coming in fourth place, but the left vote was split by anti-capitalist and Trotskyist candidates who received 1.7% between them (a Green candidate got 2.3%). In the Irish election of 2011, Sinn Fein took 10% of the vote on a fairly left-wing platform, while other left parties took around 2%.

The biggest gains for the left have been achieved in Greece, where a coalition of parties under the heading Syriza saw its vote leap from less than 5% to 16.7% in the May 2012 election, and a remarkable 27% when the second poll occurred in June.[5] This made it the second-largest party, although it refused to join the government. Its programme included a 75% tax rate, nationalization of banks, utilities and private health facilities, and withdrawal from NATO.

Yet what seems surprising, given that the 2007–8 financial collapse was perceived as a crisis of capitalism, is that left-wing parties have not made further gains. In some countries, notably Britain and Spain, centre-left parties have been expelled from office; voters were inclined to blame the party in government when the crisis hit, whether it was of the left or the right. But while resentment against the bankers is undoubtedly high, the broad outlines of capitalism still seem to be accepted; the gains for the far left have generally been outstripped by the advance of the radical right.

THE POPULIST RIGHT

It is natural that there will be more concern in Western Europe at the rise of the far right than of the far left. For much of the post-war era, communist parties enjoyed significant electoral support in both France and Italy. Given the power of the Soviet Union, and its use of Marxist parties to seize power in Eastern Europe, centrist politicians regarded the communists as a threat – Italian coalitions were deliberately organized so as to keep the communists from office. Over time, however, the Marxist parties distanced themselves from their Russian comrades and were absorbed into the political mainstream. No Western European democracy was taken over by the communists.

In contrast, of course, two Western European states were taken over before 1945 by right-wing parties operating under the fascist label, combining appeals to the economic interests of the workers with nationalist rhetoric.[6] The modern version of such parties may not carry the threat of military expansion posed by Hitler and Mussolini, but elements of their programmes are disturbingly familiar.

Although these groups are conventionally described as right wing, their programme is really a combination of social conservatism and left-wing economics, rather like the pre-war fascists. (Outside the US, it is hard to create a party with mass appeal on the free-market, extremely limited-state programme that marks out the modern Republicans.) The best way to describe the programmes of right-wing European parties is 'populist' – they claim to represent the interests of the little man against the political and economic elites. They don't tend to share the same links with business as mainstream conservative parties (for example, the populists are fairly hostile to globalization).

A Chatham House report[7] defines such groups as sharing two key features: opposition to immigration, and ethnic and cultural diversity;

and a populist anti-establishment tone that is 'ambivalent if not hostile towards liberal representative democracy'. The report found that these parties had assembled a coalition of economically insecure lower-middle-class citizens and skilled and unskilled manual workers. Support is strongest among men, and among the less educated. Analysis of the vote for Jean-Marie Le Pen of the National Front in the first round of the 2002 French Presidential election (in which he came a surprise second) showed it was remarkably uniform across age groups.

Of the 12 nations looked at by the Chatham House report, only three had far-right parties with significant electoral support (5% or more) in the early 1980s; by 2010 this had risen to seven parties, with the Austrian Freedom Party polling 25%. Even in famously liberal Sweden, the far-right Democrats took 5% of the vote and 20 seats in Parliament while in neighbouring Finland the True Finns took 19%. But these votes, high as they are, may only be tapping part of the potential for the far-right parties to prosper. A 2010 Chatham House survey[8] of six EU nations (Britain, France, Germany, Italy, the Netherlands and Spain) found that an average 61% of those polled agreed with the statement that 'illegal immigrants increase crime in society', while 58% said that immigrants were a burden on social services. Around 70% of Spaniards agreed with both statements. Forty percent of EU citizens polled, including 59% of Britons and 53% of Italians, thought there were too many immigrants.

When asked how well governments were dealing with the issues of immigration, and integration of previous immigrants, a clear majority of citizens in a survey of 12 nations[9] thought they were doing a poor or very poor job. This high level of dissatisfaction only adds to the resentment against elected politicians now that they are failing to deliver a higher standard of living to the average citizen.

The mainstream parties face a difficult dilemma. If they fail to respond to voters' worries about immigration, then they are hardly acting as democratically elected politicians, and they may increase the temptation of voters to support the extremes. But if centrist parties adopt an anti-immigration platform, they may legitimize the arguments of the right wing, as well as possibly undermining the pluralist basis of the modern state.

Workers were very mobile in the late nineteenth and early twentieth centuries, as Europeans sought new opportunities in countries like the US, Argentina and Australia. For the European continent, emigration not immigration was the issue. Mass immigration into Europe is really a product of the post-1945 era as the global empires disintegrated; the former imperial powers often gave preferential rights to the citizens of their colonies. That helps explain the disparate nature of the immigrants: many South Asians moved to the north of England to work in the textile mills and West Indians moved to London to take jobs in transport or in the NHS. French immigration came from the colonies of Algeria and Morocco. That there was an economic imperative to this shift, for host country as well as immigrants, was shown by West Germany: lacking an empire, it imported Turks as *Gastarbeiter*, or guest workers.

Anti-immigrant prejudice has traditionally focused on two mutually inconsistent points: that the new arrivals are taking jobs from the indigenous population; and that they are not working, but simply taking advantage of the host nation's unemployment benefit system. Interestingly, the Chatham House report finds that these economic concerns had been overtaken by a cultural issue: that immigrants were threatening 'the unity of their national community and way of life'.

While in the past this hostility might have been specifically targeted at Jews, or at Africans and Afro-Caribbeans, modern right-wing groups have a new target: Muslims. A survey of British National Party supporters found that 82% would be bothered 'a lot' by a proposal to build a mosque in their community, while 88% felt Islam was a danger to Western civilization.[10] These opinions are quite widely shared: a poll of citizens of eight EU countries found that proportions varying from 27% (Portugal) through 45% (Britain) to 71% (Hungary) felt there were too many Muslims in the country. The average across the eight nations that felt this way was 44%.[11]

It seems likely that a good deal of this hostility has been driven by terrorist attacks in New York, Madrid and London since the turn of the millennium. The presence of, and publicity given to, radical preachers such as Abu Hamza has added to the problem. Then there is the integration issue. Declining hostility towards Africans and afro-Caribbeans in Britain doubtless reflects their prominent role in national life, particularly in sport: it is harder to be a racist football fan when half the English team is black. There is a shared religion between West Indians and the rest of the population. Many art forms first developed distinctively by black culture (rap, hip-hop) have been enthusiastically adopted by white youth as well. With the Caribbean population resident in Britain, familiarity has bred content.

Muslim culture has not been absorbed to the same extent, although there are many examples of French footballers from Islamic backgrounds (such as Zinedine Zidane) and the British athlete Mo Farah is a very positive role model in this regard. Most significantly, many Europeans perceive Muslims as having quite distinct tastes in terms of dress, food and music – not to mention their attitudes on cultural issues such as women's rights. This adds to the sense of alienation, particularly for those living in areas where a large number of Muslims have settled – the ambience of the area alters significantly.

A CLEAR AND PRESENT DANGER

Although hostility to immigration has been a fairly constant theme in Western countries during the present era, voting support for right-wing populist parties has been fairly erratic. They have been recipients of protest votes and can be beneficiaries of the 'new kid on the block syndrome' – disillusioned voters may give them a try to see whether they are an improvement on the established parties. Sometimes, as parties become better known, some of their more unpleasant characteristics may become apparent (female voters can be put off by the thuggish attitude of the hardliners), and the party leaders can lose the freshness of their appeal. The closer they get to government, the more they become tainted by the inevitable compromises that come with office.

Nevertheless, a Counterpoint study worried about the pernicious effect that these parties could have over the long term: 'the gradual undermining of representative institutions, the impact on mainstream parties, the – related – disproportionate toll on policy-making, the increased toxicity of political discourse and, finally, the legitimisation of a set of political views through a slow but steady electoral success'.[12]

The most alarming party at the moment is the Golden Dawn Party in Greece, which has risen rapidly in popularity in the face of the country's economic problems. In 2009 the party received just 0.4% of the popular vote – it was so tiny that the Chatham House report, published in 2011, did not even mention it. Greece was occupied by the Germans in the Second World War, making it hard for neo-Nazis to play the patriotic card – at least before the effects of the current austerity started to take their toll. But now Golden Dawn does not disguise its roots. Its members have adopted a swastika-like symbol and give a raised-arm salute to its leader, and its platform includes the idea of mining Greece's borders to keep out immigrants.

In the June 2012 elections, as the country slid into economic chaos, Golden Dawn received 7% of the vote and took 18 seats in Parliament. By the autumn, its popularity had already risen significantly – it ranked third in the opinion polls, with a showing of 12%. Party members court popularity by distributing food to the needy – but only to those who can prove their nationality. Meanwhile the party harasses immigrants: in one case, it attacked market stallholders at Rafina, a port near Athens, after posing as plain-clothes police.[13] Indeed, the group appears to have strong support among the police force; there have been reports of police standing idly by while anti-fascist demonstrators were beaten up, and of a Golden Dawn MP releasing a party member after he had been arrested and placed in a police van.[14] It is all frighteningly reminiscent of the Nazi brownshirts who committed street violence in the last days of the Weimar Republic with tacit support from the authorities.

Golden Dawn undoubtedly benefits from the sense of chaos in Greece. For example, in 2012 there were so many Greek strikes and protests that the 'Living in Greece' website devoted a special page[15] to keep expats and tourists updated. At the end of September that year, there was a general strike – but the website also listed several other disputes, which meant, for example, that tourist sites might be closed, that pharmacies would only accept cash and that hospital doctors were 'going slow'. There is only a certain amount of such disruption that a democratic government can survive; if daily life grinds to a halt on a regular basis, running the country becomes impossible.

In France, the Front National (FN) was founded back in 1972 by Jean-Marie Le Pen, who has now passed the leadership on to his daughter, Marine. Its greatest success occurred when Jean-Marie made it through to the second round of the Presidential election in 2002, after a collapse in the Socialist vote; the limits of FN support, though, were shown when Le Pen received only 17% in the second round. However, Marine has tried to broaden the party's appeal, dropping her father's anti-Semitic rhetoric (although not the anti-Islamic tone), while emphasizing economic issues such as protectionism and advocating that France should leave the euro. Although she came third in the 2012 Presidential first round, her vote was higher than that of her father in the equivalent stage of 2002. As mentioned earlier, the FN may be able to capitalize on the apparent disarray of the mainstream right-wing party, the UMP, after Nicolas Sarkozy's 2012 defeat.

In the Netherlands, two right-wing parties have emerged in rapid succession – the first led by Pim Fortuyn and named after him, and the second led by Geert Wilders and known as the Partij voor de Vrijheld (PVV). Both came to the stump on a strongly anti-Islam stance but with a Dutch twist: Fortuyn, who was gay, felt that the country's history of tolerance was threatened by the arrival of a highly religious minority. Fortuyn was assassinated in 2002 (by an environmentalist, not by a Muslim). But two years later the film-maker Theo van Gogh was murdered by an Islamic extremist, providing ammunition for the rise of Mr Wilders. Although the coalition government depended on his support after 2010, Wilders failed to get his proposals for bans on minarets or burkas passed into law.

In April 2012 the Dutch government collapsed when Wilders withdrew his support for its austerity programme and adopted an increasingly anti-EU stance. This forced the Dutch prime minister, Mark Rutte, to call a September election. For a while, polls suggested that both Mr Wilders and the far-left Socialist Party would do well. But the election result was a surprise, with the two mainstream, pro-European parties gaining seats (and more than half the vote between them) whereas Mr Wilders lost ground.

The rise of the Five Star movement in Italy does not really fit into the right-wing mould; Beppe Grillo gains much of his support from voter outrage at the incompetence and corruption of mainstream politicians. The party has a strong green and libertarian agenda. But in his hostility to the EU (Five Star believes Italy should have a referendum on leaving the union), Grillo is tapping into the same issues that are being exploited by the far right elsewhere.

WHAT DO THEY WANT?

What sort of voters are these parties appealing to? In 2012 the British thinktank Demos conducted a series of surveys on the attitudes of European populist party voters, by the simple expedient of writing to supporters on the parties' Facebook pages. It found that the supporters of the Dutch PVV party were more likely to be male than female; more pessimistic that politicians would respond to their concerns; more pessimistic about the future and less trusting of institutions; more hostile towards Islam and immigration and more hostile towards the EU.[16] These last points were hardly surprising, since they were the centrepiece of Geert Wilders' campaign.

The Counterpoint survey[17] also found that as many as half of the voters for these populist parties are 'reluctant radicals' – people who are not ideologically committed to the cause but who feel that the mainstream parties do not address their concerns. The report focused on the reluctant radicals in Finland, France and the Netherlands. In 2011 Finland's True Finn Party saw a surge in its vote from 4% to 19%. This came as quite a surprise since Finland has not suffered from the economic crisis in the same way as Greece or Spain, nor has it seen the levels of immigration that have occurred in Sweden or the Netherlands. Part of the appeal of the True Finns lies in the opposition to bailouts of the southern European countries; another important element is a kind of rural, social conservatism akin to that of the Tea Party group in the US.

French reluctant radicals, the report concludes, 'are geographically, educationally and politically removed from the mainstream and thus feel a permanent sense of insecurity'. Dutch supporters of extremist parties seem to hanker for the old days of consensus politics, before the immigrants arrived.

The most significant predictor of radicalism in the three countries is not age, gender or even employment status. Radicals are likely to be less educated. This may be due to the socializing effect of attending university, where people are likely to meet others from a variety of backgrounds and cultures they had not previously encountered. Only 4% of committed Dutch radical right-wingers had been to university, compared with 31% of the electorate.

Another interesting characteristic of extreme right-wing voters is their low level of trust. It is not just that they are suspicious of politicians or the establishment: only 12% of French populist voters trusted other people in general. Even in the more open Netherlands, only 49% of PVV voters believe most people can be trusted, compared with 64% of the electorate. The populists, in other words, don't trust the populace. If you are generally untrusting of others, you are more likely to believe in the conspiracy theories outlined in Chapter 7. You are also less likely to be welcoming towards someone from a different background, religious or ethnic.

What makes this characteristic particularly important is that it plays into the trends that I highlighted earlier: the decline in turnout and mainstream party membership, and general dislike of the political class. There was a large dissatisfied constituency in the electorate even before the financial crisis; since the 2008 crash, years of austerity have made voters even less likely to be supportive of the established elites. A 2011 survey found that 80% of British National Party supporters were dissatisfied, or very dissatisfied, with the way that democracy was functioning in Britain.[18]

The BNP's thuggish reputation, though, may have prevented it from making an electoral breakthrough; it received just 564,000 votes in the 2010 general election, or 1.9%. Its thunder may have been stolen by the United Kingdom Independence Party (UKIP), a party set up to oppose British membership of the EU but which attracts supporters with remarkably similar attitudes to the BNP. The same 2011 survey found that 85% of UKIP voters felt Islam was a threat to Western civilization, that 64% would be bothered a lot by the building of a mosque near to them, and that 74% were dissatisfied with democracy.[19] Regular surveys show that the single most important issue for UKIP voters was immigration, not Europe.[20] The party's

2012 manifesto for the local elections stated it would 'end open-door immigration', 'freeze permanent immigration for five years' and 'withhold all state benefits for immigrants for five years'[21] – even though, of course, immigration is not an issue dealt with by local councils.

What gives UKIP a much greater chance of an electoral breakthrough is that it draws support from working-class ex-Labour voters as well as from anti-EU Tories, and that it is acceptable in the way the BNP is not. Nigel Farage, the party's leader, is a jolly figure who even crops up on BBC comedy panel shows, an impossible dream for Nick Griffin, the leader of the openly racist BNP. Farage is also becoming a regular face on the financial speaking circuit, something that may help the party get donations. Almost 30% of UKIP voters read *The Financial Times*.[22] All this is translating into electoral success: the party received a record 22% in the Rotherham by-election of November 2012, finishing second (and ahead of the Conservatives) in that seat and in a Middlesbrough poll on the same day. That month, a national opinion poll in November had UKIP gaining a vote share of 13%, while in February 2013 the party's candidate came second in a by-election in Eastleigh in southern England, pushing the Conservatives into third place.

In the council elections of May 2013 UKIP made a further breakthrough, getting 23% of the vote and gaining 139 seats. On top of its anti-EU and anti-immigrant message, the party also seems to be the recipient of a protest vote that previously went to Liberal Democrats and Greens. It also seems to have an appeal to the small businessman, slightly reminiscent of the Poujadist movement that had a brief success in France in the 1950s. UKIP voters are naturally conservative but have been put off by David Cameron's attempts to modernize the party on issues such as gay marriage. What is not yet clear is whether the ragbag of candidates that the party has attracted will survive the harsh light of media scrutiny that accompanies electoral success. Nevertheless, the party's rise makes the British political system look even more European, with a host of competing parties rather than the old duumvirate, and makes it more likely that further coalition governments will be needed.

CONCLUSION

Extremist parties are like those bacteria that attack people with a weakened immune system. They are most dangerous when the economy is weak and the public are dissatisfied with government. In short, at times like today. Throw in two further factors – a general sense of powerlessness in the face of globalization, and the presence of unassimilated immigrant communities in countries where voters feel the elite has not listened on this issue – and you have a potentially worrying mix. Greece may be a harbinger in more than just economics.

7

Clowns to the Left,
Jokers to the Right

*No sooner has one party discovered or invented any ameliora-
tion of the condition of man, or the order of society, than the
opposite party belies it, misconstrues it, misrepresents it, ridi-
cules it, insults it and persecutes it.*

John Adams in a letter to Thomas Jefferson, 1813

*I could not dig: I dared not rob: / Therefore I lied to please
the mob.*

Rudyard Kipling, 'A Dead Statesman',
Epitaphs of the War, 1914–1918, 1924

Back in early 2011, I was visiting Washington and, in my hotel room,
was flicking through the cable TV channels. An image suddenly
flashed up: a map of Europe in which Britain was part of an 'Islamic
caliphate'.[1] This was news to me, but turned out to be the speculative
musings of Glenn Beck, at the time a popular host on the Fox News
channel.[2] In Beck's view the 'Arab spring' was apparently the prelude
to a general Muslim takeover of much of Europe.

For the average Briton, raised on the sober tones of the BBC, it
seems amazing that such stuff can make it on air. But Fox News is a
highly successful channel in its field, with its mix of news and comment –
delivered in a much livelier style than the original cable news network,
CNN – drawing around 2 million prime-time viewers.[3] Many people
loathe it, but there are enough people who love it – and who feel that
the other networks don't reflect their point of view – to create a profitable niche. The tone is resolutely partisan – although just to wind its

opponents up, the channel's slogan is 'Fair and Balanced'. To give just one example, a Fox News poll in October 2012, a month before the US Presidential election, showed President Barack Obama five points ahead of the Republican candidate Mitt Romney in the polls; the headline on the accompanying press release read 'Voters Want Change'. Fox's more corrosive items verge on paranoia – the idea that Mr Obama was not born in America, for instance, or Mr Beck's ravings about an Islamic takeover of the West.

Such conspiracy theories are part of a long-established tendency in politics. In 1797 the Scottish physicist John Robison wrote a book with the title *Proofs of a Conspiracy Against All the Religions and Governments of Europe, carried on in the Secret Meetings of Free Masons, Illuminati and Reading Societies*. (Somehow the inclusion of the last adds a wonderfully comic touch. But have you ever wondered just what goes on at your local book club?) As with later conspiracy theories, the plotters were perceived to be the driving force behind world events, having cooked up the French Revolution. The cunning devils had a host of secret weapons, which included a tea for causing abortion and a 'method for filling a bedchamber with pestilential vapours' (perhaps an early recipe for baked beans?).[4]

Conspiracy theories are understandable in a world that we cannot control. We would like to be individually prosperous, for our economies to grow, for our nations to be powerful, and for events (such as elections) to have the 'right' outcome. When such things do not happen, we get frustrated. Rather than blame bad luck or our own inadequacies, we look for a culprit. As the historian Richard Hofstadter wrote: 'The paranoid's interpretation of history is in this sense distinctly personal; decisive events are not taken as part of the stream of history, but as the consequence of someone's will.'[5] The nature of the conspirators changes over time. Once upon a time it was freemasons or (in Protestant nations) Catholics. Right-wingers still see plots by communists or the United Nations (if only the UN was sufficiently competent to organize a conspiracy); left-wingers fear bankers or arms manufacturers; and countless conspiracy theories blame the Jews.

The details of a supposed conspiracy are always incredibly elaborate: *The Da Vinci Code*, with its secret societies dating back to the time of Christ, is a faithful fictional tribute to the genre. In a Kafkaesque touch, those who question the theory are assumed to be part of the plot. There is a strong religious element about the whole business: people are inducted into the faith, learn the liturgy required (to take the example of the JFK assassination – the grassy knoll, the man with the umbrella and the magic bullet) and then try to convert non-believers. And there is also an element of insecurity at the heart of these theories. As Mr Hofstadter noted, the typical American conspiracy theorist 'sees his own country as being so weak that it is constantly about to fall victim to subversion; and yet he feels that it is so all-powerful that any failure it may experience in getting its way in the world cannot possibly be due to its limitations but must be attributed to its having been betrayed'.[6]

Of course, there have been actual conspiracies in history, from attempts to assassinate Fidel Castro in the 1960s to, further back, Guy Fawkes's plot to blow up the British Parliament on 5 November 1605. What usually (but not always) emerges from real-life conspiracies is that the participants are incompetent and their plans ill thought out. It takes a great leap of imagination to assume that *most* events are part of a great conspiracy, or even that individual high-profile events are part of a plot that has not been noticed by the many journalists and police officers who have investigated them.

In his highly entertaining book *Voodoo Histories: How Conspiracy Theory Has Shaped Modern History*, the journalist David Aaronovitch neatly describes such theories as 'the unnecessary assumption of conspiracy when other explanations are more probable'. He cites, for example, the assumption that the Moon landing in 1969 was faked, a theory that would have required the involvement of everyone at NASA, the individual astronauts and their families, the supposed film crews who staged the event, the Navy crews who fished Neil Armstrong and company out of the sea: in total, thousands of people, none of whom 40 years later have decided to reveal the secret, even though such a story would guarantee an enormous pay day from the media.

Modern conspiracy theories are at least ecumenical. Bill Clinton was supposed to have colluded in murder (of an aide, Vincent Foster, who committed suicide); George W. Bush, in the 9/11 attacks; Barack Obama, in concealing his birthplace. In Britain, fingers were pointed at Tony Blair over the death of David Kelly, the weapons expert embroiled in the Iraq affair, and at Prince Philip over the car crash in which Princess Diana died.

My point is not, therefore, that a belief in conspiracies is a new-found phenomenon. It is simply that, in the age of the Internet, conspiracies are disseminated much more easily. Websites can be found to support almost any cause, however absurd or abhorrent. And people are getting more of their news and views online, and less from the mainstream media which – for all its flaws – at least makes some attempt to check facts and provide balance.

In 1970 more than 50 million Americans watched the nightly news on the country's three main networks, ABC, CBS and NBC. By 2011 just 22.5 million people did so – a much smaller proportion of a much larger population.[7] Some of those viewers would have switched over to Fox News or its liberal counterpart, MSNBC, but that only accounts for 3 million of the viewer shortfall. What of the rest? They are not reading newspapers. The circulation of US daily newspapers fell by around a third, from 62.3 million to 43.4 million, between 1990 and 2010.[8] The industry seems to be in chronic decline, having lost a crucial source of revenue – classified advertising – to the Internet.

The heroic period of US journalism was in the 1970s, when Bob Woodward and Carl Bernstein of *The Washington Post* uncovered the Watergate scandal that brought down President Nixon. This was a genuine conspiracy in which the president's operatives burgled the Democrat headquarters in 1972 and then covered up their trail. Every detail seemed to confirm the president's guilt, from the secret campaign funds, the tapes of White House conversations, complete with deleted expletives and missing sections, and Nixon's firing of special prosecutors who were investigating the affair.

At this time, journalists had immense authority; Walter Cronkite, a news anchor for CBS, was seen as the most trusted man in America. But perhaps journalists became too self-important, regarding themselves as the unofficial opposition to the government of the day. Many a journalist wanted to repeat Woodward and Bernstein's feat and expose official corruption. They started to treat politicians' pronouncements with more scepticism and to regard policy statements not as reasoned responses to national problems, but as tactical ploys in the search for office.

In a way, journalists seem to have adopted the philosophy of Joseph Schumpeter, who saw politics as a competition between elites for power, driven by making promises to the electorate. A media view that policies are being proposed as a tactical ploy, rather than as a genuine response to circumstances, makes it more difficult for politicians to put forward their ideas. A change in policy is portrayed as a U-turn; admission of difficulty is portrayed as a gaffe; genuine policy disagreements are a split, and so on.

In turn, this attitude has led politicians to try to manage the media. Between the two world wars, 44 people in the British government were involved in media communication; by 2008 there were 3,000 government press officers. Getting the support of press barons has been perceived as a vital part of a British politician's bid for power. In 1995, the year after his election as leader of the Labour Party, Tony Blair flew to Hayman Island in Australia to address a conference of Rupert Murdoch's News Corporation. The papers in the Murdoch stable had been aggressively hostile towards the then Labour leader, Neil Kinnock, at the previous election in 1992, with the leading tabloid declaring 'It's the Sun Wot Won It' after the Tories under John Major had scored a late victory. In 1995 Blair successfully wooed Murdoch to his cause, and the newspapers' backing helped in Labour's crushing 1997 victory.

Since press officers and public relations men do not make policy, they naturally focus on the factors they can control, which often involve the candidate's image. Margaret Thatcher was famously asked to lower her voice and change her style of dress, in order that she look like a potential prime minister. Photo opportunities will be staged to show the candidate in a caring or heroic light. These will not always work on their own terms (the picture of Michael Dukakis, the 1988 Democratic Presidential candidate, in a tank invited ridicule), but they create a level of cynicism in the journalists asked to cover them.

Staging events was followed by the development of 'news management' techniques, from the selective release of policy initiatives to friendly journalists who will present them in a positive light, to the 'background briefing' rubbishing a government member who is out of favour, to the 'rapid-response unit', which reacts to negative stories in the press or to the press announcements of the opposing party. This can involve quite aggressive lobbying of the media outlet concerned, with the press officer threatening to go over the head of the journalist in question to his editor or publisher.

All these tactics can backfire. If a journalist at one newspaper or TV channel gets favoured access, reporters at rival outlets will become resentful. They will naturally look for a new angle on the story to take it forward, pointing out for example that the policy has been announced before or is smaller in scale than suggested, or that it contradicts some previous government announcement. Negative briefing against a government member creates the impression of a government divided against itself, and increases the temptation for the media to focus on personalities rather than policies. (The British Labour governments of Tony Blair and Gordon Brown were particularly vulnerable to such criticism.) Finally, an overly aggressive approach towards the media only adds to a feeling among the latter that it is 'us against them', further contributing to a negative coverage. The respected *Financial Times* journalist John Lloyd wrote that 'the media have decided . . . that politics is a dirty game played by devious people who tell an essentially false narrative about the world and thus deceive the British people'.[9]

The net effect is a vicious cycle. The power of the media encourages politicians to try to manage the process; the management adds to the suspicion of journalists; the cynicism provokes more attempts at media management, and so on. The effect on the reading and viewing public is to make politics appear a game rather than a serious attempt to tackle a nation's problems.

Government attempts to manage the press also have their sinister side. *The Economist* Intelligence Unit found a deterioration in media freedom between 2008 and 2011 in 40 countries, of which three (France, Italy and Turkey) were European. 'Many countries have felt increasingly vulnerable and threatened and have reacted by intensifying their efforts to control the media and impede free expression,' it observed, adding that 'the concentration of media ownership has tended to increase, which has had a negative impact on the diversity of views and the freedom of expression'.[10] The reputation of the media has not been helped by its own scandals, such as the widespread hacking by tabloid newspapers of the phones of British celebrities and crime victims. The exposure of these practices provoked calls for more regulation of the press and reduced public respect for journalists. Moreover, this was not just true in Britain: a Gallup poll[11] of November 2012 found that only 24% of Americans rated the ethics and honesty of journalists as 'high' or 'very high'. This was even lower than the rating Americans gave bankers – although it was above lawyers and politicians, who, at 10%, only just outranked car salesmen.

GROUPTHINK

Some of the people who no longer read newspapers may have given up following the news altogether: a not particularly encouraging development for democracy. Some may simply not have enough time to sit down with a newspaper; others may find newspapers too bulky or messy for their liking. These latter groups may turn to the Internet for their information.

The Internet does have enormous advantages for information-gatherers. The obvious analogy is with the discovery of printing. In the absence of books, individuals had to rely on official sources for their information, such as priests and nobles. Once they could read the Bible for themselves in their own languages, they could make up their own minds as to religious doctrines. It is no accident that the Reformation followed the invention of printing in short order; Martin Luther's theses spread rapidly around Europe; one of his pamphlets was reprinted 14 times in 1518 alone and a quarter of all printed German works between 1520 and 1526 were editions of his work.[12] One of the key messages of Protestantism was that there was no need for an intermediary between the individual and God. Similarly, the Internet means there is no need for a newspaper intermediary between the reader and the news.

To many, the Internet is a welcome development. Media reporting is inevitably subject to biases, in the form of the journalists' views or the commercial interest of the proprietor. By the same token, however, the media play a filtering role, checking statements for their factual content. In most countries the Internet, by contrast, is unfiltered; disinformation is as easy to spread as information. Another double-edged element of the Internet is the ability of individuals to find others with similar tastes and ideas. If your interest is underwater hockey, visit the website of the British Octopush Association.[13] Fans of the Swedish crime writer Henning Mankell can find news about his publications and his views on world issues at the author's own site. When it comes to news, you can bypass the leftish 'lamestream media' or the mouth-piece of the corporate elite (choose your epithet) and get your news from those organizations that, like Fox News, view the world through an ideological prism.

Associating with people of a similar bent tends to cause individuals' views to become more extreme over time – and this is something that the Internet only exaggerates. Academics call this effect 'confirmation bias'. Your own view is repeatedly affirmed and never challenged; you are only presented with evidence that supports your case; you develop allegiance to people who are part of your group and you want to be liked by them; you regard outsiders not just as intellectually mis-guided, but as morally wrong. Religious cults reinforce their discipline by cutting off their members from outside influence. As the American legal scholar Cass Sunstein remarks, 'If people are told they are defined by membership in a certain group, they will be less likely to listen to those who are defined in different terms.'[14]

Mr Sunstein cites a number of examples of this phenomenon. Groups of people were asked to assess songs; without any guidance, their views tended to be quite diverse. But they were more likely to praise a song if told that other people approved of it. More seriously, Sunstein looked at the voting records of American judges on panels. American judges are elected, so can be identified as Republican or Democrat; one can also assess their judgements and grade them as conservative or liberal. On mixed panels of Republicans and Demo-crats, the votes of the former were less conservative and the latter less liberal than when the panels were one-party affairs. Hearing the other side of the argument made judges take a more balanced view.

Just being exposed to other views, other lists of facts, tends to broaden the mind and make one more inclined to compromise. For example, young people often change their political allegiance – and sometimes their religion – when they go to university and become exposed to a wider set of views than they would hear from their parents or in their particular locality.

PLAYGROUND POLITICS

Perhaps the worst part of this process is that the attitudes of the public, the media and politicians can feed off each other. The media, which is interested in sales and ratings, wants to make the coverage of politics as sensational as possible. Extremism is sensational. Extremist candidates thus get publicity, and they spend much time demonizing the other side of the political divide. This rhetoric puts off the moderate voter, who loses interest in the process. Membership of a party becomes focused on the most committed voters, who can be bothered to turn up to meetings and to deliver leaflets; often, they are the most extreme in their views. They then select extreme candidates and so the process continues.

In America, party polarization has become more extreme than ever before. Not a single Republican in the House of Representatives voted for the 2009 economic stimulus bill of the Democrats, even though the economy was in its deepest recession since the Second World War and even though the package included tax cuts of which the Republicans might be expected to approve. In part, this was out of principle; in part, tactics. Many Republicans genuinely believe that the American model is best for generating economic growth and guaranteeing personal liberty, and felt that President Obama was steering the country towards a more state-centred continental European model. But the tactical reason was that they did not wish the president to succeed. In 2010 the Senate Republican leader Mitch McConnell even said that 'The single most important thing we want to achieve is for President Obama to be a one-term president.'

This tactic is decades old. Back in 1993, the conservative strategist William Kristol urged Republicans to oppose President Clinton's health care package 'sight unseen'.[15] The idea was to prevent the Democrats from getting any work of substance done, which would thereby increase voter cynicism towards Washington and increase the electoral appeal of the Republicans as the anti-Washington party. Needless to say, such a strategy does not augur well for the future of democracy or society.

A statistical analysis[16] of voting patterns in the US Congress found that party polarization declined from around the start of the twentieth century to about the time of the Second World War. This may have reflected the peculiar coalition that supported the Democratic Party under Woodrow Wilson and later Franklin Roosevelt – northern liberals and industrial workers were allied to white supremacists in the south. That combination started to break up after the war (Strom Thurmond ran as a states' rights candidate in 1948 in defence of segregation) and completely disintegrated when Lyndon Johnson 'lost the south' for the Democrats by granting civil rights to African Americans in 1964. Now the nation is divided into red states (Republican) in the middle of the country and blue states (Democrat) on either coast, with Midwestern states like Ohio and Pennsylvania acting as the swing votes in the middle.

America is not the only country with a strong regional divide. In Britain, the Conservatives dominate the south of England but are barely represented in the north and Wales (where Labour holds sway), and in Scotland (where a combination of Labour and nationalists win most votes). Italy is divided between the prosperous north and struggling south. The Belgian government is barely functional because of the antipathy between French-speaking Walloons and the Dutch-speaking Flemish.

These divides, both regional and ideological, make it more difficult for politicians to come together and solve the very real problems that developed nations face. And the more the politicians bicker, the less the public respects them. We are demonstrating the dangers of faction that the founding fathers feared. In a letter to his great rival Thomas Jefferson, quoted at the start of this chapter, the second US President, John Adams, wrote that 'parties and factions will not suffer improvements to be made. As soon as one man hints at an improvement, his rival opposes it'. By demonizing political opponents we undermine the foundations of democracy.

8

Taking a Liberty

All those who seek to destroy the liberties of a democratic nation ought to know that war is the safest and shortest means to accomplish it.

Alexis de Tocqueville, *Democracy in America*, vol. II, 1840

Democracy isn't just freedom of opinion, the right to hold elections and so forth. It's the rule of law. Without equal application of the law, democracy is dead.

Chilean judge, quoted in 'The Great Exception' by Laurence Weschler, *The New Yorker*, April 1989

The right to vote is only one of the liberties a Western citizen has come to expect. Indeed, many would argue that it is far from the most important. Freedom of speech, freedom from arbitrary arrest, the right to trial by a jury of one's peers – all of these probably have a greater effect on the daily life of the average citizen.

Many of these rights pre-dated the universal franchise. As Fareed Zakaria noted in his book *The Future of Freedom*,[1] 'For much of modern history, what characterised governments in Europe and North America, and differentiated them from those around the world, was not democracy but constitutional liberalism.' Nineteenth-century Britain was not democratic, but it was fairly liberal. The Marxist historian Eric Hobsbawm wrote that 'The classical liberal bourgeois of 1789 was not a democrat but a believer in constitutionalism, a secular state with civil liberties and guarantees for private enterprise and government by taxpayers and property owners.'[2]

In the Western world, the notion of individual rights can be dated back at least as early as the Magna Carta (or great charter) of 1215, which stated that 'No free man shall be seized or imprisoned, or stripped of his rights or possessions, or outlawed or exiled ... except by the lawful judgment of his equals or by the law of the land.' Many later monarchs felt able to ignore many of the Magna Carta's constraints, but the document proved a useful rallying cry for later generations of theorists.

The erratic historical advance of human rights has a parallel in the advance of democracy. Once one accepts the idea that there should be a limit to the monarch's power, it is not just barons who need benefit. If one person should not have an arbitrary power over another, then barons should not have arbitrary power over others. Trial by jury did steadily become an established English right after 1215. Much later, the English Civil War and the Glorious Revolution of the seventeenth century were fought over the rights of individuals to resist arbitrary taxation or to have freedom to express their religion.

Similarly, Parliament was created to give the landed class of society a say in government, a right that was extended to the middle classes six centuries later. Once that logjam was broken in 1832, voting rights were steadily extended to other classes of society before universal suffrage was attained in the early twentieth century.

As with the rise of democracy, the advance of human rights has often been a case of two steps forward, one step back. Even modern societies have been willing to abandon their principles when under threat. Press censorship at times of war has been common, as has the rounding up of 'enemy aliens'; some German-Jewish refugees who fled the Nazis before the Second World War were interned by the British on the Isle of Man.[3] In Northern Ireland in the early 1970s, the British authorities used a number of abusive techniques on suspected members of the IRA, including sleep deprivation, prolonged periods of standing against a wall, and sensory deprivation (being hooded while listening to white noise). The British deemed these practices as 'physical ill-treatment'; the European Commission of Human Rights regarded them as torture.[4] In the same decade almost two thousand people in Northern Ireland were also interned without trial, a measure that was supposedly justified on the grounds that potential witnesses and jury members could be intimidated by the terrorist groups.

Western nations were even less scrupulous in their treatment of citizens of their former colonies than they were with regard to their own citizens. In Kenya, Britain's appalling treatment of Mau Mau prisoners (a resistance movement) in the 1950s resulted in a belated court case in October 2012, with former prisoners eventually granted damages by the British government.[5] In colonial Algeria, the French sent in shock troops to try to suppress resistance to French rule. As Alastair Horne, a historian of the Algerian War, wrote, 'what led – probably more than any other single factor – to the ultimate defeat of France was the realization, in France and the world at large, that methods of interrogation were being used that had been condemned under the Nazi occupation'.[6] In a preface to the 2006 edition, Mr Horne notes that he sent a copy of his book to Donald Rumsfeld, the then US Secretary of State for Defence, 'underscoring the evils of torture – and, not least, the propaganda value even the least substantiated rumours of it can arouse. I received a flea in the ear – courteous but a flea nevertheless – for my trouble.'

There is a cycle to these events. In moments of crisis – a war or a terrorist insurgency – governments may abandon their liberal principles. When passions have cooled, countries often regret the way they acted, although it can take a long time for apologies to be issued or redress to be made. For example, in 1942, around 110,000 Japanese Americans were interned in the wake of the attack on Pearl Harbor; the US government apologized for its behaviour as late as 1988. A Congressional report found that the internment happened in the absence of any documented acts of sabotage or espionage, and was 'caused by racial prejudice, war hysteria and a failure of political leadership'.[7]

HISTORY'S RIFT

The pattern has been repeated with an all too depressing familiarity in the so-called 'war on terror'. The terrorist attacks of 11 September 2001 were a severe shock to the American psyche. Although there had previously been terrorist incidents on US soil, notably the home-grown bombing in Oklahoma in 1995,[8] there was still a sense that such horrors only happened far away in more turbulent countries. Airline security was remarkably lax in those days.

The sheer scale of the attacks on 11 September created, naturally enough, the fear that others would follow. The subsequent capture of some Al Qaeda members in various parts of the world (together with the round-up of many people who had not committed any hostile act against the US)[9] gave the American authorities a chance to gather crucial intelligence. Under the 'ticking bomb' theory, the rights of the suspect to fair treatment were outweighed by the number of lives that might be saved if further attacks could be avoided.

In January 2002 John Yoo, a lawyer in the US Justice Department, sent a memo arguing against the use of the Geneva Conventions in the war on terror. 'You have asked whether the laws of armed conflict apply to the conditions of detention and the procedures for trial of members of Al Qaeda and the Taliban militia,' he wrote. 'We conclude that these treaties do not protect members of the Al Qaeda organization, which as a non-state actor cannot be a party to the international agreements governing war. We further conclude that these treaties do not apply to the Taliban militia.'[10] Furthermore, Yoo added, 'neither the Geneva Conventions nor the WCA [War Crimes Act] regulate the detention of Al Qaeda prisoners captured during the Afghanistan conflict'. But wasn't the US at war with the former Taliban government of Afghanistan? Apparently not, the memo stated, since 'the Taliban was not a government and Afghanistan was not – even prior to the beginning of the present conflict – a functioning state during the period in which they engaged in hostilities against the United States and its allies'.

If the captives were not prisoners of war, then surely they must be common criminals, and thus due to be tried in the US court system? But the Bush administration did not want that outcome either, since such prisoners would be entitled to their rights under US law: a series of expensive trials would follow, which might give publicity to terrorists and subject US military personnel (and CIA operatives) to cross-examination. All of which explains why the captives were detained in the legal limbo of Guantanamo Bay, a US military base on the island of Cuba – which was not on the US mainland and thus did not give the detainees any constitutional rights. In Guantanamo they could be held indefinitely, without trial.

And what would happen to the detainees while they were held there? Another memo from Mr Yoo, this time in August 2002, argued that US personnel using (undefined) interrogation techniques on prisoners would not be subject to prosecution for use of torture. It turns out that the use of waterboarding – strapping a prisoner to a board and simulating the experience of drowning – is not deemed to be torture by the US authorities. Yet this technique, first developed by the Spanish Inquisition, was used on US prisoners of war by the Japanese during the Second World War. In 1947 a former Japanese soldier was sentenced to 15 years' hard labour by the US authorities for waterboarding a US civilian.[11]

Studies later suggested that the technique was of limited effectiveness.[12] Three suspects in total were waterboarded by agents of the United States, including Khalid Sheikh Mohammed, one of the masterminds behind the attacks of 11 September. But the key piece of information that he revealed – the existence of a courier whom the US used to track down Osama bin Laden – came many years after the waterboarding finished. The trouble with torture is that while people will say anything to make it stop, the information they reveal may be neither accurate nor useful.

That the torture occurred under the presidency of a man who made much of his Christian faith and who campaigned on a slogan of 'compassionate conservatism' was an unintentional irony. Neither did reports of the technique dent President George W. Bush's support among his Christian base: he was re-elected in November 2004. It seems unlikely that waterboarding is the answer to the question posed by the popular US bumper sticker 'What would Jesus do?'

But the more serious impact on the US's moral authority came from the revelations of prisoner abuse at the Abu Ghraib prison in Iraq. Here it was the pictures that caused the damage. Prisoners were shown naked or attached to dog leashes, with grinning US soldiers standing by. Although senior politicians expressed horror at the events, many commentators argued that official policy, including the bypassing of the Geneva Conventions, must have contributed to the soldiers' attitude.

In terms of preventing further acts of terrorism, these actions were surely counterproductive. By adding to a sense among Muslims that the 'war on terror' was in fact a 'war on Islam', the West's abusive behaviour must have persuaded many angry young men to pursue a path of violence.

Other countries, including Britain, were implicated in the process thanks to a policy of 'extraordinary rendition', under which prisoners were captured by US authorities and transported to third countries, bypassing the legal process. Sometimes the prisoners were taken to American bases; at other times, they were taken to prisons run by allies of the US, where torture might well have been used. These flights often passed through the airspace of European countries. A European Parliament report detailing the saga condemned:

> the practices of extraordinary rendition, secret prisons and torture, which are prohibited under domestic and international legislation stipulating respect for human rights and which breach *inter alia* the rights to liberty, security, humane treatment, freedom from torture, non-refoulement, presumption of innocence, a fair trial, legal counsel and equal protection under the law.[13]

Human Rights Watch, a charity that bravely tackles abuses of individual rights wherever they occur, reported in June 2012 that 144 countries had enacted or revised counter-terrorism laws since the attacks of 11 September. The charity managed to review 130 of those laws and found that all contained provisions creating the potential for abuse. It concluded that these laws 'represent a broad and dangerous expansion of government powers to investigate, arrest, detain and prosecute individuals at the expense of due process, judicial oversight and public transparency'.[14] A particular problem is that the broad sweep of these laws allows governments to arrest peaceful dissenters. Human Rights Watch cited one egregious example in Turkey, a democracy that would like to join the EU. Two students who unfurled a banner that read 'We want free education, we will get it' were convicted of membership in an armed group and sentenced to more than eight years in prison.[15]

As many commentators have pointed out, the war on terror is a conflict that has no apparent end. One cannot really triumph over a tactic. The battle is also, disturbingly, global in scale: terrorist attacks have taken place in Africa, Asia, both American continents and Europe. The cycle is well described by Mr Horne in Algeria: an act of violence provokes a reaction from the Western forces; their subsequent crackdown only motivates more militants, leading to more attacks. In Algeria, it led eventually to complete French withdrawal – but withdrawal into separate spheres of influence is not really a practical option for Western and Islamic forces.

Admittedly, Western troops have already left Iraq and most are scheduled to leave Afghanistan in 2014. But, as the Libyan and Syrian civil wars have demonstrated, there will still be plenty of arenas in which the West will be tempted to intervene in the affairs of Muslim nations. And there are, of course, substantial Muslim minorities living in many Western nations.

Wars usually involve the demonization of the enemy, which must be portrayed as particularly evil or, worse still, as subhuman. The early stages of wars are often marked by stories of atrocities that were committed by the other side: following Iraq's invasion of Kuwait in 1990, for example, there were reports of Iraqi troops removing babies from their incubators. Such stories were never verified.

All this is deemed necessary to persuade a democratic nation that a given conflict undertaken in its name is just and good. Hence the publicity driven by the US and UK governments about 'weapons of mass destruction' in the lead-up to the second Iraq war of 2003. Most armies also now use volunteers, rather than conscripts, and they too must be taught to think of the conflict as a just war in which it is vital for 'us' to prevail against 'them'. Medieval kings had only to dream up some spurious familial claim to a particular piece of territory for their noblemen to go along with the process. Nowadays, neither voters nor soldiers will easily be swayed by a war motivated by naked conquest.

Once one has demonized the opposition, however, it is very hard to accept a compromise peace. This is particularly the case with terrorist groups which will, in the course of their campaigns, have killed many innocent people. (It is not impossible, however: Martin McGuinness, a former Provisional IRA commander, is now deputy prime minister of Northern Ireland. But it took 30 years before a deal could be done.)

There is also the sunk-cost problem, which occurs frequently in business and in finance. Executives are reluctant to close down subsidiaries or operations that they themselves have founded: such actions would amount to an open admission that they were wrong, and would lead people to question other aspects of their leadership.

Usually, it is up to the successor executive to clear away the dead wood left by the previous incumbent. Similarly, investors are reluctant to sell a share and take a loss. They are much more likely to sell a share in order to realize a profit. The problem is psychological – hanging on to the loss-making share allows the investor to hope that he or she might be proved right in the end.

When it comes to wars, any politician who brings an end to a conflict without victory is open to the accusation that the sacrifice of military personnel will have been in vain. The sunk-cost syndrome may have prolonged the First World War and the Vietnam conflict. It may be prolonging the 'war on terror' too. As de Tocqueville predicted, 'There are two things which a democratic people will always find very difficult – to begin a war and to end it.'[16] But as we have seen, wars inevitably hurt the health of a nation's democracy at home, as well as its reputation abroad.

ACTION AND REACTION

It is the kind of ethics question that a teacher might set a 17-year-old student: Should we tolerate those who do not believe in toleration? Western societies broadly respect the concept of free speech. But what happens when free speech offends a minority? Which right is paramount: the right to speak or the right not to be offended? The problem has been well illustrated by the various bouts of violence, or threats of violence, that have resulted from critical and satirical works about Islam.

Western liberals have been tied in knots by this issue. Over the last 40 years or so, Christianity has become a regular subject for satire; the Crucifixion scene at the end of Monty Python's *Life of Brian*, as the victims sing 'Always Look on the Bright Side of Life', is seen as a comedy classic. But Muslims are offended at any depiction of their Prophet or at any denigration of their religion. The result of such clashes is that two cultures regard each other with mutual incomprehension and suspicion. The first major clash followed the *fatwa* issued in February 1989 by the Ayatollah Khomeini, then the supreme leader of Iran, against Salman Rushdie, author of *The Satanic Verses*. The *fatwa* called for Rushdie's assassination; the author was forced into hiding. He was never attacked directly. But Rushdie's Norwegian publisher and Italian translator both survived assassination attempts while his Japanese translator was stabbed to death.

While Mr Rushdie's magical realist book was not intended to offend, later incidents – such as the series of Danish cartoons or the video entitled 'The Innocence of Muslims' released in 2012 – were designed to provoke. These various episodes both highlighted and increased the gap in understanding between the Western and Islamic worlds. Brought up on a belief in freedom of speech, Westerners were largely baffled by the outrage. In their eyes, the violent reactions to this provocative material only reinforced the negative image of Muslims that, in some cases, it had been designed to satirize. The linguist and cognitive scientist Steven Pinker, in his hopeful book about the decline of violence, points to the challenges that religious justifications pose to rational debate: 'Since one cannot defend a belief based on faith by persuading skeptics it is true, the faithful are apt to react to unbelief with rage, and may try to eliminate that affront to everything that makes their lives meaningful.'[17]

In Islamic countries, the insulting Danish cartoons and other material like them have been construed as part of a general Western plot against Muslims, along with the lengthy and destructive Western military interventions in Iraq and Afghanistan. Many Arab countries have blasphemy laws that override free speech (as did, until relatively recently, Christian nations). Furthermore, Arab media are also heavily state-dominated; little will be published of which the government disapproves. So it can be hard for people in the Middle East to understand that the American government cannot control the making of a YouTube video and that the First Amendment of the US Constitution upholds freedom of speech.

Many Western Muslims are embarrassed by the extremists and their protests. But some feel alienated from societies that allow insults to their religion while negating other elements of free speech (incitement to racial hatred or Holocaust denial, for example). In turn, these feelings of alienation may lead Western Muslims to join in with protests that make their whole community seem more threatening to the rest of society. In turn this leads to demonization of the Muslim population and thus a greater feeling within it of alienation.

The divide was highlighted by the 'Ground Zero mosque' affair, which erupted in the American media in 2010. The plan to build an Islamic centre at Park 51 in New York (two blocks away from the 'Ground Zero' site, the centre was intented to replace a former clothes shop) was seized on by conservative commentators as an insult to the memory of those who died in the World Trade Center attacks of 11 September 2001. Rudy Giuliani, the former mayor of the New York, called the idea 'a desecration. Nobody would allow something like that at Pearl Harbor'. Bloggers talked of the 'Islamization of America'; in an over-reaction, the state of Oklahoma later passed a law preventing the use of sharia law in its courts.[18]

Democracies have often found it difficult, at times of stress, to deal with minorities within their midst. Whether it is the British with the Catholic Irish, the 1930s Eastern European states with their German minorities, or Yugoslavia in the 1990s – enormous tension is created if it is believed that a minority owes an allegiance to another state or to another power. Even America, widely seen as a successful example of a melting pot of many races, is not immune from this problem.

Francis Fukuyama, whose book *The End of History* celebrated the triumph of liberal democracy over its ideological rivals,[19] did speculate on how it might be undermined. One flaw is the very system of tolerance that makes democracies so attractive for people to live in. We start by accepting that people have the right to follow alternative ways of life, and then move to regarding those ways of life as essentially equal to our own. Those who think otherwise are accused of racism or cultural imperialism.

Even in seemingly minor matters, Western nations have struggled to deal with the challenges presented by the integration of their Muslim minorities. A classic example is the French ban on the wearing of veils, or *niqabs* and *burgas*, in public, which took effect in 2011 – women are forbidden to cover their faces on the bus or in a shop. This is part of the French tradition of banning displays of religion in public places; the ban has been defended as a means of preventing the subjugation of women. Many people feel uncomfortable with the idea that women should be hidden from view, while to the modern eye the *burqa* (full-body covering) has a distinctly medieval look.

Nevertheless, there is something fundamentally illiberal about legislation that prevents people from wearing what they like. Westerners need to remember that, until the post-war era, most people would wear a hat in public.

Other issues might prove even more fraught. Say, for argument's sake, that religious parents demand that their children be excluded from biology lessons, because they will be exposed to teaching on the theory of evolution. Is that a parental right? Children can be excluded from sex-education lessons, and from religious instruction. But at what point does a child's right to be informed about the world override the rights of a parent to restrict its knowledge? And does the state have a right to dictate the detailed content of the curriculum, when many issues – such as interpretations of historical events – are not a matter of absolute truth?

If we allow all interpretations to be equally respected and represented, we end up giving the cranks and bigots publicity (and risk turning more people into cranks and bigots). Mr Fukuyama worries that 'relativism must ultimately end up undermining democratic and tolerant values as well. If all values are culturally determined, then cherished principles like human equality have to go by the wayside as well.' If this seems a little over the top, remember that many people argued in the 'Arab spring' that Muslim countries were not 'ready' for democracy, and it therefore should not be forced upon them. Democracy is a culturally determined value as well.

The danger is clear. Western countries may talk of freedom of speech and freedom of religion, but their commitment is less strong when it is a religion they don't like or when people say hateful things. Not only is this hypocrisy well noted in the Islamic world, but it brings into question the whole basis of the Western multicultural model.

RELIGIOUS MINORITIES AND HISTORY

This is an age-old issue. Europe went through its own religious wars after the Reformation, as Catholic powers tried to oust the rulers of 'heretic' Protestant nations. Eventually, after the particularly destructive and complex Thirty Years War ended in 1648, a compromise was reached in the Treaty of Westphalia: a country or territory would take the religion of its ruler, and other rulers would not interfere.

This still left the problem of what to do with religious minorities within a territory. Louis XIV expelled his Protestants, the Huguenots, thereby giving a boost to the English textile industry. In turn, dissenters from England – who were Protestants, but of a radical hue at odds with the state Protestantism – were the early emigrants to America. Those religious minorities that remained were often excluded from society. Roman Catholics were not given the vote in Britain until 1829. The growth of trade helped the process of toleration: merchants tend to be ecumenical about who they do business with.

Cities are centres of trade and by definition tend to be more cosmopolitan than the countryside. Similarly, economic growth requires innovation, and innovation is often linked to scientific knowledge. The Enlightenment, a term used to describe a process of intellectual development in the eighteenth century, emphasized reason and the scientific method. All assumptions, even religious ones, were open to question.

In the nineteenth century, the theory of evolution, as described by Charles Darwin, showed that a literal interpretation of the Bible was incompatible with science. People came to understand that 'acts of God', like lightning strikes and earthquakes, had no supernatural origins at all, but could be explained in terms of electrostatic discharges and tectonic-plate movements.

Many Christians simply adapted, focusing on the moral principles of their religion and rationalizing biblical stories as parables rather than literal truths. As European countries retreated from their empires, there was also a change in attitude towards other cultures and other religions. No longer was there an arrogant assumption that the peoples of Africa and Asia were 'savages' who needed civilizing and converting.

Religion thus became a purely private matter that had little to do with the state. Indeed in Western Europe, there was a sharp decline in religious observance. But the modern secular society is only the result of a long historical process and is still not universally accepted, most notably in America. Even in Europe, the Catholic Church still fights rearguard actions against secular ideas on contraception and homosexuality.

The Islamic religion has never had the equivalent of a Reformation, nor has it fully come to terms with the Enlightenment. Islamic countries have snapped up the technological advances of the West – from mobile phones to, less happily, rocket launchers – but the sprit of free inquiry is not accepted. There is a stark contrast with the reaction of the Japanese in 1853 when four menacing US gunboats appeared off their shores; the shock caused a rapid rethink of Japanese culture, and an attempt to copy the West.

Of course, it is dangerous to oversimplify when talking of a religion with a billion adherents. Plenty of Muslims do accept Western science and work in technological fields. These generalizations apply only to governments and to religious leaders.

But the problem remains: two cultures divided by mutual incomprehension, where suspicion leads to aggression, and aggression leads to a greater level of hostility. For the West, the danger is not of an Islamic takeover, but the erosion of long-cherished liberties in the course of the 'war on terror'. These liberties were created for a reason: the state can arrest the innocent as well as the guilty and can use its powers to harass dissenters as well as genuine terrorists.

If long-established rights – free speech, the right to a fair trial – become secondary considerations to issues such as security, it is easy to imagine that other rights might also be overridden. Section 76 of the British Counter-Terrorism Act 2009, for example, appears to make it an offence to photograph policemen;[20] some press photographers have had their cameras seized and pictures deleted.[21] Other historical episodes have shown that security concerns can slide into hysteria. In the 1950s academics and workers in the US entertainment industry were hounded from their jobs because of their supposed links with communism. Today, elected politicians may find they are unable to stand up for basic rights, for fear of being seen to be unpatriotic or soft on terrorism. The more rights we sacrifice in the name of security, the less distinctive our democracies become.

9

Europe Divided

Europe is in trouble. The risk that the EU will disintegrate is more than a scare story that politicians are using to force austerity measures on unhappy voters. It is a clear and present danger.

Ivan Krastev, chairman of the
Centre for Liberal Strategies in Sofia,
Journal of Democracy, October 2012

If there is one region of the developed world where democracy seems most threatened, it is Europe. America has its problems, as the next chapter will argue. But Europe's economic difficulties are greater than those of the US, reducing its chances of growing its way out of the debt crisis. Furthermore, Europe is conducting a tricky political experiment, one in which trans-continental governance structures are being grafted onto a system that is based on the nation state. In addition, individual European countries have slipped out of the democratic ranks on a number of occasions in the past one hundred years.

Greece, Spain and Portugal all emerged from dictatorships in the mid-1970s. Greece went through a long civil war between monarchists and communists in the aftermath of 1945 and then saw a coup by an anti-communist group of junior officers (the Colonels) who governed from 1967 to 1974. Spain and Portugal had almost forty and fifty years under the respective rules of General Francisco Franco and António Salazar before becoming democracies in the mid-1970s.

Ironically, given the current antagonism towards the EU in much of southern Europe, all three nascent democracies felt that it was a benchmark of their maturity that they be allowed to join the European

Union, as they did in the 1980s. All three countries have been net recipients of EU transfer payments during their membership.

The tensions that are now emerging within the EU reflect the wider problems that afflict Western democracy. Just as individual citizens expect democracies to deliver higher living standards, countries thought that joining the 'rich men's club' of the EU would guarantee prosperity. But the current crisis has seen living standards decline, and the price of EU membership is now adherence to austerity programmes that are resented by voters. The result has been political turmoil. The euro crisis broke in early 2010. By May 2012, with the defeat of Nicolas Sarkozy in the French Presidential elections, nine of the 17 leaders of euro-zone nations had been forced from office.[1]

The problem is not just that Europe is no longer delivering significant growth. Individual European countries no longer command the confidence of international financial markets to the extent that they did in the past – not when there are more attractive bolt-holes for capital in Asia and Latin America. Europe's political problems are all the worse because governments have often overridden the wishes of electors in their zeal to promote the federal ideal. This has resulted in a loss of legitimacy for the European project at the very moment when Europe's leaders are asking voters to make economic sacrifices.

In a bid to solve its economic problems, Europe now appears to be heading towards ever greater political and fiscal union. This may involve a further loss of democratic control, as economic decisions previously taken at the national level are decided by the heads of government acting in unison (in practice, Germany and France nearly always get their way, if they agree). The trade-off is that, in return for losing budgetary freedom, the poorer countries get tax subsidies (or cheap loans) from the better-off nations. But if countries refuse to go down this path, the strains on the European economy may eventually lead to a break-up of the euro zone.

Voters may yet sabotage this plan. In the struggling countries, such as Greece and Italy, we have already seen extremist parties gain in strength as voters revolt against the austerity that is the price of EU aid; in the rich countries, they may revolt against the cost of subsidizing their neighbours. This conflict has its roots in the very beginnings of the EU.

THE DREAM

At its heart the European Union has always been a utopian project, founded with the aim of preventing the calamitous wars that scarred the continent in the twentieth century. Between 1870 and 1945 the European problem was that Germany could not be militarily contained by the other continental powers without help from Britain or America. Two world wars ensued. The Common Market, as the EU was originally known, may have had economic roots, balancing German industry with French agriculture – but the political desire was to steer German development in a peaceful direction.

In that respect, the EU has been remarkably successful. A European war is now unthinkable. But political leaders have been unwilling to let the union remain a purely economic arrangement. They have consistently pushed forward the project of unification in the face of widespread indifference, or sometimes outright hostility, from their populations. And the process of integration has illustrated the difficulty in reconciling economic and political efficiency, financial stability and democracy.

Meanwhile the crisis of the single currency has shown that nationalism is still a powerful force in Europe. We have recently witnessed the sick irony of Greek demonstrators donning Nazi uniforms to protest at the visit of Angela Merkel, the German chancellor, while genuine neo-Nazis have been elected to the Greek Parliament.

These events would not have taken place without the creation of the euro, which was in part the result of political pressures. Back in the 1980s and 1990s, committed federalists like Jacques Delors, a French socialist minister, thought that the European project was like a shark: it had to keep moving forward or it would sink. The single currency, they thought, would make political union more likely by allowing European citizens to feel less nationalistic and more European. However, a single currency was not something that would happen naturally, from the bottom up: it had to be pushed through by political leaders.

A second motivation was economic. As any pre-1999 tourist can recall, travelling across Europe was a cumbersome business, involving the need to change currency at every border. I still have a collection of now-useless Belgian francs, Portuguese escudos and Italian lire. Different national currencies made it more difficult to create a single European market for goods and services; it was hard to compare prices when they were denominated in different currencies. By the same token, life was inconvenient for businesses which might be producing goods in several countries and selling them in several more. A company might get invoices from suppliers in French francs, pay its workers Deutschmarks, only to receive Dutch guilders when it sold the finished products in the Netherlands.

These costs were grit in the wheels of the European economy. The only beneficiaries were currency traders at banks and the operators of bureaux de change. Trade and tourism would increase, economists believed, if a single currency was introduced. A common currency became all the more sensible once money became largely an entry on a computer, rather than physical notes and coins. Changing Deutschmarks into French francs became the equivalent of changing a number from base 10 into base 8 – purely a matter of form.

A related benefit came from pooling the continent's financial markets. Individual European capital markets were quite small: few Americans wanted to lend money in Belgian francs, for example, because of the currency risk. As a result, the market of potential investors was quite small and borrowing costs were high. By pooling their currencies into the euro, European companies created a much more liquid market, thereby reducing the costs of servicing their debts.

The third motivation was a combination of political and economic reasoning. Under the Bretton Woods system, which lasted from 1944 to 1971, exchange rates were fixed against the dollar: they changed only when countries were forced to devalue, a process that was normally (like Britain in 1967) a subject for national humiliation. After Bretton Woods collapsed, the world moved towards 'floating' currencies, in which exchange rates changed day by day – indeed minute by minute.

Some economists, led by Milton Friedman, welcomed the change. They regarded fixed exchange rates as artificial, as government interference in the market process. Economies are not static. Over time, some become more competitive than others and that should lead their exchange rate to increase. Indeed, this process explained why the Bretton Woods system broke down: exchange rates that were sensible in the aftermath of the Second World War, when the American economy was dominant, were no longer appropriate once the West German and Japanese economic miracles had occurred in the 1950s and 1960s.

But the Europeans resisted the idea. They have never been as enthusiastic as the Americans about free-market economics. To European leaders, having markets set the exchange rate meant that a key measure of economic policy was set by 'speculators', who could upset carefully laid financial plans. So the Europeans tried to tame the markets by introducing a series of systems for managing exchange rates. The first was the 'snake', in which European currencies traded in narrow bands with each other and the group of currencies moved in tandem with the US dollar. The dollar link disappeared in 1973 and the whole system collapsed in 1977.

Undaunted, the Europeans tried a second time, in 1979, with the Exchange Rate Mechanism (ERM). Again, currencies traded in narrow bands against each other. But the system was dogged with persistent crises, as countries were forced to devalue against the Deutschmark, the linchpin of the system. The need to maintain the link against the mark constrained economic policy, as in 1983, when François Mitterrand, elected President of France in 1981 on a left-wing programme of nationalization and higher taxes, was forced to reverse policy and adopt a more market-friendly attitude.

The underlying cause of these crises was that other countries tended to have higher inflation rates than Germany. Over time, this made their goods more expensive and thus less competitive in international markets, leading to wide trade deficits. Devaluing the currency was another way of bringing prices back in line. The downside of this approach was that a devaluation raised the prices of imported goods, thereby giving inflation a further push. If workers demanded higher pay to compensate for such higher prices, the economy could get stuck in a cycle of high inflation, forced devaluation and more inflation.

The death knell for the Exchange Rate Mechanism came in the early 1990s. The reunification of Germany resulted in a construction boom, which in turn prompted the Bundesbank, the German central bank, to raise interest rates to reduce inflationary pressures. Higher rates increased the attractiveness of the Deutschmark, pushing it up against the currencies of other European countries. Those countries were forced to increase interest rates in order to keep their currencies within the ERM bands. In some cases, as in Britain, the result was a sharp recession. Speculators, led by the Hungarian-American hedge-fund manager George Soros, bet that Britain would not be able to stand the pain and would let the pound devalue. Soros was proved right – but not before the Bank of England had spent billions defending the pound in 1992. Britain opted out of the ERM; other countries, including Italy, stayed within the system, but with wider bands for fluctuation against the Deutschmark.

The whole episode confirmed the suspicions of European leaders that speculators like George Soros could cause chaos in fixed-exchange-rate systems. Individual central banks did not have sufficient resources to fight back. The answer was to deprive such speculators of a target: if all European countries had the same currency, there would be less scope to speculate. Even if traders targeted the new currency, the euro, European countries would have more ability to fight them if they pooled their resources. These countries pushed ahead with their plans, which involved launching the euro in 1999.

THE DOUBTERS

There were some, however, who doubted whether the European currency could possibly work. They pointed to the persistent crises in the ERM as evidence, not that speculators were at work, but that European economies had fundamental differences. Such differences made it very difficult for a single currency to work.

Let us go back to the idea that, if inflation rates vary between countries, the high-inflation economy will eventually become less competitive unless the exchange rate adjusts. In a single-currency area, there is no exchange rate to adjust. So what will happen instead? Business in the high-inflation countries will fail and workers will lose their jobs; either wages will fall or people will move to other areas of the single-currency zone in search of work. That is exactly what happens in America, where workers have historically moved from the old industrial areas of the northeast and Midwest, in search of jobs in southern and western states like Texas and California. Some states suffer from persistently high unemployment: their workers get benefits from the federal government in Washington DC to tide them over.

So a single currency works in the US because it is combined with a fiscal union (a single tax and spending authority), a political union (making New Yorkers happy to bail out those in Louisiana), and a single language that allows workers to move easily across borders. None of this was true of Europe before the single currency was set up; none of it is true now.

Yes, the EU does have a central budget – and sends grants to impoverished regions of the zone – but it is tiny by the standards of national budgets, around 1% of euro zone GDP, while many governments spend 40–50% of their national output. And yes, workers do move between countries in the EU – spot the Polish builders and the French bankers in London – but not on the same scale as intra-US migration.

Without the features that define the US, the risk was that euro zone countries would become less and less competitive. They would be forced to take perpetual subsidies from the richer nations – or, if such subsidies were not forthcoming, to quit the currency altogether. No previous currency union between sovereign nations had survived.

European leaders realized that some of these problems might occur. The 'snake' and the ERM had failed because other European countries could not match Germany's low inflation and export success – and, as the early 1990s showed, this made them vulnerable to a change in policy by the Bundesbank. The French hoped that the new European Central Bank (ECB) would be less German-dominated and less obsessed with inflation; the Germans feared that they would swap the strong Deutschmark for a weak euro and would end up subsidizing the profligate nations of southern Europe.

So the Germans insisted on several conditions. The new ECB would be based in Frankfurt and, so the Germans hoped, would be a clone of the Bundesbank. Countries could only join the euro if they met economic conditions concerning their inflation rate and their debt-to-GDP ratio; once in the euro, a 'stability and growth pact' would prevent national governments from being too profligate. In practice, however, countries were able to fudge their way to meeting the economic conditions (most notoriously, in the case of Greece) and the stability and growth pact was ignored more than it was enforced.

Despite these looming problems, the early years of the euro went remarkably smoothly. Citizens gave up their old notes and coins and adopted the new currency with enthusiasm. The new currency did bring some economic advantages, as international investors were more willing to buy bonds denominated in the highly liquid euro than they were in the smaller currencies like the Portuguese escudo. European companies found it easier to get finance.

The euro lost ground against the dollar in its early days but eventually recovered as investors developed confidence in the policies of the ECB. There was no Soros-style speculative attack with the aim of driving individual currencies out of the euro. Quite the reverse. The fringe countries like Italy, Spain and Greece had always faced much higher borrowing costs than Germany; investors feared that such countries would have higher inflation or would devalue their currencies, fears that were all too often fulfilled. But once it became clear that the euro was going ahead, bond yields started to fall to German levels in a process known as 'convergence'.

In retrospect, however, this fall in borrowing costs sowed the seeds of the current crisis in the euro zone. In some countries, notably Greece, the fall in costs gave politicians a free ride, providing them with no incentive to tackle underlying problems in their economies (cartels, uncompetitive industries, etc.). Greece's debt was all the higher by 2009 because it had not faced the fierce discipline of the markets. Far-sighted democratic leaders might have tackled the problems anyway – but Greek leaders were not far-sighted.

In other countries, notably Spain and Ireland, low financing costs led to a speculative bubble in property financed by the domestic banks. Had such economies maintained their own currencies, central banks might well have increased interest rates to pop such bubbles. But the ECB set interest rates with its eyes on Europe-wide conditions, rather than the property market in Dublin. This 'one size fits all' approach was another flaw in the euro zone's design: because the

European economy was not uniform, the right interest rate in Munich was not necessarily the right rate in Madrid.

A whole economy can be transformed when speculation is unchecked. In Ireland and Spain, property developers bought land and raced to erect houses, confident that a steady supply of buyers would be found; the banks became heavily exposed to such developers and the labour market became more heavily weighted towards construction. Democracies do not deal well with speculative booms. Rising house or equity prices look like a victimless crime: people are getting richer. Property developers and bank traders are happy to keep speculating; the banks are happy to keep lending; politicians see rising markets as a testament to their own skills. Central banks can, in theory, play the role of the party pooper but the ECB had no remit to tackle property booms in Spain and Ireland. It was simply concerned about the overall inflation rate for the euro zone, which stayed low.

Over the years, therefore, a series of imbalances built up within the system. A key measure of productivity is unit labour costs; the wages needed to produce a given amount of goods and services. Between 2000 and 2012 unit labour costs rose by less than 10% in Germany but by more than 30% in Italy and by 35% in Greece. As their businesses became steadily less competitive, both Italy and Greece ran persistent trade deficits. As a result, they steadily owed more and more to foreign investors. By the end of 2011, Portugal, Ireland and Spain owed more than 90% of their GDP to international investors; Greece and Cyprus owed around 80%.

This debt was owed by a combination of the public and private sectors. In Greece, it was largely a government issue, the result of its system of 'clientilism' under which rival parties handed out jobs and benefits to their supporters when they took office. When I visited Greece in early 2010, economists told me of a number of strange restrictions: very few truck licences were granted, for example, making it more expensive to transport goods from nearby towns in Greece than from faraway Italy. In her book *Greekonomics*,[2] the Greek-born economist Vicky Pryce (since better known for her role in the fall of her ex-husband cabinet minister Chris Huhne) cites a number of examples of waste and featherbedding. Many jobs were cited as 'hardship professions' that allow employees to retire early on full benefits: tuba players and hairdressers were on the list. Employees of the electricity utility who knew how to send faxes got a bonus of €870 a month. And thanks to various rules and regulations, it costs six times as much to build a road in Greece as it does in Germany.

By contrast, the budget positions of Spain and Ireland looked fairly sound. However, the banking sectors of both countries were taking on huge debts that would eventually come back to haunt their governments. Everyone seemed to be getting rich as their property rose in value; few dared to question the soundness of the boom. An Irish professor who raised some doubts was ridiculed by the country's prime minister.

THE CRISIS HITS

The trigger for the Greek crisis was the revelation, in February 2010, by the recently elected government of George Papandreou that the country's 2009 budget deficit was not 5% of GDP but a staggering 12.7%. Even this turned out to be an underestimate: the eventual shortfall, according to Eurostat, the European statistics agency, was 15.6% of GDP.

When a government spends more than it receives in taxes, it must borrow the difference. If it owes money to its own citizens, the task of refinancing debt is a lot easier; habit, national pride or regulations usually ensure that a lot of domestic investors are willing owners of their government's debt. But if the country also has a trade deficit, then it must borrow part of the money from foreign investors. Such investors need to be convinced that the country is a good credit: that it will pay back the debt in full and in the same currency in which it was borrowed. Up until 2008, this was no problem, for international investors made little distinction between lending to the Greek or German governments. But the restatement of Greek finances shattered the confidence of foreign investors; the cost of Greek borrowing soared. To put it another way, Greek bond yields increased sharply.

This revealed yet another flaw in Europe's plans to defy the speculators by instituting a single currency. The financial markets are like a bouncy castle: if you suppress them in one corner, they will pop up somewhere else. Speculators might not be able to bet against the Greek currency, but they could bet against Greek bonds. Just as damaging as speculation is a buyers' strike. Naturally enough, pension funds and insurance companies, with fiduciary duties to safeguard the funds entrusted to them, were reluctant to lend money to Greece.

A crisis of confidence in the bond markets can be a self-fulfilling prophecy. As it becomes more expensive for the government to borrow money, it becomes harder to close its budget deficit. Lack of progress in shrinking the deficit alarms investors, leading to a further rise in borrowing costs, and so on. A rule of thumb is that governments get into trouble when their cost of borrowing is higher than their nominal economic growth rate. So if government bonds yield 7%, but the economy is growing by 5% a year (say 2% real and 3% inflation), then the debt problem will get steadily worse. Any government that falls into such a hole will need to run a budget surplus[3] if it wants to get its debt-to-GDP ratio down.

But eliminating a deficit is extremely difficult when an economy falls into recession. When economic output shrinks, tax revenues tend to fall, since people are earning less and spending less and corporate profits are lower. Government spending is also likely to rise during a recession, particularly on unemployment benefits.

Governments initially responded to the 2007–8 financial crisis in classic Keynesian fashion, allowing their deficits to widen sharply. But the Greeks provided an awkward test for the Keynesian approach, which assumed it was always possible for governments to finance their deficits in the markets. Greek bond yields quickly surged into the double digits, making the country's finances look completely unsustainable. The country's debt was downgraded to junk status by the rating agencies, making it virtually untouchable by mainstream investors.

What happens when governments can no longer get private sector credit? In such a situation, they have to borrow money from other governments or from global lenders like the International Monetary Fund (IMF). But such lenders can be just as hard-headed as any hedge fund when it comes to getting their money back. The effect is that governments, and therefore citizens, lose control of economic policy.

The first bailout package for Greece was arranged in May 2010.

The lenders (a combination of the EU and the IMF) agreed to lend Greece €110 billion, provided that the government adopted an austerity programme, reformed its economy and raised €50 billion through privatization. This is where the tricky issues for democracy start to emerge. Just as the Germans resented the idea of lending money to the Greeks, the Greeks resented the conditions imposed by the more prosperous Germans. This antipathy had a historic basis: the Germans occupied Greece in the Second World War. However, it seems likely that bad feelings would also have arisen had, say, the French been setting the rules.

Had the EU truly been a single country, the attitude of the creditors might have been different. After all, many countries provide subsidies to their depressed regions; the difference between these subsidies and lending money that will never be paid back is purely a matter of semantics. But Greece is a separate country from Germany, with separate tax and benefit rules. It was natural for the German public to resent subsidizing the Greeks when the Greek state was so poor at collecting taxes from its own rich. Naturally, therefore, the creditor countries looked for signs that the Greeks would mend their spendthrift ways in the medium term, and would not become permanent dependants.

There is more to it than nationalism. The American tax and benefit systems are organized on a national basis: people from Mississippi and Nebraska pay the same Federal income tax rate and get their pensions at the same age. In Europe, however, tax rates vary from country to country, as do retirement ages. This further reduces the sense of solidarity. The French mutter bitterly about the low Irish tax rate on corporate profits, which causes multinationals to site their corporate headquarters in Dublin. Germans, facing a retirement age of 67, resent sending subsidies to Greeks so they can retire at 62.

By 2011 it was fairly clear that the first Greek bailout package would not be enough. The Greek economy was collapsing, sending its debt-to-GDP ratio higher, not lower. A combination of minimal investor enthusiasm and a lack of political will meant that there had been no privatization. So Greece received a second bailout, and this time the EU insisted that the country's private sector creditors should suffer a write-off, so that the debt burden could be reduced. Official creditors were unaffected. The aim was to restrict Greece's government debt-to-GDP ratio in 2020 at a still-high 120%. More austerity was required. The practical effect of these loan conditions was that Greece's economic policy was being set not by its voters, but by outsiders. This looks anti-democratic to the Greeks. In addition, it may well be that German voters disapprove of the decision to lend Greece money on any conditions. Democracy is therefore negated in both creditor and debtor nations.

Those fears were brought into sharp relief by the events of November 2011. Faced with widespread protests over the country's austerity programme, the Greek prime minister, George Papandreou, announced that he would hold a referendum to allow voters to approve, or reject, the latest loan package. This caused consternation in other European nations: the leaders of France and Germany said that if Greece were to hold a referendum, it would have to be on EU membership, not the loan conditions. They also talked for the first time about the possibility of Greece abandoning the euro. Mr Papandreou was forced to back down. He resigned, to be replaced by Lucas Papademos, a former central banker, at the head of a coalition government.

Conspiracy theorists will have a field day with this episode for decades. Was the whole event a cunning ploy by Mr Papandreou to ensure that his Pasok (socialist) party did not take the entire blame for the austerity package? (If so, it wasn't successful: Pasok's support plunged in the 2012 elections.) A more benign interpretation might be that Mr Papandreou recognized that only a coalition government could muster enough support to push through the deal.

The most damning interpretation of the affair is that the elected leader of a sovereign state, who wished to get voter approval for a major change in economic policy, was removed from office by foreigners in the equivalent of a coup, and replaced by an unelected banker who was willing to accede to the demands of foreign creditors. In the same month, Silvio Berlusconi resigned as Italy's prime minister after broad hints from German and French politicians that they would be happy to see him depart.

However, it is worth noting that Greek voters still had the option of rejecting those politicians who agreed to the loan; indeed, Greece had two general elections in 2012, which revolved around the loans and the resulting austerity packages. Although Greek voters flirted with extremist parties, a coalition led by the New Democracy Party was able to form a government. Similarly, the German voters have the chance to reject Angela Merkel, the chancellor who agreed to the loans, when she next offers herself for election in 2013. German opposition parties have not been calling for the Greeks to be abandoned. The underlying structure of representative democracy has been maintained.

THE DEMOCRATIC DEFICIT

Nevertheless, the Greek affair has reinvigorated the debate over whether Europe has a democratic deficit. The EU has a separation of powers, rather like the US. It has an administration – the Commission – based in Brussels. It has a Parliament, full of directly elected MEPs, which travels between Brussels and Strasbourg. It has a Supreme Court, the European Court of Justice, based in Luxembourg.[4] And it has an executive, the Council of Ministers, which comprises the 27 national governments meeting together.

The Commission doles out posts to prominent citizens of various countries. While Commission members are all nominated by their home governments, the task of parcelling out the jobs arises from a combination of horse-trading between the big powers and the desires of the Commission president. The former British prime minister Gordon Brown famously lobbied for the foreign minister's job for his own nominee, Baroness Ashton, leaving Britain's cherished financial sector at the mercy of a French appointee.

The executive, in the form of the Council of Ministers, is the most powerful force within the EU. Nothing can get done unless the individual governments agree amongst themselves, and that was a problem in the era when decisions could be held up by a veto of a single state (broadly speaking, from 1965 to 1986). In the latter year, the Single European Act introduced Qualified Majority Voting (QMV) to areas of cross-border trade (the single-market programme) and it was extended into other areas such as education and employment in the 1990s.[5] The admission of more countries into the EU required more detailed negotiations about how QMV would work, culminating in the Treaty of Nice of 2001. The current system allows decisions to go ahead if 74% of the countries by 'voting weight' or 62% by population agree. This means that, in theory, the EU could go ahead with a decision even if France and Germany were both opposed; in practice, France and Germany tend to dominate.

Although democratically elected governments have been involved in driving forward European integration, the process has not been particularly democratic. The elites have led the way, often without consulting the voters. Decisions have been made at late-night summits, with national leaders under pressure not to block an EU-wide deal. Horse-trading is implicit; block the EU in one area and a dissident country might suffer retaliation in another.

On those occasions when the voters have been consulted, their response has tended to range from indifference to outright disapproval. After the 1992 Maastricht Treaty, which set out the path to the euro, French voters were allowed a referendum on the deal: they approved it by just 51% to 49%. Danish voters rejected the deal by a similar margin; they were made to vote again the following year, a process that should make any democrat deeply uncomfortable (although Denmark, like Britain, did not join the euro zone) – and this time they approved it.

After the Treaty of Nice (which allowed for the admission of ex-communist nations in Eastern Europe), Irish voters rejected the deal in a referendum; they too were asked to vote again in order to come up with the 'right' answer (which they did). Then came the new Constitution for Europe in 2005. When that was rejected by both French and Dutch voters, EU leaders displayed a modicum of shame and did not make either country vote again. But many of the Constitution's provisions reappeared in the Treaty of Lisbon, which was signed in 2007; when this too was rejected in an Irish referendum in 2008, the Irish were again forced to vote a second time – voting for the treaty in 2009, bringing it into force the same year.

It is true that referenda can be blunt instruments: electorates may use them to express disapproval of the government of the day, rather than to answer the question before them. Nevertheless, the habit of making voters reconsider, like naughty children, is profoundly undemocratic. What is the point of voting if only one answer is acceptable?

European leaders seem to have adopted the argument of 'output legitimacy' – that provided integration plans enhanced prosperity, voters would approve them in retrospect. That might just have been plausible in the early days of the euro, when the main effect of the currency seemed to be to lower borrowing costs. But as *The Economist* commented, 'Output legitimacy is a hard sell when the outputs voters use to reach a judgment are a crisis they didn't create and austerity they didn't want.'[6]

There have been various attempts to address the democratic problem by, for example, boosting the powers of the European Parliament. Ironically, as the powers of the Parliament have increased, voter enthusiasm has dwindled; turnout in European elections fell from 63% in 1979 to 43% in 2009. Charles Grant of the Centre for European Reform argues that the Parliament has done a good job in monitoring the legislation produced by the Commission. But he admits that such monitoring has done nothing to restore the body's public reputation, which is still dogged by issues such as MEPs' expenses, for which no receipts are required.

One problem is that voters in European elections aren't really choosing a European government. In a national election, a vote will change the prime minister or president, and policies will change as a result; this is not the case with an EU poll. Perhaps this will change in future. The various political parties have formed loose federations – the Socialists, and the Alliance of Liberals and Democrats, and the right-wing European People's Party, although this does not include Britain's Conservatives, who dislike the federalist policies of the other groups. The seventh Parliament, elected in 2009, has asserted itself more vigorously, particularly in areas such as the budget and on financial regulation; it will be interesting to see whether its higher profile sparks a higher turnout when European voters choose the next Parliament in 2014.

The Parliament gets to approve the choice of Commission president, but only after the Council of Ministers makes its own choice – another opportunity for horse-trading. Direct election of the president has been mooted, but one can foresee problems with the idea: German voters would outweigh several of the small nations and British voters would feel alienated, since a UK candidate would never receive enough support from other EU nations to be chosen. Some sort of electoral-college system would be needed.

By itself, the lack of democratic legitimacy has become a block to reform. As the current crisis developed, many commentators argued that what the EU needed was more integration – for example, of fiscal policy. But any changes would need to be put to voters in a referendum, in the middle of an economic crisis when EU institutions were very unpopular. Politicians were understandably unwilling to risk it.

Just as democracy has been challenged at the European level, it has also faced a crisis at the national level. For a short while, the prime ministers of Greece and Italy were both unelected. In Greece, Lucas Papademos, a former central banker, ruled from November 2011 to May 2012 and oversaw the negotiations that led to the write-off of around €100 billion of Greek debt. Democracy was not abolished: Mr Papademos depended on the support of the two main parties in Parliament and acted as the 'Dirty Harry' of the crisis, doing the nasty job for which no elected politician wanted to take the blame.

Papademos's appointment was followed by that of Mario Monti, a former EU commissioner, as prime minister of Italy. He was brought in to replace Silvio Berlusconi and, in order to take his post, he was appointed senator for life by the Italian president. Like Papademos, Monti depended on elected MPs to get his measures through Parliament. But unlike Papademos, he was still in office a year later – even though the popularity of his government had fallen by 32 percentage points.[7] Again, Monti seemed to be there to do the dirty work: he pushed through reforms of pensions and labour laws and raised taxes. In December 2012 the parties linked to Silvio Berlusconi withdrew their support on the grounds that Monti had pushed austerity too far. In the election that followed in February 2013, Mr Monti's bloc came only fourth – a sign that his reforms had made him unpopular – while depressingly, Mr Berlusconi's group received as much as 29% of the vote.

The decision to appoint Messrs Papademos and Monti can be justified by results; reforms were pushed through and debt was restructured. But the whole episode leaves a nasty taste. European democracy has to turn away from elected politicians in the face of a deep economic crisis, and those politicians were able to absolve themselves from responsibility for all the difficult tasks that had to be performed. But if politicians cannot take the tough decisions, voters might ask, why do we need them at all?

AIDED BY ACRONYMS

After the financial crisis broke, the EU was in a dilemma. Outright aid to EU countries would seem to contravene the 'no bailout' clause (article 125 of the original Rome Treaty) that was built into the EU project to reassure Germany that other countries would not be allowed to go on a spending spree and leave Germany with the bill. So the leaders came up with a variety of ingenious devices, marked by their use of acronyms and a degree of wishful thinking.

The fundamental issue was whether the various EU countries had a liquidity problem or a solvency problem. A liquidity problem means that the country has a temporary difficulty in getting access to credit, usually because the market has been disrupted. When the market returns to normal, such a country will have no difficulty paying its creditors back. A solvency problem means that the country is broke; it simply does not have the resources to pay back its debts. Helping a country with a liquidity problem is not a bailout; helping a country with a solvency problem is.

The EU decided to treat the issue as a liquidity problem. It set up the European Financial Stability Facility (EFSF) in 2010 and its successor, the European Stability Mechanism (ESM) to lend money to countries whose borrowing costs had shot up. The EFSF was backed by guarantees from the richer sovereign nations. In a sense, it allowed Greece and Spain to piggyback on the better credit ratings of Germany, the Netherlands and the rest.

The first Greek bailout was undertaken before the EFSF was established. But the EFSF did take part in the €85 billion bailout of Ireland in November 2010, the €78 billion package for Portugal in May 2011 and the second Greek deal in late 2012. With all these demands on its funds, it quickly became apparent that the €440 billion backing for the EFSF might not be enough; it was beefed up to €780 billion.

The ESM, which started in October 2012, had a slightly different approach. The better-off nations put up capital for the ESM, something which will allow it to borrow money from the markets at a cheap rate, with a total capacity of €500 billion. It was designed to replace the more temporary EFSF and act as a permanent lender within the EU.

As well as helping countries, the ESM can also be used to recapitalize the region's banking system. As was made very clear in the 2007–8 credit crunch, the fates of governments and banks are closely tied together. No government can afford to see a major bank collapse for fear of the effect it will have on consumer confidence and business lending. Goverments step in to rescue banks taxpayer money. But banks have also been significant buyers of government bonds, which they are allowed to treat as 'risk-free' assets on their balance sheet.

Countries that apply for help from the ESM must agree to a memorandum of understanding with the fund, covering the austerity programmes and structural reforms that will be required. The country must also have ratified the 'fiscal compact' – the treaty that was agreed in early 2012 by all nations in the EU except the Czech Republic and the United Kingdom. The fiscal compact is a reincarnation of the stability and growth pact that failed to keep government finances in order before the debt crisis. It requires countries with debt-to-GDP ratios above 60% to bring them down, and those with budget deficits to limit the structural element (that which is unconnected with the economic cycle) to 0.5% or 1% of GDP.[8] In theory, countries can be brought before the European Court of Justice, and fined 0.1% of GDP if they do not honour this commitment. The rules sound pretty harsh but the devil, as always, is in the details. There is nothing that forces the nations to do these things immediately: analysis suggests it may be four to five years before the rules of the fiscal compact begin to bite.[9]

Whatever the formal nature of the rules, the practical implications of the ESM are that countries applying for a loan will have to surrender some degree of sovereignty over economic issues, just like countries that get a deal with the IMF. They may have some latitude over how they get their deficit down, but they are expected to reduce it some-how. They will, in practice, have latitude over the pace of economic reforms but they will be expected to sign up to a reform programme. Nevertheless, the potential loss of a degree of sovereignty makes countries reluctant to apply to the ESM for help; as of May 2013 none had done so. As noted earlier, further loss of sovereignty will occur under the so-called two-pack deal; countries will need to get their budgets pre-approved by Brussels.

Of course, those countries (Greece, Ireland and Portugal) which had bailouts from the EFSF have had to pursue austerity in any case. A fourth, Spain, has had help for its banks and has been desperately trying to avoid a formal bailout; it has pursued austerity as part of that strategy. All four have largely been successful in reducing their structural deficits. But economic weakness has meant that cyclical deficits have remained, adding to their debt totals.

BRING IN THE CENTRAL BANK

Big though the lending capacity of the ESM might be, it is only big enough to deal with relatively small economies like Ireland, Greece and Portugal. Italy has almost €2 trillion of government debt. So when Italian and Spanish bond yields started rising sharply in 2011, it was clear that more had to be done. The authorities had to turn to the euro zone's central bank.

In its early years, the ECB was seen as pretty strict and unimagina-tive, focusing on its inflation target and on the money supply, a topic that was no longer mentioned by the central banks of the US and UK. But when the financial crisis first erupted in August 2007, the ECB was swift to act, pumping €95 billion into the market as inter-bank lending started to dry up. An old central-banking adage (coined by Walter Bagehot, a nineteenth-century editor of *The Economist*) was that in a crisis a central bank should lend freely to solvent banks, pro-vided they could offer good collateral. But as the crisis dragged on, the ECB became less and less strict about the collateral it would accept, leading one commentator to describe it as the 'soup kitchen' for Europe's banks.[10]

Lending to banks was one thing – lending to governments was another. The original Rome Treaty on setting up the EU (or European Economic Community, EEC, as it was then) had two clauses that should have made it difficult for the ECB to buy government bonds.[11] The first (article 123) was the prohibition of monetary financing – in other words, the creation of new money to fund a government's deficit. That was what the Reichsbank did in 1923, leading to the hyperinflationary episode that is seared into Germany's folk memory. The second was the no-bailout clause.

So given these clauses, how could the ECB start to buy Spanish and Italian government bonds, as it did via yet another acronym, the SMP (Securities Market Programme)? Technically, the rules were met. The ECB was not bailing out the countries; it expected them to pay back the bonds. Nor was it buying the bonds with new money; it was 'sterilizing' the purchases by withdrawing the same amount of money from the markets. And the SMP could be justified as part of its monetary policy remit. The ECB has the responsibility for setting interest rates across the continent; the sell-off in Spanish and Italian bonds was affecting short-term rates in those countries.

If the SMP programme seemed big (about €200 billion at the time of writing), the ECB's next acronym, the LTRO (Long-Term Refinancing Operation), was even bigger. Launched in late 2011, the programme was designed to deal with the same problem that erupted back in August 2007: banks were having problems getting financing, because they were reluctant to lend money to each other. The danger was that struggling banks would cut finance from consumers and businesses and send the European economy into freefall. So the ECB stepped in and provided cheap financing (around 1%) to banks for a three-year period. In Spain and Italy, the banks took that money and invested it in their own government's bonds, earning a nice turn in the process. Here again, no rules were broken. The ECB was not bailing out governments; it was bailing out banks, which were bailing out governments. In all, the ECB handed out €1 trillion in loans; it took collateral, of course, largely in the form of government bonds.

So what happens if the banks don't pay the money back? The ECB gets to keep the government bonds. And what happens if the governments default? Then the ECB will be left with a big hole in its balance sheet – a balance sheet that has expanded from well under €1 trillion before the financial crisis to almost €4 trillion by March 2012. Almost certainly, the governments of northern Europe will have to subscribe new capital to repair this hole.[12]

In content, if not in form, all this certainly looks like a bailout – and it looks a lot like monetary financing as well. It will be remarkable if the ECB ever does shrink its balance sheet down to pre-crisis size: when will the European economy be strong enough to absorb a sale of the ECB's government bond holdings? The same goes for the Federal Reserve and the Bank of England, with their quantitative easing programmes.

The equity markets rallied in response to both the SMP and the LTRO. The big hope was that the crisis for the euro zone might be over. Lower financing costs would allow the banks to start lending and the troubled economies to recover. But both rallies petered out.

So in the summer of 2012 the ECB president, Mario Draghi (who hails, coincidentally or not, from Italy, one of the debtor countries), pledged that the bank would do 'whatever it takes' to save the euro. His plan, unveiled almost five years to the day since the ECB's first intervention in the crisis, was to buy potentially unlimited amounts of short-term Spanish and Italian government bonds. Needless to say, a new acronym was needed – the OMT (Outright Monetary Transactions) programme. If only the European economy were as productive in areas like technology as it is with acronyms!

Once again, Mr Draghi wasn't breaking the rules – any bond purchases would be sterilized (no monetary creation) and the conditionality of the loans meant that the programme would not involve the funding of spendthrift governments. But the ECB was starting to resemble one of those problem drinkers, who started off life teetotal. One day they try a small sherry, then before you know it they are on the scotch, and they end up sleeping on a park bench with a bottle of lighter fluid.

Again the markets rallied, although there were a couple of catches. The first was that the Bundesbank, under its leader Jens Weidmann, was against the plan. In the circumstances, it seems remarkable that Mr Draghi went ahead, given the ECB's perceived role as a European Bundesbank and Germany's clout as the largest economy and biggest creditor within the zone.

This was an irony on many levels. First, as already noted, the ECB was intended to be a replacement for the Bundesbank – assurance for the German people that their sound money would not be destroyed by inflationary southern Europeans. And here was an Italian head of the ECB pushing through a bond purchase deal that would benefit his home country. Second, what stands behind the credit of the ECB? In the end, it is the wealth of European taxpayers. And since several European countries have their own credit problems, German taxpayers are the main guarantors of ECB debt. But the views of their own bank were overruled. As the *Financial Times* columnist Gideon Rachman noted shortly after the launch of the OMT, the ECB cannot be overruled by the German Parliament, or by German courts; at the ECB council, the president of the Bundesbank has the same vote as the president of the central bank of Malta.

The ECB was not offering a blanket guarantee to buy bonds: countries would have to agree to an ESM rescue programme, with policy conditions attached. So responsibility for Spanish or Italian economic policy would pass from Madrid and Rome to Frankfurt. As Mr Rachman pointed out, 'As a result of the ECB's actions, voters from Germany to Spain will increasingly find that crucial decisions about national economic policy cannot be changed at the ballot box.'[13]

Maybe this programme will work, or maybe it will not. But let us step back and look at it from a democratic point of view. Two rescue schemes have been set up which can dole out money to governments across the euro zone; European taxpayers stand behind them. But these proposals have not been put to a vote in any European nation, even though they appear to circumvent the terms of the treaty which is the basis for countries to join the EU. The ECB, an unelected body, is also taking risks on behalf of the European taxpayer without any democratic mandate. That is a problem for voters in the creditor countries; in the debtor countries, they face the prospect that decisions about the level of taxes, of social spending and the structure of local industries will be made at the European level and not simply confined to voters within their borders.

The European Central Bank was expressly set up to be free of democratic influence, on the grounds that politicians are too tempted to meddle with monetary policy, with inflationary results. But the head of this undemocratic body, Mario Draghi, is arguably the most powerful man in Europe, just as his counterpart Ben Bernanke of the Federal Reserve is the second most powerful man in the US after the president.

NEEDS MUST WHEN THE DEVIL DRIVES

The defenders of the EU will argue that the ESM and the EFSF were established with the approval of national governments and that they represent the only practical way a financial rescue plan could have been accomplished. In the midst of a financial crisis, there is no time to submit detailed proposals to a referendum. Governments make financial decisions all the time, some of which involve other countries – the granting of foreign aid, for example.

One can also argue that the economic consequences of a euro zone break-up would be so huge that the EU and the ECB prevented much hardship and unemployment by acting the way that they did, and this excuses any minor rule-bending to the provisions of a treaty which very few voters will ever have bothered to read. (Of course, by the same token, European ministers might have avoided a lot of problems by not setting up the euro in the first place.)

Nevertheless, it seems extraordinary that taxpayers can be committed to underwrite some very large sums without their explicit consent. Three trillion euros (the expansion of the ECB's balance sheet) is almost as large as Germany's entire GDP. A commitment to stand behind another nation's debts is easily as important as the governance changes in the Nice Treaty that were put to referenda and rejected by French and Dutch voters.

German opponents of the bailout plan took their case to the country's constitutional court in September 2012 and lost. The court acted very cautiously, insisting only that the German Parliament give consent to all the various proposals. It seems the judges do not want to be accused of sabotaging the European economy. Nevertheless, we have ended up with a situation where no one seems very happy: neither voters in the creditor nations, who resent subsidizing the debtors, nor voters in the debtor nations, who resent having austerity imposed upon them.

The dilemma was highlighted again in March 2013 when Cyprus, one of the smallest nations in the EU, turned to the EU for a bailout. As part of the conditions for the deal, the EU insisted the Cypriots raise €6 billion from their own resources, in the form of a levy on the banking sector. The Cypriot banks were around eight times the size of the country's GDP, having been inflated by the use of the island as an offshore home for Russian money. The Cypriots initially tried to recover the cost by imposing a levy, not just on uninsured deposits (those with over €100,000) but on insured depositors too. This caused outrage and was quickly withdrawn in the face of public demonstrations. A second deal placed all the burden on uninsured deposits, leading to heavy losses for small businessmen as well as the Russians. The plan required limiting the amount of money Cypriots could remove from cashpoints as well as capital controls to stop funds leaving the country. The effect is likely to be a deep recession with output falling by as much as a third.

Again, the crisis illustrated the problems of the EU structure; the Cyprus government did not have the financial strength to back its own banks. It thus implicitly relied on other EU nations to provide the financial support. But the rest of the EU saw no reason to penalize their own citizens to bail out Russian investors, especially when they had no say in regulating Cypriot banks.

REALITY BITES

Never mind the politics of austerity: many people think that the economics of austerity are also misguided. The euro zone economy is desperately weak, recording six successive quarters of falling output up to the spring of 2013. The outlook for the rest of the year seemed no better; in April, the IMF forecast that output in the euro area would fall 0.2% over the full year. The public are deeply unhappy, as manifested by repeated strikes and protests, including a Europe-wide day of action in November 2012.

Keynesians like Paul Krugman think that government deficits are the inevitable consequence of decisions by the private sector (particularly business) to stop spending and accumulate surpluses. Government finances will return to normal when the economy recovers. As Krugman put it in one blog post:

> Shaving an extra couple of points off the structural deficit will make very little difference to long-run solvency, nor will it do much to accelerate the pace of internal devaluation. It will, however, depress employment even further and inflict a lot of direct suffering too through cuts in social programs. In effect, the policy is to inflict pain for the sake of inflicting pain.[14]

When governments raise taxes, the income of consumers obviously falls; when they cut spending, this usually means lower payments for benefit recipients or fewer jobs for government workers, something that also hurts demand. This lower demand hurts businesses in the private sector, which may also cut back on investment or jobs.

There have been a few examples of countries that have cut their way to prosperity, most notably Canada in the 1990s. But Canada benefited from the fact that its neighbour, the US, was enjoying a boom at the time. Canadian businesses were thus able to export more and simultaneously maintain wages and employment, even as the public sector was shrinking. The problem in the current crisis is that many countries are pursuing austerity at the same time. Greek businesses cannot offset weak domestic demand with higher orders from Spain or Portugal. Furthermore, a usual benefit of austerity programmes is that government bond markets react positively. Lower interest rates thus support the economy. But in much of the developed world, interest rates are already very low. There is no boost to come from this direction.

The IMF has traditionally been a supporter of austerity programmes. But in its 2012 World Economic Outlook, it showed signs of changing its mind. The key measure is the 'fiscal multiplier': how much does a cut in the government budget affect overall GDP? Back in 2010, the IMF thought that the multiplier was 0.5; in other words, a deficit reduction of 1% of GDP would result in a GDP fall of 0.5%. But when the IMF looked at what actually happened, it reckoned that the multiplier might even be higher than 1 (the estimated range was

0.9 to 1.7). If the latter number is correct, then austerity makes the economy and the debt-to-GDP ratio deteriorate.

That seems to be the case in Greece, where the economy has consistently underperformed the projections of the IMF ever since the fund became involved in 2010. Gabriel Sterne of the research firm Exotix says that Greek GDP in 2013 is likely to be 22% lower than the IMF's November 2010 forecast, while government revenues are expected to be 15% lower. The debt-to-GDP ratio will be 38% higher than the IMF originally thought.

In late October 2012 a Greek coalition government led by Antonis Samaras announced new economic projections. These foresaw a budget deficit of 5.2% of GDP in 2013, a further decline in GDP of 4.5% and a likely peak debt-to-GDP ratio of 192% in 2014. In theory, Greece was supposed to be getting its debt down to 120% of GDP by 2020, something that looked highly unlikely without help. To illustrate the problem: the Greek budget assumed that the country would be running a primary surplus in 2013, in other words, its revenues would exceed its expenditure, before interest payments. But the debt mountain was so high that the country was still running a big deficit after interest payments. The economist Vicky Pryce concluded that 'The time frame for Greek reform was too short, technical assistance came too late and the austerity measures were too harsh and did not take into account the impact they would have on the economy and the inability of the Greek system to reform in a hurry.'[15]

A further Greek austerity programme was agreed in November 2012, but there must be doubts over whether it can succeed where previous efforts have failed. It seems very likely that other euro zone governments will have to forgive Greek debt. Capital Economics forecast that governments will have to take a loss of more than 50% on their Greek debt holdings. But that might not be acceptable to the electorates of creditor countries and would, in effect, add to the debt burdens of those countries. The ECB was also indicating that it would not accept a write-down of its holdings, since that would amount to the kind of Weimar-style 'monetary financing' forbidden in the Treaty of Rome.

Spain seems like another case of a downward spiral in which

austerity leads to economic weakness, bigger deficits, and thus more austerity. In early 2013 Spanish unemployment was running at 27%, with (excluding students) one in two young people unable to find a job. Some of those people may have jobs in the informal or black-market economy – nevertheless, the figures are remarkably high. A September 2012 budget protected social spending but raised taxes in a variety of ways, including a wealth tax and a tax on lottery winnings.

Ironically, the Spanish government actually ran a budget surplus in 2006 and 2007; it was only after the crisis broke that the deficit shot up to 9.7% of GDP in 2010. The housing boom created a false sense of security, since high property prices (and strong bank profits) brought in tax revenues. As a proportion of GDP, Spanish tax revenues fell more than 5 percentage points between 2007 and 2012, the worst performance in the EU.[16] Falling tax revenues were one reason why Spain struggled to get its budget deficit under control: instead of falling to 6% of GDP in 2011 (the official target), the deficit was still 9.4%. The target for 2012 was 6.4% and the government calculated a final figure of 6.7%; however, the EU's statistical arm, Eurostat, came up with 10.6% when the cost of supporting the banks was included.

Spain's devolved structure has caused trouble, with its 17 regional governments responsible for one-third of all public spending. The regions have tended to spend more than they take in, and to rely on central government to make up the shortfall. As of autumn 2012, Andalucia, Castile la Mancha, Catalonia, Murcia and Valencia had all applied for aid from the central government. Their combined requests totalled €14.9 billion, out of an €18 billion fund put aside for the purpose.[17] The crisis has also provoked a separatist campaign in Catalonia, the northeastern region that includes Barcelona. Catalans feel that they contribute more to the central government than they get back (despite the bailout). An opinion poll in October 2012 found that 81% of Catalans wanted a referendum on secession and that 53% would vote in favour.[18]

In Portugal, the centre-right government unveiled a tax-hiking budget in September 2012, with the administration hoping to raise €4.3 billion, or 2.6% of GDP, in extra revenue. The average income tax rate was pushed up to 13.2% from 9.8% in an effort to reduce the budget deficit by 1.6% of GDP and meet the targets set by the EU under Portugal's €78 billion bailout programme. The plan was opposed by the Socialist opposition and by the trade unions, which called a general strike. Portuguese unemployment was already 16% and is expected to head higher.

The trade position of the struggling countries has improved. Ireland, for example, has managed to get its current account in surplus and its exports are worth more than 100% of GDP.[19] Spain has also eliminated its trade deficit. But in the case of Greece, the decline in the trade deficit is largely down to the slump in the economy – 2013 is expected to be the sixth successive year of falling output – that has caused demand for imports to collapse.

FORWARD MARCH

In the face of these problems, many commentators say that the EU cannot dither any longer. It must either go back or go forward. Going back means dissolving the euro zone or at least jettisoning some of the weaker members. This would be very difficult in political terms, given all the effort that has been put into the euro's creation. It would be very difficult in financial terms, given the amount of government debt owned by the ECB, the rescue funds and the commercial banks of the creditor nations. And it will be very hard to draw the line and decide which nations should stay and which should leave: on some criteria, France does not belong in the premier league.

Going forward means a closer union, in political and financial terms. One proposal is for a banking union in which a single body (probably the ECB) stands behind all banks in the euro zone and all banking deposits are guaranteed. In short, if a Portuguese bank goes bust, German or Dutch depositors have to meet part of the bill. To safeguard those depositors, Europe will need an international regulator. But this means someone in Brussels or Frankfurt can tell a French or Italian bank to stop lending, even if that means hardship for Italian businesses and consumers. That will be tough to swallow. Traditionally, European banks have had a close relationship with their business sectors: supporting the corporate sector has been seen as more important than maximizing profits.

Another proposal is for the issue of common eurobonds, in which one country's debts are guaranteed by the rest. This would eliminate the problem of high bond yields in the peripheral countries, but at the cost of pushing up yields in Germany and France. Germany is understandably reluctant to go down this road.

In a book called *For Europe*, Guy Verhofstadt, the former Belgian prime minister, and Daniel Cohn-Bendit, a German MEP,[20] call for a federal Europe as the only solution to the crisis. In an interview they argued that 'there is no alternative. All other options have been exhausted over the past three years and to no avail. The intergovernmental approach, where unanimity rules, has been utterly discredited by the financial crisis.'[21] They want the next European Parliament – elections are due in 2014 – to draw up a constitution which will be subject to an EU-wide referendum, followed by referenda in individual countries over whether they want to join the super-state. This will, they admit, result in a split Europe, but they argue that this is already the case. Some countries are in the euro, some are not; some share border controls, some do not.

The common difficulty in all these proposals is how to reconcile them with democracy. Europeans think of democracy in national terms; they pay little attention to events in the European Parliament, and vote in lower numbers than they do in their national elections. There is little evidence that they want to be part of a federal Europe. But economics points to federal solutions as the only way out of Europe's mess. If Europeans do not get a democratic version of federation, they may get an undemocratic version, as all the key decisions are taken out of the hands of voters. This may only increase their feeling of powerlessness and their alienation from the political elites.

10

All Men are Created Unequal

The true patriot in a democracy ought to take care that the majority of the community are not too poor for this is the cause of rapacity in that government.

Aristotle, *Politics*

Where the riches are in a few hands, these must enjoy all the power and will readily conspire to lay all the burden on the poor, and oppress them still further to the discouragement of all industry.

David Hume, *Philosophical Works*, vol. IV, 1748

The year 2012 was the hundredth anniversary of the sinking of the *Titanic*. The loss of the ship continues to fascinate us, as the great success of James Cameron's 1997 movie demonstrated. The tale seems to have so much resonance, both as an example of human pride brought low (the ship was deemed unsinkable) and as an awful omen of the much greater carnage that was to occur in the First World War.

But, in a wonderfully unsubtle fashion in the Cameron film, the *Titanic* is also used as a class parable: a world in which happy-go-lucky fiddle-playing third-class passengers drowned as snooty, fur-coat-wearing aristocrats scrambled into the lifeboats. Thank goodness, we are meant to feel, that we have left behind such ridiculous class prejudice and extremes of wealth.

But perhaps things are not so different after all. The Occupy Wall Street movement with its slogan of 'We are the 99%' tapped into a feeling that the world is once again being controlled by an aloof elite.

Rather than everyone being in the same boat, the rich have escaped on to their luxury yachts and private jets. We pay taxes; they avoid them. We vote, but they finance the politicians' campaigns. They speculate, and we bail them out when the banks fail. Moreover, this is not just a left-wing view. A recent book by Ferdinand Mount, a former aide to Margaret Thatcher, decried the emergence of a British oligarchy, stating that 'Instead of democracy widening and deepening as had been hoped, power and wealth have, slowly but unmistakably, begun to migrate into the hands of a relatively small elite.'[1]

From the late 1920s to the late 1970s, the share of wealth of the top 1% of the population generally fell quite steadily in most Western countries.[2] This 'great compression', as it became known, had a number of different causes. The growth of university education allowed more children to be socially mobile; the Great Depression destroyed the capital of many wealthy people; and very high tax rates, particularly in wartime, did the rest. When governments were not confiscating and redistributing wealth through taxes, they were eroding it through inflation, penalizing those who had patriotically bought government bonds to support the war effort. At the other end of the scale, the welfare state supported the incomes of the elderly and the unemployed. During these years, the world of the *Titanic* and its class divisions increasingly seemed consigned to the history books.

But in the 1980s everything started to change. First of all, the very wealthiest began to enjoy enormous income gains. One survey[3] found that the average annual earnings of the top 0.1% of Americans increased by 362% between 1979 and 2007. Contrary to the assertions of those who believe in 'trickle-down' economics, these gains were not shared by the average citizen. Workers in the bottom 90% of the population saw their earnings rise by just 17% over the same period. And the effect was even worse for those at the bottom of the ladder. In 1978 the average incomes of American households in the poorest fifth of the population was the equivalent, in today's money, of $11,659; by 2011 it had fallen to $11,239. By 2007 the top 0.1% of American earners were receiving 200 times the average of the bottom 90%.[4]

There are many ways of slicing the data, but the economist Joseph

Stiglitz calculated two striking statistics: the top 1% of Americans received 40% more in a single week than the bottom 20% received in an entire year; the top 0.1% (a thousandth of the population) only took a day and a half to receive what the bottom 90% earned in a full year.[5]

Moving from income to wealth, in 2004 the average net worth of the top 1% of American households was $15 million; the bottom 80% had an average of $82,000 (including their houses). The top 1% owned a third of all American assets. Individuals in the bottom 40% of the population had seen their wealth decline; their average wealth in 2004 was just $2,200, compared with the equivalent in real terms of $5,400 in 1983. And 17% of households had zero or negative net worth: they owed more than they possessed. Between 1983 and 2004 only 10% of all wealth gains went to the bottom 80% of Americans.[6] These figures were almost designed to prove the truth of the old music-hall song: 'In this life, nothing's surer, the rich get richer and the poor get poorer.'

The British data are almost as striking. As Downton Abbey fans will know, incomes in the Edwardian era were extremely unequal – which is why Lord Grantham could afford to live in a large house with all those servants. Income taxes, death duties, a fall in agricultural income caused by global competition: all these reduced the traditional sources of British wealth. The great country-house estates were weakened during the First World War (with a shortage of labour, servants could find higher wages elsewhere) and almost wiped out during the Second World War. Between 1945 and 1974 a further 250 British country houses were demolished.[7]

The top 0.01% of the population (1 in every 10,000 households) received 4.25% of the national income in 1913;[8] this share fell pretty steadily to 0.28% in 1978 (a time, not coincidentally, when the top rate of tax on investment income was 98%). Margaret Thatcher took office in the following year, and the share of the wealthiest began to rise again, peaking at 1.44% in 2007.

A broader measure is to compare the top 10% of the population versus the bottom 90%. In 1913 the former group's share of total income was 47.5%, rising to 48.6% in 1923. Once again, 1978 was the 'most equal' year in recent times, with the top 10% getting 27.8% of the income. By 2007 their share was back at 42.6%, a proportion not seen since 1929.

THE AMERICAN DREAM

Extremes of wealth might be tolerable in a meritocracy: the American dream, after all, is that anyone can rise to the top. Research shows that, at the time of the American Revolution, income in the 13 colonies was probably more evenly distributed than anywhere else in the world.[9] But it seems to be getting harder, not easier, to move up the social scale. In 2004, 1 in 10 of the richest 1% of Americans had started life in the bottom 80% of the population; in the 1970s the proportion had been 1 in 7.[10]

Education may be the key. The cost of an American college education is prohibitive and while universities do offer scholarships, they do not offer enough to make a significant impact. In the 1970s US private-university tuition fees were 20% of median income; by 2009 they were 45%. American men aged between 25 and 34 are now less likely than their fathers to have a university degree.[11] A survey of the American colleges deemed most competitive (such as Harvard and Stanford) found that 74% of students came from families with earnings in the top quartile and just 3% from those in the bottom quartile.[12] Only 29% of poor students with high maths scores in national tests go on to get a degree, whereas almost 75% of rich students do so. In addition, with more women now attending university, marriages are increasingly taking place within the same social group, leading to less mobility within the population. In the top 5% of the population by income, 75% of married couples each have university degrees; in the general population, the proportion is just 25%.

The level of US parental income explains 50% of the future income of their children; in Scandinavia, it explains only 20%.[13] The World Bank has an 'inequality of opportunity' index which assesses what share of inequality is explained by accident of birth – race, gender or parents' education. In Britain, the proportion is more than 20%; in the US, it is just under. In Norway, by contrast, it is only 2%. So in the

US and Britain at least, the better off get their children into the best colleges; graduates of those colleges then earn more, marry each other and perpetuate the cycle.

The British and American economies may be extreme examples of inequality, but the general trend in the developed world has been in the same direction. In the 27 countries of the OECD (the rich economies' club), the real average income of the top 10% of the population rose by 1.9% annually between the mid-1980s and the late 2000s, whereas that of the bottom 10% rose by only 1.3%.[14] Only Belgium, Chile, France, Greece, Ireland, Portugal, Spain and Turkey saw the gap close. Yet even the achievements in these countries seem a little double-edged. By 2010–11, four of them (Greece, Ireland, Portugal and Spain) were ensnared in the euro zone debt crisis. A disturbing implication of their failure is that the drive towards greater equality may (by raising social benefits and discouraging entrepreneurship) have played a part in making such economies uncompetitive. Certainly, the austerity resulting from the debt crisis will probably cause inequality in these countries to rise again.

Cast your mind back to the 1970s, and you will recall that conservatives argued economies were too egalitarian. Taxes were far too high on the top earners, discouraging them from starting new businesses or expanding their companies. Much was made of the Laffer curve, an American professor's theory which showed that the tax take would be zero with a tax rate of either 0% or 100% (because nobody would bother to work in the latter scenario), and that therefore there must be a point beyond which higher taxes are counterproductive.[15]

The argument that high tax rates on top earners damage growth is still being made today. In 2012 Edward Conard, a friend of the US businessman and Presidential candidate Mitt Romney and a partner of the asset management firm Bain Capital, wrote that 'The high price for talent is essential to properly allocating what limited supply of talent we do have to the most valuable investment opportunities. Given their enormous contribution, it should be obvious that small increases in the supply of talented risk takers will produce significant increases in GDP.'[16] But even on growth, the evidence is not particularly supportive of his thesis. The 2000s were much less equal than the 1970s, yet real US growth in the first decade of the millennium was just

1.6% per year compared with 3.2% in the 1970s – dismal as that decade may seem in retrospect.

A 2012 paper by the Congressional Research Service found that 'changes over the past 65 years in the top marginal tax rate and the top capital gains tax rate do not appear correlated with economic growth'.[17] In other words, cuts in marginal tax rates for the rich do not lead to a burst of entrepreneurship and increases in the rate do not stifle business. The study did find that 'top tax rate reductions appear to be associated with the increasing concentration of income at the top of the income distribution'. In other words, the pie does not get bigger; rather, the rich get a bigger piece of it.

TOP TAXES

Other studies point to the same conclusion. A paper by Thomas Piketty and Emmanuel Saez,[18] the academics who have probably delved deepest into the issue of inequality, found that the average tax rate paid by the top 0.01% of the American population fell from 74.6% in 1970 to 34.7% by 2004. The average tax rate paid by the top 0.01% of Britons fell from 91.7% in 1970 to 42.5% by 2000. In more egalitarian France, the average tax rate for the ultra-rich rose from 48.8% to 61.5% between 1970 and 2005.

Of course, the rise in inequality means that the rich pay a larger share of total federal income tax than they used to. But it seems a pretty good trade. Jacob Hacker and Paul Pierson calculate that in 2000 the top 0.1% had about 7.3% of total national after-tax income, up from 1.2% in 1970; had tax rates stayed the same, they would have had just 4.5%.[19] When you consider all taxes, the share of the tax take contributed by the richest 1% of Americans is around 21.6%, close to their share of pre-tax income.

In the US, the reduction in tax rates for the rich has been accompanied by a sharp rise in the government's take from payroll taxes, from 6% of labour income in the early 1960s to more than 15% in the 2000s. While many ordinary workers escape income tax, payroll taxes fall on pretty much all employees. It is generally assumed by economists that employers compensate for the cost of their payroll contribution by paying lower wages or by employing fewer people. Piketty and Saez conclude that 'The progressivity of the US federal tax system at the top of the income distribution has declined dramatically since the 1960s.'[20]

Clearly, as Arthur Laffer pointed out, there is some point at which the marginal rate on tax is too high. But most developed countries seem to have set taxes below that level. When in 2009 Britain raised its marginal tax rate from 40% to 50%, there were dire predictions that lots of wealthy people would leave the country; a few did so, but most decided that the cultural appeal of London was rather greater than that of Geneva or Singapore. While most people would accept that the 90%-plus rates that applied in Britain in the 1960s were too high, the big kink in the Laffer curve might turn out to be well above 50%, and therefore higher than the American or British systems currently impose.

The better off also get explicit government handouts. In the US, mortgage-interest payments are tax-deductible, no matter how large the loan, while employer-provided retirement schemes give tax relief on contributions. In 2004, 69% of the benefits from mortgage interest deductions went to households earning $100,000 or more, while the same group received 55% of the benefits of the retirement tax break.[21] Another benefit is the tax subsidy of employer-provided health insurance: only 16% of those in the lowest-earning households were able to take advantage of this subsidy, compared with 55% of those in the highest-earning quintile. All told, in cash terms, the average subsidy for those earning between $200,000 and $500,000 was three times that received by those earning between $10,000 and $20,000.[22]

Professor Suzanne Mettler of Cornell regards these subsidies as part of the 'submerged state', which distorts perceptions of the government among average voters: many people who think they are not beneficiaries of government policy turn out to be so. 'People are easily seduced by calls for smaller government,' she writes, 'while taking for granted public programmes on which they themselves rely.'[23] A 2008 poll by the Cornell Research Institute found that 57% of respondents said they had never used a government social programme, but when taken through a list of 21 actual programmes – such as social security and the home interest mortgage deduction – 94% of the deniers admitted they had actually done so.

This perception gap may be down to the difference in programme design. It is easy to see that a direct grant from the government is a handout, but less easy to see that a tax subsidy acts in the same way; and even harder to see how a government guarantee (such as on US student loans), by reducing the cost of borrowing, is also a social programme.

As Ms Mettler points out, some of these programmes are deliberately designed to obscure the government's role. They were the result of a compromise between a Democrat desire to benefit individual groups and a Republican distaste for government bureaucracy. The growing popularity of 'nudge' strategies – designed to alter individual behaviour by tax breaks, or rule changes like auto-enrolment in pension schemes that take advantage of individual inertia – may only add to the state's submerged nature.

Some would argue that there is a genuine difference between a subsidy and a tax break – that is, a decision not to tax a particular activity. But most economists agree that the best tax system is as neutral as possible between various activities, treating all income on an equal basis. Any other approach tends to distort incentives, makes the system more complex, and creates more work for accountants and lawyers.

Differential tax rates for different kinds of income can also benefit the rich more than the poor. Capital gains tax rates are lower in many states than taxes on earned income. This is usually cited as a way of encouraging entrepreneurship; but capital gains tax rules usually do not distinguish between the profits made from building up a business and those made from passively holding a diversified portfolio of shares. Either way, the vast majority of the gains from this break go to the wealthy (since the wealthy own most of the capital). Furthermore, capital gains taxes are not normally levied on the family home: another tax break for the better off, since the poor tend to be tenants rather than owners.

The capital gains tax exemption is also relevant to the debate over inheritance tax. In a meritocracy, one would want inherited wealth to be limited, because such wealth means that all citizens do not have 'equality of opportunity'. But inheritance taxes have always been resisted, since most people have a natural desire to pass their wealth on to their children. Some argue that an inheritance tax (in the US, conservatives dub it a 'death tax') is an instance of double taxation. But while this may be true in some cases, the biggest element of many bequests is the family home, on which no capital gains tax has ever been paid. In most countries, there is a high threshold before tax is due on bequests. The result is that children of middle and upper-class parents can look forward to a tax-free lump sum that is not available to their poorer compatriots.

A further bone of contention is that of 'carried interest', the performance fee received by private-equity managers when they earn high returns. (Private-equity managers invest in companies that are not listed on the stock market.) This fee usually represents the bulk of the return earned by the individual managers, many of whom are very wealthy; the return is taxed as a lower capital gains rate, rather than the higher income-tax rate. This, as one British private-equity manager was honest enough to admit, leads to the strange situation where millionaire managers are taxed at a lower rate than the office cleaners. Since private equity is a controversial business on other grounds (some believe the managers are asset-strippers, selling off the profitable parts of the companies they buy and sacking lots of workers in the process), this tax break has been the subject of heated debate on both sides of the Atlantic.

Then there is the accounting treatment of share options. In the 1980s academics were very worried that the corporate sector suffered from a classic principal-agent problem: the agents (managers of the company) did not have the same interests as the principals (shareholders). The executives had every incentive to feather their nests with perks (executive jets, expense account lunches) and to build their empires rather than to create 'shareholder value' in the form of better dividends and a higher share price. The answer to this conundrum was to give executives share options – the right to buy shares at a set price. If the share price went up, both executives and shareholders would do well.

All that sounded good in theory. In practice, there were two flaws. The options certainly helped executives become much better off in the equity bull market of the 1980s and 1990s. But this was because share prices rose, rather than because of any particular managerial brilliance on the part of the executives concerned. From the point of view of the executives, it was a one-way bet; if the share price rose, they became rich; if it fell, the options expired worthless but they lost nothing. Those were not the same odds that faced shareholders.

The ratio of American chief-executive compensation (including share options) to that of the average worker increased from 26.5 times in 1978 to a mind-blowing 411.3 times at the height of the technology boom: it was still 209.4 times in 2011. Total compensation for chief executives increased by 725% in real terms over the same period, compared with a gain of just 5.7% for private sector workers. By contrast, the S&P 500 index, a broad measure of the US stock market, increased between four- and fivefold over the same period.[24]

Secondly, a share is just that: a share in the profits and assets of the company. If the executives are given more shares, that leaves less of the pie for the original investors. Such a cost ought to be reflected in a company's accounts. As the investor Warren Buffett said, 'If stock options aren't a form of compensation, what are they? If compensation isn't an expense, what is it? And, if expenses shouldn't go into the calculation of earnings, where in the world do they go?' But technology companies fiercely resisted any accounting treatment which would reduce their stated profits; they lobbied Congress in protest, which in turn threatened the independent accounting board in charge of making the rules. These rules were not tightened during the hi-tech boom.

Another factor that has helped the rich get richer is globalization. As China and (in the 1990s) Eastern Europe entered the capitalist world, hundreds of millions of people were added to the global labour pool. This clearly had an impact in holding down wages in developed countries – although these were under pressure in any case, as the heavily unionized sectors (coal, steel, cars) declined and service industries took their place. Service industry workers are dispersed in smaller units and have proved harder to organize.

While the wages of blue-collar workers were squeezed, at the other end of the scale a 'war for talent' developed. This is most obvious in the fields of sports and entertainment, where the most successful athletes and artists have a 'franchise' that enables them to attract multi-million-dollar salaries. People want to see Kobe Bryant play basketball, Tiger Woods play golf and Lionel Messi play football, and they buy the T-shirts, shoes or other equipment associated with the 'brands' of those players. In less glamorous fields, the growing use of personal computers and other technologies made skilled workers more attractive to employers; some of those workers were also highly mobile, switching countries in search of work. It is striking that the greatest relative gains for the top 1% occurred in English-speaking nations (the US, UK, New Zealand and Canada), where workers are able to shift locations without experiencing any language difficulties. Top computer programmers, top accountants, top management consultants: all can and do ply their trade in many different parts of the world.

Although many of the new wealthy have college degrees, education cannot be the only factor behind the rise in inequality. After all, while many more people go to university than they did fifty to sixty years ago, income gains have been focused not on the top 40–50% but on the top 10%. The incomes of college graduates have risen quite slowly. An American entry-level worker with a bachelor's degree earned only $1,000 more in real terms for a year's full-time work in 2006 than their equivalent did in 1980.[25]

In the long run, one might think that lower social mobility would be more economically inefficient. The best university places and the best jobs will be taken, not by the most able, but by the best connected. Conversely, free-market economists argue that the prospect of getting rich persuades individuals to invest in their own (and their children's) education, to set up new businesses and to come up with inventions. Economists who have analysed the data have yet to conclude that there is a close correlation between inequality and growth.

BIG MONEY

The credit boom also played a significant role in widening inequality, by pushing up asset prices and bolstering the finance sector. In America, around 60% of the top 0.1% of income earners in 2005 were corporate executives (who earned the bulk of their wealth in the form of share options) or worked in finance.[26]

For anyone below 40, it might seem natural that many of the brightest minds at college hanker after a degree in finance. As someone who was at university in the late 1970s, I can attest that it wasn't the case back then. Finance was seen as a very boring profession, a dreary matter of checking numbers and approving loans.

Finance sector salaries took off from the early 1980s, as deregulation kicked in. A recent academic paper[27] examining this trend showed that this rapid rise in income could not be explained in terms of the skills of those employed in finance, nor by the increased use of technology: the pay rates of engineers with similar education levels did not increase anything like as rapidly. The paper estimated that 'rents' – an economist's term for excess returns due to special factors – were responsible for 30–50% of the finance sector's wage differential. What explains these rents? Over the last three decades, those who work in finance have benefited from explicit or implicit government guarantees. Banks enjoy a cheap cost of funding because, since the 1930s, deposits have been insured: if they had not been, weak banks might have to pay a high rate to attract funds from consumers and would be vulnerable to runs of the kind that Northern Rock suffered in 2007. The financial crisis of 2007–8 showed that governments felt obliged to rescue banks to prevent the wider economic consequences of their collapses.

Fund managers have also benefited from the so-called 'Greenspan put', the tendency of central banks to cut interest rates whenever the market falters. The managers' fees are based on a percentage of the money they manage: as the markets rise, their remuneration goes up. So fund managers really prospered in the long equity bull market from 1982 to 2000 – but were given a further boost when central bank rate-cuts (and quantitative easing) helped equities to rally in 2009 and 2010.

A further factor is the information asymmetry between those who work in finance and their customers. Individuals and companies are affected by financial variables like interest rates and currency movements, and often wish to buy protection against such shifts. They purchase such insurance from the finance sector. But just like a second-hand car salesman who has painted over the rust on an old banger, the financier may have a better idea of the risks involved than the customers. Modern financial products are very complex, and the client may simply be unable to comprehend the scale of their potential losses, or calculate the implied level of fees involved. There have been a whole series of mis-selling scandals, in which taped conversations have indicated the willingness of bankers to put one over on their clients.

To protect these rents, financial firms have lobbied hard to get regulations on their industry removed. According to the Center for Responsive Politics,[28] the industry was the third-highest spender of all US sectors on lobbying between 1998 and 2012; all told, the figure was a staggering $5.1 billion. One of the sector's most notable American successes came with the abolition of the Glass–Steagall Act in 1999. The act had been introduced in the 1930s after the Wall Street Crash. It was designed to separate commercial from investment banking, so that the deposits of ordinary Americans were not put at risk by market speculation. The line between commercial and investment banking had become blurred in the 1980s and 1990s, however, and American bankers argued that the Glass–Steagall rules put them at a competitive disadvantage compared with their foreign counterparts.

Simon Johnson, a former chief economist at the International Monetary Fund, noticed that many governments in developing countries were seduced by businessmen who had the president's ear and who used this influence to maintain their monopolies. Looking at the US, he felt that the finance sector played the same role. In his book *13 Bankers*[29] he recounts the story of how Brooksley Born, chairwoman of the Commodity Futures Trading Commission, wanted to regulate financial derivatives in 1998 and was told by Larry Summers, the distinguished academic and then deputy Treasury secretary, 'I have thirteen bankers in my office and they say if you go forward with this you will cause the worst financial crisis since World War II.'

When the financial crisis broke in 2007 and 2008, the complex structure of financial derivatives made it very difficult for investors to assess which banks were safe and which were risky. Although it is hard to give a definitive answer (since regulators are often outflanked), the lack of derivatives regulation may have contributed to the scale of the debt crisis.

There is no doubt that the low standards of lending in the American housing market played a very big part in the crisis. And here lobbying also played a significant role. A paper[30] by economists from the IMF found that those mortgage lenders that lobbied most offered riskier loans, offloaded more of those loans to other investors via the securitization market,[31] and subsequently had higher default rates and poor stock-market performances. As the economists remark, one possible explanation is that 'lenders take up risky lending strategies because they engage in specialised rent-seeking and expect preferential treatment associated with lobbying'.

Important though lobbying may have been in the enhanced influence of the financial sector, politicians and regulators may well have been subject to 'cognitive capture' – the belief that the financiers really did know best. After all, the heads of investment banks and hedge funds were immensely wealthy: surely this must be down to their ability. (There is a probably apocryphal exchange between a hedge-fund manager and an academic. 'If you're so smart, why aren't you rich?' asked the manager. 'If you're so rich, why aren't you smart?' retorted the professor.)

The belief that financiers were the most able men of their generation prompted both Democratic and Republican presidents to appoint heads of Goldman Sachs (Robert Rubin and Hank Paulson) as their treasury secretaries. In a previous era, manufacturing was seen as the most important sector; in 1961 John F. Kennedy had turned to the head of a car firm and a master of systems analysis, Robert McNamara, to run his defence department.

PUBLIC OPINION

Whatever the causes, the extremes of wealth and income are now the subject of much debate. It seems as if the public was more tolerant when the general economy was doing well. And people also seem to have a different reaction to the money made by entertainers or genuine entrepreneurs, such as Mark Zuckerberg of Facebook fame or Sir Richard Branson, than they do to that made by bankers.

The problem is not just that few people understand what bankers are doing when they trade frantically on their screens all day or when they create complex derivatives, but that there is a feeling there is one law for the bankers and one law for the rest. If the local plumbing or building firm gets into trouble, it will be allowed to fail, whereas a bank will be rescued at vast cost to the taxpayer. If the average worker leaves his job under a cloud, he or she will be lucky to get paid before the end of the month; the banker will get a six-figure payoff and a gold-plated pension.

In Britain, this dichotomy became personified in the saga of the then Sir Fred Goodwin, head of the Royal Bank of Scotland. Sir Fred, generally perceived to be an autocratic leader of the retail bank, went on a spending spree that included the building of a new head office at a cost of £350 million and the purchase of NatWest – one of the big four English clearing banks – and culminated in the bid for ABN Amro, a Dutch investment bank, in October 2007. RBS and its partners outbid Barclays for the bank, and were almost immediately subject to what economists dub the 'winner's curse': by definition, the successful bidder in an auction is likely to overpay.

The £49 billion bid was approved by the board, even though a subsequent report by the UK Financial Services Authority found that the bank had performed little in the way of due diligence, its research consisting of two lever-arch files of notes and a CD.[32] When the financial crisis broke in 2008, RBS was overwhelmed by the debts it had taken on; in the autumn of 2008 the then chancellor of the exchequer Alastair Darling received a phone call from a senior RBS executive telling him that 'It was quite clear the bank was going to fail in a couple of hours and he said "what are you going to do?"' Mr Darling added that 'They were going to have to close the doors. They couldn't get the cash out of the machines.'[33]

Had the automated teller machines at RBS (and its NatWest subsidiary) failed, there would probably have been a run on all the British banks: financial and economic chaos would have ensued. Fred Goodwin thus bore a heavy responsibility, and he resigned days after the bank's collapse. Crucially, he was not formally fired, a process that, thanks to labour laws, would have involved a lot of time and unwelcome publicity. As a result, he claimed his contractual rights – which included an annual pension of nearly £700,000 a year.

This caused outrage. Had RBS been allowed to go bust, then Goodwin's pension would have fallen under the insurance scheme known as the Pension Protection Fund; under that system, the maximum payout was £27,000 a year. In effect, by making the bank so big and its collapse so potentially calamitous, Goodwin had ensured that his bank needed a rescue, and thus protected his own pension rights. Such a system hardly seems the ideal incentive structure, to say the least.

In the face of adverse publicity (and an attack on his house), Goodwin agreed to accept a reduced pension of £342,500 annually – but only after taking a £2.5 million tax-free lump sum. Eventually, he was stripped of his knighthood on somewhat dubious grounds (he had committed no crime), on the long-standing British principle of shooting the occasional admiral – as Voltaire put it, '*pour encourager les autres*' ('to encourage the others').

Goodwin was not alone in presiding over a collapse: similar events occurred at HBOS (a combination of the old Halifax building society and the Bank of Scotland), which was forced into the arms of Lloyds TSB. The HBOS purchase, apparently encouraged by the prime minister, Gordon Brown, proved a hospital pass for Lloyds, which subsequently needed a government rescue. In the US, Lehman Brothers and Bear Stearns were hit by the same liquidity squeeze, the former going bankrupt, the latter being rescued by J. P. Morgan. On top of all this, there were bank scandals with rogue traders losing billions, other banks being caught out because employees had helped tax evaders or money launderers, and a big scandal in which various banks were fined for inaccurately reporting a key interest rate known as Libor.

Often, the executives of the banks concerned argued that they were unaware of the abuses that were going on among junior employees, and that they could not possibly have anticipated the collapse in the US housing market or the severe funding squeeze that followed. Such arguments are not entirely without merit: banks are large, complex organizations and economies are very hard to forecast. But bank executives were not so keen to emphasize the corollary of their argument. If they could not be held fully responsible for events at the bank when things went wrong, they could not claim credit for events when they went right. In other words, they were not entitled to vast rewards that were merely the result of fortunate economic circumstances or the work of junior employees they did not understand.

To the ordinary person, not just the Occupy Wall Street protesters, these rewards seemed monstrously unjust. The bankers made their millions, then they wrecked the economy, then the taxpayer bailed them out. This narrative is a slight exaggeration: government policy helped as well, for example in encouraging the relaxation of lending standards in the boom, and the formal cost of the bank bailout could eventually be limited by profits made from reselling the banks to the private sector.

But there is some truth in the account of Occupy Wall Street. Voters had been told by free-market economists that the private sector, left to its own devices, would create prosperity, and they went along with the deregulation of the banking sector, including (in the US) the end of the separation between retail and investment banking. The result was a mess. To continental Europeans, the crisis was clear evidence that the Anglo-Saxon liberal model did not work. Europeans argued for more regulation and for a financial transactions tax designed to curb some of the trading excesses. Neither the Americans nor the British were willing to agree, but the authorities did impose higher capital requirements on the international banking system through the Basel III accords (agreed in 2010 and taking effect by 2019). Over time, such requirements should lead to a less risky sector, lower returns on equity and lower bonuses for staff.

Such technical provisions did not seem enough to many people. After all, the bankers were still earning salaries many times the national average. Meanwhile, the crisis they helped cause was resulting in austerity in many parts of the developed world – a process that was creating a general increase in taxation, drastic cuts in social benefits and widespread layoffs of ordinary workers.

MONEY, LOBBYING AND VOTING

If the last 30 years have seen democracies become more unequal, why haven't voters rebelled? After all, in the Second World War and after, governments pursued highly distributive policies: the top US tax rate was 94% at one stage, while the theoretical top tax rate on British investment income reached 98%. It is entirely within the power of electorates to support politicians who favour such policies.

Their failure to do so may be down to a number of factors. One possibility is that many people believe that they, one day, will be wealthy: this is famously true of Americans even though, as we saw earlier, their chances of climbing the social ladder have been vastly reduced. Another possibility suggested by Thomas Frank in *What's the Matter with America?*[34] is that conservatives have persuaded Americans to vote against their economic interest by focusing on cultural issues like abortion and gun rights.

But a simpler explanation is to refer to the theory of Mancur Olson, as described in Chapter 5.[35] Olson argued that subsidies and tax breaks are very valuable to those who receive them, while the cost is shared out between the millions who do not. As a result, it is worthwhile for the beneficiaries to lobby for their retention, whereas there is less incentive for those who pay the bill to oppose them.

According to the Center for Responsive Politics, the total amount spent on lobbying in the US has risen from $1.44 billion in 1998 to $3.55 billion in 2011.[36] Becoming a lobbyist in the famous K Street area of Washington is the pathway to a lucrative career. Lobbying is not merely a matter of making a persuasive case. If you want access to a politician, it helps if you are willing to fund him. A campaign contribution of $1 million or so is small change if the potential gain from a favourable tax treatment is several hundred million dollars.

Since control of Congress, and the key agenda-setting committees, can pass from one party to another, smart firms often fund politicians on both sides of the aisle. Both parties are keen for the cash. The result is a political arms race. If your opponent raises a lot of money, he can blanket the airwaves with advertisements denigrating you; you must raise a similar amount to fight back. Get-out-the-vote campaigns, involving phone calls and door-to-door canvassing, also cost money.

Suzanne Mettler[37] found that the average amount spent by winners of elections to the House of Representatives roughly doubled in real terms from $697,000 to $1.36 million between 1990 and 2006, while Senate spending rose from $5.4 million to $9.4 million. (Senatorial candidates have the whole state to cover; House members are elected from smaller districts.) Total spending in the 1976 Presidential election was $66.9 million. By 1988 that figure had tripled to $210.7 million. Although there was a dip in 1992, spending passed the $1 billion mark in 2008 (actually reaching $1.3 billion).[38] Total spending in the 2012 election was around $2.4 billion.[39]

This financial requirement means that House of Representatives candidates, in particular, must spend much of their time in office on fund-raising. Inevitably, people will give money to the candidate that most closely supports their views; this gives wealthy voters more influence than poor ones. Voters recognize this: one poll found that 75% of Americans believe that campaign contributions buy results in Congress.[40]

Furthermore, wealthy people are canny with their money. Ideally, they would like to see their contribution go to a winning candidate, so that he or she will then be able to influence government policy in Congress. This gives an enormous fund-raising advantage to incumbents. The better off are also more inclined to vote. In the 2008 Presidential election, 25% of voters came from households with incomes of $100,000 or more – although only 16% of the electorate falls into that category.[41]

There is also a feedback process at work. If politicians enact policies that favour the rich, the rich will have more money – which they can use to finance supportive politicians and so on. The very broad caricature that Democrats favour the poor while Republicans favour the rich turns out to be right. Research by Larry Bartels,[42] a political scientist, found that under Democratic presidents the real post-tax income of the poor grew by 1.56% a year between 1952 and 2004; under Republicans, it declined by 0.32% a year. The income of the richest group, however, rose under both parties.

Back in 1861 John Stuart Mill was already suspicious of the cost of political campaigns. 'What must an elector think when he sees three or four gentlemen, none of them previously observed to be lavish of their money on projects of disinterested beneficence, vying with each other in the sums they expend to be enabled to write MP after their names?' he wrote. 'Is it likely that he will suppose that it is his [the voter's] interest that they incur all these costs?'[43]

Even if one accepts that candidates will pay more attention to those who fund them, the findings of Larry Bartels are quite remarkable. Analysing the voting patterns of US senators, Mr Bartels compared them with the political preferences of their constituents. If senators were representing their entire electorates, then you would expect there to be a close match between their voting patterns and the views of their voters. But instead, Mr Bartels found that the views of constituents in the upper third of the income distribution were given 50% more weight than those in the middle third. And voters in the bottom third of the income distribution? Their views carried no weight at all.[44] To give one example, Bartels examined the voting record of senators on the issue of an increase in the minimum wage, a matter of great significance to the poor. If high-income voters in their state were against the measure, then senators were likely to oppose it, whatever the views of the rest of their constituents.

Some of this may simply be unconscious bias. Senators mix in a certain social milieu, particularly when they are fund-raising. They spend little time wandering around low-rent housing projects. Better-off people are more likely to have fully formed political views; poor people may be too consumed with their daily struggle to worry too much about events in Washington. So the latter will spend less time writing to, emailing or phoning their representatives. Mr Bartels found that 'the average levels of knowledge and contacting among low-income respondents were less than half the average levels among high-income respondents'.[45] Even when he allowed for these factors, however, senators were still more responsive to the views of the better off.

Money seems to be the main driver of senators' voting patterns. A survey of campaign contributors found that three-quarters of all money was donated by those in the top 25% of income earners, whereas just 2% of all contributions came from those in the bottom 20%. As Mr Bartels points out, these numbers are consistent with the hard-headed view that senators pay most attention to their donors. Since the poor don't donate, they don't get heard.

Various attempts have been made to limit the influence of campaign finance, dating all the way back to Teddy Roosevelt, who helped push through the Tillman Act of 1907. The Watergate scandal led to another round of reform, including the establishment of the Federal Election Commission and a limit on the campaign contributions by individuals. A further bipartisan reform effort, from Republican John McCain and Democrat Russ Feingold, tried to limit the 'soft money' that has been used to get round the contribution limit.

All these restrictions have run into the problem of the First Amendment to the US Constitution, which bans any restriction on free speech and which (curiously to European eyes) has been interpreted by the courts as ruling out restrictions on campaign spending. (Perhaps American judges should come to Britain and enjoy the rough-and-tumble of a general election, which is not noticeably restricted by the impact of spending limits.)

A 2010 Supreme Court decision allowed for the creation of Super-Pacs, political action committees, which can raise unlimited amounts of money to campaign for, and against, political candidates or their positions. The SuperPacs must report their donors to the Federal Election Commission, and must not pay money directly to the candidates. In the 2012 election more than $630 million was raised by such bodies, with around three-quarters backing the Republican candidate, Mitt Romney – who, not coincidentally, argued in favour of low taxes for the better off.[46] The satirist Stephen Colbert took aim at this development, setting up his own SuperPac (Americans for a Better Tomorrow, Tomorrow). Candidates and SuperPacs are supposed to be independent of each other: in practice, as Newt Gingrich demonstrated in his campaign for the Republican nomination, candidates could suggest that a SuperPac should follow a certain course of action, without breaking the rules.[47]

All told, the 2012 election season may have seen some $6 billion in campaign spending. The result was that the incumbent president was returned to office, while both the Senate and the House were controlled by the same parties as before.

Contrast these huge numbers with the money that is spent at British general elections. In 2010 the parties spent just over £30 million on their campaigns, a figure that was well down on the combined £40 million cost of the 2005 campaigns.[48] (The discrepancy was largely because of a huge drop in spending by Labour.)

No doubt the campaigns would have liked to have spent more. But rules set down by the Political Parties, Elections and Referendums Act 2000, and monitored by the Electoral Commission, limit total spending in the year running up to the election to £30,000 per constituency, or £19 million for the whole country.[49] The broadcast networks, meanwhile, are required to provide the main parties with airtime for broadcasts during the campaign. This is a huge cost saving, set against the enormous expenditure on TV ads incurred in the US.

Does this cap on spending mean that rights of free speech in Britain are more restrictive than in the US? Surely not. Anyone interested in a general election campaign can hear all the main views by watching TV news or listening to the radio, while the flourishing British press will devote much space to the election during the – mercifully brief – campaign season. Thanks to the Internet, anyone with a computer can get access to the parties' manifestos and can express their view in an online forum.

Campaign finance rules vary sharply from country to country. In Germany, the six main parties spent around €1.8 billion (roughly £1.5 billion) in the electoral cycle from 2006 to 2009, and the main parties (the CDU and SDP) spend around €200 million in an election year. But it is worth noting that German parties are given quite a lot of money by the state (just under a third of all total spending) and that corporate donations are fairly limited and subject to strict transparency rules that make the names of the donors public.

THE THREAT

The danger is clear. Democracies can pay more attention to the wealthy because the rich fund the politicians. This may result in implicit and explicit government subsidies for industries such as finance or sugar farming.

The tension between political equality and economic equality has always been present. 'Democratic institutions awaken and foster a passion for equality which they can never entirely satisfy,' de Tocqueville observed back in the 1830s.[50] I argued earlier in the book that voter enfranchisement in the nineteenth century was a response to the growing power of various elements in society: first, the middle classes were given a greater say in Parliament, then the industrial workers. This was a complex process in which politicians sought allies for their own positions from within the newly enfranchised male voters and then had to adapt their policies to appeal to those voters later on. Once the franchise began to be widened, other sections of society – notably women – resented the fact that they were excluded from the vote.

Now economic power has shifted decisively to the rich, particularly in the US. If electoral power follows economic power, as I have suggested, then political influence should have shifted massively to the rich. Sure enough, that is what we have found. In the US, every political campaign involves an epic process of fund-raising that, inevitably, relies heavily on the rich. Better-off people may be less numerous than the poor – but they punch well above their weight.

Democracy is a good idea in its own right. But it was originally adopted as a means to an end: a means of national liberation in some parts of Europe and a means of economic betterment in others. It was based on the idea that all lives were of equal value, even though, as on the *Titanic*, citizens may have paid different fares and slept in different cabins.

Now we may have not 'one person, one vote' but 'more dollars, more votes'. The chances of the typical individual – the man on the Clapham omnibus or the Brooklyn subway – influencing policy are much less than those of the man in the executive jet. It may seem odd to argue this when President Obama was re-elected in the face of opposition from significant parts of corporate America. But note that two of his top three contributors were Microsoft and Google, while lawyers and lobbyists paid $25 million to his campaign, and the finance and communications sectors nearly $18 million each.[51]

The risk is of a vicious cycle. The poor are ignored so they lose interest in the political process, and so they are marginalized to an even greater extent. Policy decisions are made against their interest, and so their plight worsens. Faith in democracy declines still further. Perhaps this doesn't create the conditions for a revolutionary uprising in the style of 1789 – but it is disturbing all the same.

And now we are facing an era of austerity, in part to clean up the mess that the much-protected finance sector has created. In his book *Ill Fares the Land*, Tony Judt argued that welfare states were set up in the wake of the Second World War as a kind of insurance policy against a repeat of the Great Depression, when the abject poverty of many had driven voters to political extremes and the world to war.

For the middle and upper classes, higher taxes were a price worth paying to avoid a repeat. But this bargain may now be broken. Some of this, as has already been discussed, may be unavoidable because of the economic imbalances that have been built up over preceding decades. Nevertheless, the political task of reforming government finances has been made much more difficult by the inequalities described in this chapter.

Having argued in Chapter 5 that the state can be overwhelmed by the claims of ordinary citizens, in the form of benefits like pension and health care, this chapter's focus on inequality may seem rather odd. But as I have stressed, this is not a book designed to appeal to the right or the left of modern politics. The point is that modern governments have attempted to appease both the poor and the rich – and, in the last 40 years, have faced few financial constraints on their ability to pull off the trick. The emphasis has been different on the two sides of the Atlantic, with the US being more favourable to the rich, and continental Europe, in general, being more favourable to the average citizen. But now, with money running short, the choices are harder.

In theory, the voting power of the rich in a democracy should be overwhelmed by the sheer numerical power of the voting bloc of the other 99%. But this may not come about if the key influence on voting patterns is the effect of campaign spending, and the ability to raise funds from the better off. And that may only increase the alienation of the poor.

11

Defining the Problem

Democracies in which there are no significant political choices to be made, where economic policy is all that really matters – and where economic policy is now largely determined by nonpolitical actors (central banks, international agencies, or transnational corporations) – must either cease to be democracies or accommodate once again the politics of frustration or populist resentment.

Tony Judt, *Ill Fares the Land*, 2010

The picture that has emerged from the last ten chapters is quite alarming. Our democracies are facing economic crises at a time when voters' faith in politicians is very low and turnout at elections has been falling, while support for extremist parties has generally been rising. Terrorism has caused societies to restrict long-established liberties and to become suspicious of minorities within their midst. The issue of immigration is already being explored by the radical right. The gap between rich and poor has been widening, particularly in America, and there is a fear that government has been captured by special interests. The long-term challenges of ageing populations, which will inevitably weigh on economic growth, are yet to be faced. The developed world faces a financial crisis, and power is passing to the hands of its creditors, both official and unofficial.

In aggregate, voters may have demanded too much. We have asked politicians to deliver rising standards of living, generous social safety nets, enhanced employment rights for workers in the face of global competition, and taxes which, if not low, nonetheless fall on someone else (the rich, the corporate sector) rather than on ourselves. We also ask politicians to listen to our personal concerns, run the administration efficiently, keep our streets safe and our borders secure. They have to do all this in the face of relentless media criticism and public cynicism. If our leaders listen to experts, they are the tool of special interests; if they don't, they are both foolish and aloof. We do not want to join political parties any more, nor to pay for them via our taxes – but we complain when they raise funds from lobbyists and bankers. Perhaps we can blame politicians (and economists) for promising too much, and not delivering. But we failed to be sufficiently sceptical, falling for the argument that all would be well if only we eliminated waste, or benefits to the feckless, or aid to foreigners – or any number of easy targets.

We have accumulated, as my last book, *Paper Promises*, pointed out, vast debts – not just at the government level, but at the banks, at companies and in our own personal lives. These debts have to be repaid out of future wealth. But if the economy does not grow fast enough, these debts cannot be repaid in real terms – either the borrowers will have to default or the debt will have to be inflated away. In the process, there will be big losers, as the Cyprus crisis of early 2013 illustrated; those with deposits of over €100,000 faced big losses. In different countries, the bill will fall in different places; high debts may force governments to cut benefits, for example. Whoever pays the bill will be aggrieved.

Meanwhile, although capitalism 'won' the ideological battle with communism, many voters are not content with the outcome. There is attitudinal blindness on both sides of the Atlantic. In Europe, the profit motive is often derided and the notion that a nation has to pay its own way seems to have been lost. Meanwhile, the American rich tend to assume that anyone who is not wealthy, or at least not in a high-paying job, lacks either talent or a willingness to work hard. They seem not to consider that there are plenty of people who work hard – a nurse in a care home or a waitress in a diner – but receive scant reward at the end of the week. And the rich also fail to consider that only the efforts of millions of such people ensure that the economy can function. Voters on both sides of the Atlantic have to understand that a healthy economy needs a flourishing private sector as well as supportive government policies.

The current debt crisis, and the absence of rapid economic growth, has left the public and its representatives with some unappealing choices. Should government push up taxes to reduce the deficit and maintain social spending, and risk losing business and skilled labour to other countries? Should it keep the welfare state affordable by eliminating middle-class benefits and costly subsidies to special interests? Should it reform the welfare state totally, hoping that such reform will lead to a rise in labour participation, but at the risk of causing suffering for the poor and sparking social unrest? These are very difficult choices which any society might struggle to make. It would help if we could make those choices in the context of a rational debate. But Western politics has been poisoned by an atmosphere of distrust and name-calling, and by the failure of the politicians and the media to present the choices facing the electorate in an open and honest fashion.

OTHER VOICES

Is my view that democracy is under threat an extreme or sensationalist one? Have I followed the familiar journalistic template of 'first simplify, then exaggerate'?

In my defence, I am far from alone in making the case. In March 2013 the Council for Foreign Relations, a respected US thinktank, launched a book called *Democracy in Retreat: The Revolt of the Middle Class and the Worldwide Decline of Representative Government*. *The Economist* Intelligence Unit report for 2011 was headed 'Democracy under Stress', while *The Independent* declared in 2012 that 'Our Democracy is Desperately Sick' – indeed, barely a week went by during the writing of this book without someone making a comment that supported my thesis. For example, Michael Portillo, a former British Cabinet minister, argued that the broad extension of democracy 'is a post-Second World War phenomenon. During that brief period, democracy has been inextricably linked with steadily growing national wealth. Democratic politicians have little experience in managing decline. Instances where they have had to do so offer little encouragement.'[1]

Mr Portillo also pointed out that the link between rapid economic growth and democracy is no longer so obvious. South Korea made rapid economic advances under the military dictatorship of General Park Chung Hee in the 1960s and 1970s; Singapore's economic growth has occurred despite the absence of an opposition with any hope of taking power; and China's rapid growth of the last twenty years has occurred in a one-party state. South Korea is now democratic, but the citizens of Singapore and China may consider that political stability and rising standards of living are much more important than the notional ability to unseat the political leadership every few years.

Another worrier is Raghuram Rajan, an Indian citizen who has been chief economist of the International Monetary Fund (IMF) and now teaches at the University of Chicago. 'Democracy treats individuals as equal, with every adult having an equal vote, whereas free enterprise empowers individuals based on how much economic value they create and how much property they own,' he wrote.[2] Mr Rajan sees capitalism as having two problems with legitimacy. The first is inequality of opportunity. Success depends on having a high level of education, something that is becoming unaffordable for all but the upper middle classes and the rich. The second issue relates to the selective enforcement of property rights. Because of their accumulated debt burdens, governments may have to choose between paying off creditors and maintaining the promises made to voters in the form of pensions and health care. They are likely to favour the creditors, Mr Rajan believes, because they have a continuing need to borrow. By favouring the rights of creditors over the rights of those who rely on government benefits, the effect will be to cause great resentment among the public; there will be demands for punitive taxes on wealth and business.

I am not sure he is right that creditors will always win. History is littered with examples of monarchs defaulting on debt, or debasing their currency to pay back creditors with 'funny money'. Such a strategy might be a lot more electorally popular than letting down pensioners. After all, Greece has already defaulted to its private sector creditors.

Samuel Rines of Chilton Capital,[3] a fund management group, talks of the creation of debt democracies, in which power 'lies not with elected leaders, but in an extra-national or non-governmental entity with the de facto power to impose its will on the debtor. Sovereignty of the mass citizenry is lost to the power of the outside few.' He worries that 'the temptation will be to elect a powerful, nationalistic executive' as a way of resisting this foreign power.

So what might make democracy lose ground? Samuel Huntington, who cited three waves of democracy's advance,[4] suggested the reverse waves that occurred when democracy retreated were the result of seven separate factors. The first was the weak hold of democratic values among the elite and the general public. The second was an economic crisis or collapse. The third was sharp social or political polarization. The fourth was the existence of a middle class or conservative grouping that was determined to prevent leftist parties from seizing power. The fifth was a general breakdown in law and order. The sixth was the impact of intervention or conquest by a non-democratic power. And the seventh was the 'snowball' effect of democratic collapse elsewhere, analogous to the copycat effects seen during the 1848 and 1989 revolutions.

Not all these effects can be seen today. Outside the confines of the old Soviet Union, it seems unlikely that any country in the developed world will be conquered or intimidated by a foreign power. On Huntington's seventh point, the snowball effect cannot start until one country falls outside the democratic camp.

But several of Mr Huntington's factors are observable in Greece, which has suffered an economic crisis, sharp social polarization and a large number of strikes and riots. And the first two factors may still be gaining momentum across the rest of the developed world. It is more than five years since the debt crisis began and a solution is nowhere in sight; central banks have bought governments time by buying their bonds, but it is not clear whether this tactic can work in the long run. The public, if not yet disillusioned with democracy, has certainly lost faith in politicians. Economic inequality, and the sense that the financial sector is still profiting from a crisis of its own making, is creating social polarization – as shown by the Occupy Wall Street movement.

The political danger might come from populism, a term that sounds benign in theory but can often be unpleasant in practice. A populist ruler speaks the language of serving the people. This mantra can then be used to justify all sorts of actions, from penalizing minority groups, to nationalizing business, to restricting freedom of the press. Elections are held under populist rulers, but in a climate in which the odds are tilted heavily towards the government in power.

Latin America has seen many populist rulers from Juan Perón in 1950s Argentina to Venezuela's Hugo Chavez. Mr Chavez (who died in March 2013) was a fascinating case in point. He won several elections and referenda and was undoubtedly popular among his nation's poor. But he used his power to boost his electoral chances. In October 2012 Mr Chavez won re-election by 55% to 45%; during the campaign, national TV was deluged with adverts extolling the government's achievement, whereas his opponent, Henrique Capriles, was limited to three minutes' airtime a day.[5]

This was a relatively mild restriction by Mr Chavez's standards. After a coup attempt against him in 2002,[6] he closed down independent radio and TV stations and claimed the right to interrupt domestic TV on any occasion he chose. During the 2012 campaign the Supreme Court ordered the seizure of the assets of the last remaining independent TV station, Globovision (the company saw off the threat by paying a $2.1 million fine, imposed for its coverage of a prison mutiny).[7] The electoral authority ruled that 23,000 expatriate (and largely opposition-supporting) Venezuelans living in Miami would have to register their votes in New Orleans, several states away.[8] When Mr Capriles was selected as the opposition candidate in a primary, the government instructed its own workers to boycott the poll.

All this shows the huge power that a populist can exercise while still keeping the appearance of democracy. One can argue that Mr Chavez is only practising openly what many politicians in developed countries do covertly: using the financial and regulatory power of government to bribe voters in order to maintain his hold on office.

Mr Chavez was lucky to run an oil-rich state during an energy boom. He was able to dole out goodies to his supporters, while his 2012 re-election campaign involved subsidies for consumer goods prices and a programme of public housing. But the nationalized oil company has not been run well and production has declined: in late 2012 inflation was running at 20% and the currency, the bolivar, was devalued in February 2013 by 32%. The effect was a cut in the standard of living of Venezuelans; imported goods like TVs suddenly cost a lot more.

DOUBLE DELEGATION

The rise of a Chavez or a Putin (or even a Berlusconi) is an obvious danger for democracy, as is the emergence of extremist parties like Greece's Golden Dawn. But there are more subtle dangers. Modern societies are incredibly complex. When Athens developed democracy, it was feasible for all the interested citizens to gather at a public meeting and make decisions. When democracy revived in the mid-eighteenth and nineteenth centuries, such a system was no longer considered possible. Instead, legislative democracy developed a system allowing citizens to elect the people who make decisions on their behalf.

Countries in the twenty-first century have taken the process a step further. Our elected politicians have delegated many of their powers to bureaucratic and technocratic bodies. Central banks are perhaps the most powerful of these bodies. They were set up precisely to limit the level of political control. The European Central Bank, established in 1998 to govern the new single currency, has formal independence with the aim of keeping inflation low. Members of the executive council are appointed by their home governments, but have eight-year terms to shield them from political interference. In the US, the Federal Reserve chairman has to testify to Congress. But provided he is reasonably civil in such meetings, the worst he has to suffer is embarrassment in the form of rude or critical questions.

As their power has risen, many central banks have become more transparent, publishing the minutes of their rate-setting meetings and issuing reports on whether they are meeting their policy goals. This has undoubted economic advantages, making the banks' intentions clear to savers and borrowers, and thus reducing uncertainty. It also makes clear to voters (and politicians) what the central bank is doing and why.

But striking the balance between independence and democracy is extremely difficult. In practice, a government has three sanctions against a central bank it dislikes. It can dismiss the head of the bank; it can take away the bank's powers altogether; or it can amend the terms under which the bank operates. The first two are a bit like nuclear options: they might be used in theory, but the result would be mutually assured destruction. A government that sacked its central bank governor or closed down the bank altogether because of a disagreement over economic policy would lose the confidence of the markets. Investors would assume that the country was ready to let inflation rip. The currency would decline and the cost of finance would soar. Using the third option – changing the bank's remit – is feasible if the proposed change is simply technical (the Bank of England has changed inflation targets since it was given independence in 1997), but a drastic change would probably be greeted adversely by the markets.

Currently, some feel the problem is that central banks are being too generous to governments – using newly created money to buy government bonds, thereby enabling governments to finance their deficits more easily and cheaply. Arguably, this strategy is anti-democratic in that it favours governments over political oppositions: the incumbent administration has an unlimited credit card with which to bribe the voters.

Central banks are only one example of a technocratic organization, but such bodies are everywhere. In Britain they are known as quangos, or quasi-autonomous non-governmental organizations. Many of them do vital jobs but, like weeds, they seem to spread remorselessly. In October 2010 the new coalition government announced that it had reviewed 901 quangos and had marked 120 for closure; by August 2012 it claimed to have closed or merged a hundred, including the Hearing Aid Council, the Teenage Pregnancy Advisory Board and British Waterways.[9]

But when these bodies are axed, their work has to be done by somebody else. So the effect may simply be that a surviving quango gets bigger. In theory, quangos are subject to democratic control – governments can take their powers away, MPs can question their activities. But there are so many of these bodies that it is hard for elected politicians to keep track of what they are doing. And a modern minister rarely stays in his or her post for long: they get promoted or demoted, or simply reshuffled, every year or two.

It is also hard to see how individual voters can influence a quango's decisions. Elections are not won and lost on the role of quangos in general, let alone a single authority in particular. Nor are these organizations subject to the discipline of the market: if they are bad at their job, they will not necessarily lose their revenues and go out of business. At the national level, then, one can say that many decisions are taken without direct reference to the electorate.

In the US, frustration at the deadlock inherent in the political process has prompted suggestions that fiscal decisions should be taken out of politicians' hands. Writing in the *New Republic* in 2011, Peter Orszag, the former budget director of President Obama, argued that:

> To solve the serious problems facing our country, we need to minimize the harm from legislative inertia by relying more on automatic policies and depoliticized commissions for certain policy decisions. In other words, radical as it sounds, we need to counter the gridlock of our political institutions by making them a bit less democratic.[10]

One suggestion from Mr Orszag is fairly uncontroversial, in democratic terms at least. The government could expand its automatic 'stabilizers' which help rebalance the economy. Current stabilizers include progressive tax rates (as people's incomes fall, they pay proportionately less tax) and unemployment insurance (which supports workers' incomes, and thus consumption, when they lose their jobs). But this could be expanded to include payroll taxes – the levy on workers' salaries used to pay for pensions. Payroll taxes could be raised when the economy is booming and reduced when unemployment picks up.

But the more controversial proposal is for fiscal policy to be shifted to an independent commission, as happened with proposals to cut military bases in the 1980s. The democratic role would still be kept, since Congress would be given a yes/no vote on the commission's proposals. But politicians would not be allowed to cherry-pick individual proposals and remove them from – or indeed add them to – the commission's list.

One such commission was set up under two elderly politicians, Alan Simpson and Erskine Bowles; it included Congressmen from both parties and reported in 2010. The report was a complex document containing a number of alternative plans.[11] The basic idea was to reduce tax rates by eliminating, or cutting, various exemptions, like the mortgage-interest deduction. The result, as well as raising extra revenue, would be a much simpler system. But the commission failed to get enough votes from its members (14 out of 18 were needed) for a 'supermajority' to endorse the report. The seven who voted against the final deal included members of both parties – one of whom, Paul Ryan, later became Mitt Romney's vice-presidential nominee in the 2012 Presidential election.

The plan was criticized on both sides: by the Democrats for cutting spending on social security and Medicare, and by the Republicans for cutting defence spending and for raising some taxes. Being criticized by both sides is usually a good sign that the proposal is a reasonable compromise. However, even before the commission had been set up, the Senate had rejected the idea of a yes/no vote on the outcome, and the report never made it into law. But it did crop up as a debating point in the 2012 Presidential campaign.

Such commissions are needed more in the US system than they are in European parliamentary structures, where governments can usually be guaranteed to pass their budget proposals into law. Perhaps they are the only way round the US gridlock. But one can see some dangers. Lobbying groups will be just as active in targeting commission members as in targeting Congressmen. And to the extent that the better off can afford more lobbyists, their case might get more of a hearing than that of the poor. Critics noted that the Simpson-Bowles report contained no proposal for a tax on the financial sector, even though such a proposal has often been included in European deficit-reduction plans.

GLOBALIZATION AND DEMOCRACY

If citizens feel that it is hard for them to control decision-making within their own country's borders, the problem is even greater when it comes to international bodies. As discussed in Chapter 9, this problem is glaringly obvious with regards to the EU.

But many of the decisions that affect our lives are taken by international bodies. Here the difficulties of aggregation are made very clear. The interests and philosophies of the big powers differ enormously, and the likes of the US, Russia and China are naturally unwilling to see their interests overridden. The really big decisions at the United Nations are taken in the Security Council, on which all three big powers have a veto. The General Assembly, which comprises all nations, is more democratic but has less power. The effect is that very little gets done in the General Assembly and (with the exception of relief, peacekeeping and health agencies) the UN is dismissed in many quarters as a talking shop.

The real power resides in the global institutions that were set up by agreements between nations, like the IMF and the World Trade Organization (WTO). Once established, these institutions acquire a life and power of their own; their democratic credentials are very thin.

The International Monetary Fund was set up during the Second World War as a body to provide financing for governments. It has enormous power to set the conditions for the loans it supplies; by convention, its claims for repayment take superiority over all others. The IMF is controlled by member countries but voting power is determined by a combination of historical accident and economic size: the US has 16.8% of the votes to be cast, Japan 6.2%, Germany 5.8%, France and Britain 4.3% each, and China just 3.8%.[12] The Americans and Europeans can outvote the others. Hence the custom that a European always heads the body, while an American also heads the World Bank, which deals with lending for development. When Dominique Strauss-Kahn was ousted from the IMF in a sex scandal in 2011, he was replaced by another French politician, Christine Lagarde.

The IMF played a significant role in British history, being the cause of (yet another) national humiliation in 1976, as the Labour government had to turn to the fund for help. In a sense, the fund provided cover for the centrist leaders of the Labour Party, Jim Callaghan and Denis Healey, to turn the tables on the left-wingers in the party. Public spending was cut and monetary targets were introduced. The stage was set for Margaret Thatcher's more sweeping reforms.

But the IMF had an even more controversial role in the developing world in the 1980s and 1990s, first in Latin America and then in Asia. Countries that accepted aid had to agree to impose on their own populations a package of policies that were dubbed the 'Washington consensus', including privatizations, public spending cuts and the abolition of capital controls. The recessions that followed provoked public protests. Asia's experience in submitting to IMF demands persuaded countries to adopt more mercantilist policies – pursuing bigger trade surpluses – so as never to be dependent on foreign creditors again. A picture of Indonesia's President Suharto signing an agreement, with the IMF managing director Michel Camdessus standing behind him, arms folded, was perceived as a symbol of Western colonialism.

What is striking in retrospect is that even the IMF is no longer convinced about the policies it insisted on at the time. It is more willing to accept that capital controls may be needed to limit the destabilizing effect of hot money flowing into, and out of, a country's banks and financial markets. On austerity, the IMF now thinks that the multiplier effect of spending cuts may be more than 1 – in other words, that they may make the economy worse, not better. Here is the danger: an unelected body can insist on policies that a country's citizens dislike, on the basis of economic theories that prove later to be incorrect. As has already been stated, economics is an art, not a science: dogmatism is unwise.

The World Trade Organization was established in 1995 as part of the Uruguay round of trade negotiations. Based in Geneva, it is run by yet another Frenchman, Pascal Lamy (he is due to be replaced by Roberto Azevedo of Brazil in September 2013). Its role is to settle trade disputes between member countries and to see whether previous agreements have been adhered to. When the WTO makes a decision, countries are obliged to abide by it, something which has led to much criticism that it is anti-democratic. As with other examples of its type, it was set up by democratically elected national governments which could, if they wished, withdraw from its orbit. But such withdrawal might carry with it a heavy economic cost, in that WTO members might feel free to discriminate against the goods of a non-member country.

The WTO is unpopular on both the left and the right, the subject of street protests by those who feel that it emphasizes free trade over workers' rights and the subject of nationalist fears over its power to rule against governments. One fringe 2012 Republican candidate for president, Buddy Roemer, called for US withdrawal from the WTO, arguing that:

> The WTO is also a terrible deal for American sovereignty, for American democracy. We've given these useless judges over in Geneva the right to tell us what laws we can and can't have, based on what some foreign company or investor in the U.S. doesn't like. Somebody called

the WTO 'the constitution of the world economy'. We don't need somebody else's constitution to run our economy; we already have our own. That's the whole point of having a free country that we govern ourselves. Why are we throwing that away?[13]

A particularly sensitive issue for Americans is that the US has only one WTO vote, the same as other countries. But how else should an international body be organized? Weighting votes by population size would give China and India well over a third of the total. The Americans would not like that either. If each country were given a veto, like the UN Security Council, then nothing would get done: every country would veto any decision that conflicted with its interests.

There isn't a 'right' answer to the question of reconciling democracy and efficiency. But a retreat into isolationism, along the lines favoured by politicians like Mr Roemer, would leave many issues untackled. First, there are plenty of subjects that do require international cooperation; second, as the 1930s showed, isolationism only encourages an attitude of hostility towards foreigners that ends up hurting democracy. A cynic might say that international bodies are always set up by the existing international powers and are designed to impose their belief systems on the rest of the world. That was certainly the argument of Germany and Russia against the interwar League of Nations.[14] The cynic might add that, in practice, such agreements will only work if this is the case, since only the established powers can enforce them: to misquote Stalin, 'How many divisions has the IMF?'

Could the answer be to get rid of national self-determination? Possibly, the whole idea of nationalism may turn out to be a temporary concept, like the city states of the Middle Ages. It was a powerful dream in the nineteenth and twentieth centuries when peoples were struggling to escape from outside control, whether from dynasties like the Hapsburgs in Austria-Hungary or colonial powers like Britain and France. Nationalism owes its potency to the idea that a 'people' are entitled to their own government. But what exactly does the notion of a people mean these days? The world's most powerful country, the US, is a melting pot. Immigration means that previously homogeneous European countries, such as Sweden, now have much more diverse populations. We can no longer say that the population of a country looks the same, dresses the same, shares the same religion or speaks the same language. The result is that many of us have mixed loyalties. Should an Indian-born shopkeeper in Cardiff feel Welsh? Or British? Or European? Or Indian?

Nevertheless, getting people to accept that decisions can be made at the global level – where their own ethnic or religious group can be outvoted – is a much bigger step. Perhaps we are as far from that point as the Athenians were from a modern social democracy. Without international agreement, for example, a truly multinational issue – global warming – is not being tackled. The challenge of reducing carbon emissions involves a classic 'free rider' problem: if nation A cuts backs its emissions, it bears the economic cost but nation B shares the benefit. Some politicians have been reluctant to acknowledge the problem at all, while those in the East argue that it is up to the West – which has higher carbon emissions per capita and which is much wealthier – to deal with the issue.

The power of international bodies like the IMF and the WTO has been a key target of criticism by the anti-globalization movement, which has occasionally disrupted summits of global leaders. Like the Occupy Wall Street movement, the agenda of the anti-globalizers can be incoherent, but their cause has attracted some heavyweight intellectual backing.

With all this in mind, Dani Rodrik of Harvard argues[15] that there is a 'trilemma'. Countries cannot simultaneously pursue democracy, national self-determination and economic globalization. The problem, as Mr Rodrik sees it, is that voters are not willing to put up with an economy in which competitive shifts can cause industries to up sticks and move overseas in search of lower costs. In the past, voters would have demanded trade barriers against such low-cost competition, but these tariffs are against international trade treaties. The democratic rights of voters are overridden in the name of globalization.

The economic benefits of globalization arise because resources are transferred to where they can be used most efficiently. Just as it makes no sense to grow bananas in Alaska, it makes no sense to produce low-value items in high-wage countries. It makes more sense for high-wage countries to produce goods where the skills used to create them can be reflected in the price. Technology is an enormously important factor in this equation. Modern communication devices like smart phones can make producers and consumers instantly aware of the best available price for goods, making it harder for inefficient producers to survive. Jobs that would once have had to be done locally, such as the preparation of legal documents or investment research, can now be outsourced to Bangalore. A modern factory can consist of little more than two technicians keeping watch over an automated production line. Nevertheless, this process usually creates losers in the form of low-skilled workers in the high-wage countries. Some of those workers can be re-employed in the service industries; some services (haircutting, restaurants) are not tradable across borders. But those positions may be lower paid and less secure than the old blue-collar manufacturing jobs.

Up to now, governments have cushioned the effects of globalization via the welfare state. Mr Rodrik cites research showing that the more exposed a country is to international trade, the higher the level of government intervention in the economy: 'People demand compensation against risk when their economies are more exposed to international economic forces and governments respond by erecting broader safety nets.'[16]

The debt crisis, however, has weakened the ability of states to provide that protection. The result may be to weaken support for globalization and to turn nations against foreigners. Trade barriers could be erected with the inevitable effect, as in the 1930s, of slowing economic growth and leading to more unemployment. Domestic minorities may be targeted because they are taking 'our' jobs or living off 'our' benefits. Again, mainstream politicians may be damned either way. If they respond to these fears, they may only legitimize them. But if they ignore them, they will be accused of elitism and will drive voters into the arms of anti-immigration extremist parties. And in many countries, immigration is one of the biggest single concerns of voters.

THE PROBLEMS DEFINED

Having described the practical threats that face democracy, it seems worth taking a step back and thinking in conceptual terms: this may help when it is time to consider some potential solutions in the next chapter.

The first issue is the difficulty of *aggregating* the choices of various individuals. Back in the 1950s an American economist called Kenneth Arrow posited a theory stating that, where voters have choices between more than two possibilities, no voting system can produce an ideal outcome. In practice, this occurs very frequently. How does one balance the right to free speech with a consideration for the feelings of those who are caused offence? How does one balance a desire to help the poor with the right of the wealthy to enjoy the fruits of their labours? How does one balance the right of one individual to enjoy life (by playing loud music, for example) with the rights of others who might be adversely affected? This trade-off is clear in the debate over America's gun laws, where the right of individuals to own guns is set above that of children to be protected from deranged killers. 'This is a republic, not a democracy,' said one pro-gun enthusiast, arguing that even if 99.9% of all voters wanted gun controls, the Constitution would still protect the gun owner.[17] These issues occur in all societies, of course – democratic and non-democratic. But by claiming to represent 'the will of the people', democracies have not really defined how the rights of the majority are balanced with those of the minority. Liberals who assert the rights of gays to marry, or women to wear the burka, struggle with the right of homeowners to own semi-automatic rifles; for conservatives, the struggle is in the opposite direction.

Nor are we really certain whether democracy is a means to an end, or an end in itself. Would we trade our right to vote for prosperity, economic equality, freedom from terrorism or the liberty to ignore the morality of other citizens (the right to smoke, for example)? Each of us would have to make some trade-off. As Joseph Schumpeter wrote, 'There are ultimate ideals which the most ardent democrat will put above democracy ... no more than any other political method does democracy always produce the same results or promote the same interests or ideals.'[18]

Aggregation is also a problem because of the nature of representative democracy. We tend to vote for an individual, or a party, not for an issue. Many voters may have a hazy notion of what a candidate thinks about the various issues, or may approve of their stance on some subjects and not others: voters may prefer, for example, Barack Obama's social attitudes and Mitt Romney's fiscal approach. But they cannot express their vote that way. As a result the 'mandate' of a winning candidate is not as clear as it might be: some voters may have backed him, while still disliking large parts of his programme.

Aggregation is also a problem for democracies at the international level. The relationship between creditors and debtors is hardly a democratic one: a large country can hardly insist that a small country lend it money, just because the large one has more voters. And what happens if the desires of two democracies clash? If one country wants to build a nuclear power station on the borders of another, or dam a river that the second country depends upon?

The biggest financial aggregation problem, of course, is the balance between a society's demand for services and its willingness to pay taxes. The sums have not balanced and developed world governments have squared this circle by the expedient of borrowing money. In the long run, that has created two problems. It has given power to creditors (an undemocratic concept) and it has placed a burden on the next generation.

Indeed, the *inter-generational problem* is another issue. Voters take decisions that affect not just their lives but those of their descendants. For example, they may promise themselves pensions which have to be funded out of the earnings of future workers. But there are broader issues such as pollution and global warming. By continuing to burn carbon fuels in such large amounts, we may be adversely affecting the lives of generations to come. The outcome is not certain, however: the climate models may be wrong and future generations may be able to adapt. What cost is the current generation willing to pay to insure against this uncertain future? It is not clear that democracies have worked out a good way of analysing this issue. In addition, this problem has its aggregation dimension: when carbon fuels are burned by one country, they affect the climate of all countries.

Another problem is *the balance between accountability and efficiency*. The most accountable decisions are usually the most local. But devolving power to localities will inevitably result in different decisions being made in different areas. The result may be what is dubbed a 'postcode lottery' – better schools or health care in one area than another. Many find this dissatisfying. It may also be economically inefficient. If every locality uses a different computer system, each one will find it hard to communicate with the others (and with central government), and the overall cost will be higher than if a single government purchaser had taken advantage of its financial muscle.

Local decision-making also leads to the problem of 'nimbyism' – that the building of prisons, power stations, long-distance rail links and the like should be 'not in my back yard'. But these things have to be built in somebody's back yard, so a national government has to step in. Even where it does, the process of consultation can delay projects for years, adding to the expense and delaying the benefits for other citizens.

Conversely, national governments can seem too remote from the concerns of the ordinary person. Political analysis becomes a kind of game, in which one team has to be seen to be beating another: newspapers and TV programmes focus on scandals involving politicians, on campaigns to unseat a party leader, and so on. In the US, people talk of events 'inside the Beltway' (Washington's ring road), while the British focus is on the Westminster village. In France, many leading politicians have been to the elite schools and colleges and are dubbed '*énarques*' after the prestigious École Nationale d'Administration. As of early 2012, seven of the past 12 French prime ministers had been *énarques*.[19] A sense of being governed by a remote elite only adds to voters' alienation.

The terrorism threat has placed a further barrier between voters and their representatives. Traffic stops in any town that the US President sweeps through, as an armed motorcade protects him; there is an eerie resemblance to the medieval monarch sweeping past in his golden carriage. Other politicians travel in private cars or first-class train carriages. Visitors to the British Houses of Parliament must pass through metal detectors. Such precautions are understandable nowadays – but still add to the impression that 'they' live a different life from 'us'.

That brings us to the final problem – *the lack of trust or enthusiasm among the voting public*. The contrast with the 'Arab spring', where thousands demonstrated for democracy, or the 1989 revolutions, when totalitarian regimes were swept away, is striking. Those people were desperate to get the vote; those of us who have it cannot be bothered to use it.

Enthusiasm will not necessarily be generated by people voting more often. Rather, voters need to care about the outcome, and to think that their participation will make a difference. In the 2008 US Presidential election, young people and African Americans showed genuine enthusiasm for the personality of Barack Obama, and the change he represented from the regime of George W. Bush, another in a long line of white well-to-do males.

In the 2012 election, although overall turnout was down, enthusiasm among African Americans may have been sparked by Republican efforts to exclude them from the electoral roll, on the grounds of preventing fraud. An attempt to deny them the vote resulted in an increased appreciation of its value. Women may also have turned out in greater numbers because of fears that Republicans might try to restrict their access to contraception and abortion, an issue that mattered to them very deeply.

THE CASE FOR MUDDLING THROUGH

Despite all these problems, some may say that there is nothing – fundamentally – to worry about. Yes, the democratic system is not perfect, but no system is. Some people are always discontented; some can always be relied upon to pronounce that 'the end is nigh'. Just as stock markets are said to climb a 'wall of worry', democracies negotiate through an endless obstacle course. They stumble occasionally, but they also stay upright. Moreover, rich countries tend to be democracies and, even if they may be slightly less rich than they were, citizens are better off than they were a century ago.[20] There are very few examples of a democracy collapsing once it has been in place for a few decades. No Western European country has been lost to democracy since Spain exorcised the ghost of Franco.

Voter turnout has declined, but enough voters turn out to show that the system has broad public support. In May 2012 power passed seamlessly in France from Nicolas Sarkozy of the right to François Hollande of the left. That November, there were long lines waiting to vote in Florida as the polls for the US Presidential election closed; people were concerned to see their vote count in what looked like a genuinely close race. Around 122 million people across the country voted, with 63 million supporting Barack Obama and 59 million Mitt Romney. These are not the signs of a system on its last legs.

My case for concern is inevitably circumstantial. But the historical evidence for democracy's robustness is based on a very short time period, during which the global economy has been doing rather well. If we go back to Samuel Huntington's 'reverse wave', the period when democracy retreated, the most significant reversal was in the 1920s and 1930s, when the world economy last faced a crisis of the current magnitude.

The waves of democratization are also indicators of how another reverse wave could occur. The 1914–18 war destroyed the legitimacy of the Hohenzollern, Hapsburg and Romanov dynasties. Those regimes had promised military glory to their citizens, but instead had unleashed four years of slaughter, followed by defeat and economic collapse. The same goes for the regimes that failed in the Second World War. The third wave of democracy described by Mr Huntington began in 1974, just one year after the oil shock, which exposed the weakness of the Portuguese and Greek economies and caused plenty of problems else-where. In the same year the US President was forced to resign because of the Watergate scandal, while Britain held two elections amid talk that the nation was 'ungovernable'. Similarly, the 1989 revolutions in Eastern Europe followed a long period of sluggish economic perform-ance, as it became clear that the communist model was not working. Mikhail Gorbachev was aiming to reform the Soviet system, not to end it – but it proved too unstable to allow for modest adjustment.

If economic failure can result in a revolt for democracy, it can also result in a revolt against it. In a way, my thesis revolves around human nature. We are a constantly dissatisfied species, striving for something better. Of course, this explains man's great achievements, from popu-lating the entire world, through building skyscrapers and bridges, to visiting the moon. We are also impatient, a characteristic that has been dubbed the 'Diet Coke' syndrome, in which we want sweetness without calories, benefits without taxes – and we want them now.

We have a tendency to be over-optimistic about our own abilities, attributing our successes to skill and our failures to bad luck. If we suffer a long run of failure, it becomes implausible to put it down to bad luck, so we look for someone else to blame. One of democracy's many uses is that it gives us a chance to vent our frustration by the simple expedient of ejecting the office-holders. In a monarchy or dictatorship, violent revolution would be needed to achieve the same aim.

But what happens when we throw out one set of office-holders only for the new set to follow exactly the same set of policies? This has happened in Greece, where political leaders have been faced with the unappetizing choice of exit from the euro – with the inevitable chaos that would accompany such a move – and submitting to the demands of foreign creditors. It is only natural that some voters will turn to parties that appear to offer an easy way out: blaming foreigners, blaming immigrants, blaming capitalism. It is only natural that voters will think that all politicians are corrupt or incompetent, and that an outsider with fresh ideas – a businessman or a general – will run things much better. The chart below shows that economic growth and trust in politicians are closely linked.

Figure 11.1 Economic growth and trust in government

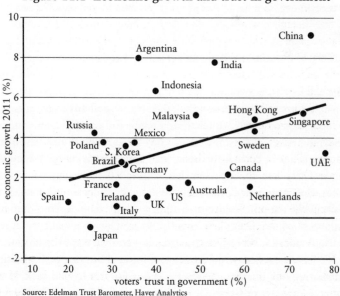

Source: Edelman Trust Barometer, Haver Analytics

In this regard, Greece may be the canary in the coalmine. Other countries are not that far behind, as we saw in Chapter 6. In Britain and America, we may be lucky that the outsiders who have emerged so far are so easy to dismiss: that Nick Griffin, the leader of the British National Party, looks like a thug and that Donald Trump, who flirted with a run at the US Presidency, is so ridiculous.

But I do not think that we can afford to be complacent when the public view of politicians is so negative. We know that the public is not completely passive – mass demonstrations take place over issues that people care about – and we know that riots can also flare up. These riots may not be politically motivated but they can have political effects, if only to increase the public's desire for law and order. During the riots of August 2011, the British police appeared to lose control of the streets: voters will not put up with many episodes of this kind. Similarly, the ability of terrorists to strike in spectacular fashion can have short-term political consequences – the Madrid bombings probably decided the Spanish elections of 2004 – and may have profound longer-term effects. That old Hobbesian bargain – citizens are happy to surrender their liberty in return for the sovereign's protection against the forces of violence – might still seem a good one.

THE SCORECARD

The theorist Robert Dahl[21] says that a democracy requires effective participation (can everyone make their views known?); voting equality (can all people vote, and do their votes count equally?); enlightened understanding (do they have the chance to learn about policies?); and control of the agenda (can voters' real concerns be raised?). How do our modern democracies meet these criteria? Certainly, all people can vote, while anyone who makes a reasonable effort should be able to learn about the policies of the various parties, to the extent that manifestos are a genuine guide to their likely conduct in office.

But doubts can be raised about the ability of all voters to have their voices heard, as seen in the findings of Larry Bartels (see Chapter 10) on the lack of influence of the poor. The power of lobbyists and, in the US, campaign contributors means that the voices of the corporate sector and of the well-off carry more weight than those of others. Control of the agenda is in the hands of the few rather than the many. And the tone used by the modern media may not be conducive to enlightened understanding of the issues.

Most of the time, the gaps in voter knowledge or information don't really matter. People have a broad impression of what is happening from what they experience in their daily lives. They can tell whether prices are rising, whether the government is taking a bigger chunk from their pay cheque, whether the standard of provision in schools and hospitals is improving or deteriorating, whether it is easier or more difficult to find a job, and so on. The way that they process that information into a vote for one party or another may not resemble the workings of a supercomputer, but who cares? It is their pay, their job, their services and they have the right to decide. The 'wisdom of crowds' argument applies.

However, it is possible that this rough-and-ready system does not work as well in two circumstances: a deep short-term crisis or a long period of stagnation. Take, for example, the financial crisis of 2008. The US authorities were frightened that the freezing of the money markets would lead to the collapse of the banking system. Even though the president (the younger George Bush) was strongly in favour of free markets, as was the Treasury secretary (Hank Paulson), the government felt obliged to intervene.[22] When Congress originally debated the $700 billion bailout plan, the public reaction was over-whelmingly hostile: complaining voters outweighed supportive ones by a margin of nine to one. The bill was duly defeated in the House of Rep-resentatives, causing one of the largest one-day stock-market declines in history. A revised bill eventually passed, but there was a danger that a visceral hatred of bankers among voters might have led to the kind of economic calamity that would have harmed the voters most of all.

Had the bill been put to a referendum, it would undoubtedly have been defeated. In addition, the time needed to hold such a vote – several weeks, at least – would have been a period of immense uncertainty in the markets, during which several banks might have gone under. In such emergencies, voters have to delegate decisions to their elected representatives – but this carries with it the possibility that those representatives may vote against their wishes.

We are faced with getting a quart into a pint pot. Our democracy needs to be fair, to be affordable, to encourage growth and to reflect the majority view – all at the same time. It is hard to meet all these criteria at the moment. What is fair may not be affordable, and the majority view may not encourage growth. So if we fall short of the ideal in theory, and if we have lots of problems in practice, what can we do to address the issue? That is the subject of our final chapter.

12

A Way Forward

If the underlying conditions are highly favourable, stability is likely with almost any constitution the country is likely to adopt. If the underlying conditions are highly unfavourable, no constitution will save democracy.

Robert Dahl, *On Democracy*, 2000

It is all very well to point out the problems that democracy faces. By now, I hope the reader will feel, if not alarm, then at least concern about the challenges ahead. The combination of voter disillusionment, austerity economics and antagonistic political rhetoric means that democracy faces its greatest challenges for decades. To assume that the system will always prevail just because it is better than all the others, or because it has been around for a century, is the height of complacency.

But what can be done to improve the prospects for democracy's survival? We must be practical as well as thoughtful. A complete overhaul of the political system is unlikely to happen, save in the case of the type of revolution we are anxious to avoid. We can start by describing the elements that we want to preserve.

One person, one vote. John Stuart Mill felt that the voices of the better educated should carry more weight in society, and the idea lived on after him. My father was able to vote in the 1945 general election for a constituency representing Cambridge graduates as well as in his place of residence. Owners of businesses also had two votes. Such additional votes were only abolished in 1948. However, any system that gives more votes to the 'better educated' smacks of the Jim Crow laws of the old American south, which were designed to exclude

African Americans from the electorate by imposing general-knowledge tests that were not applied to white voters. We need to stick to the principle that, since all people must obey the laws, so all people should have an equal say in their making.

But we have to recognize that there are many policy areas in which unelected bodies (central banks, for example) have huge power. In such contexts, these technocrats effectively have a vote that carries much more weight than that of the man on the Clapham omnibus or the New Jersey turnpike. We need to find ways in which experts can deliberate – subject, of course, to the final approval of the voter.

Local representation. Voters need to have a representative who is responsible for their particular area, so they can put a face or name to their vote. That rules out any system based on party lists. But it does not rule out proportional representation (PR) in other forms, such as the single transferable vote or the French two-round voting system. First-past-the-post systems lead to a feeling of wasted votes, with many constituencies electing the same parties year after year. While the British may have rejected PR at the national level, Londoners use a single transferable vote to elect their mayor and, in the last election, still had a clear choice between two quite different leading candidates, Boris Johnson and Ken Livingstone.

Regular, but not too regular, elections. Back in the 1840s the Chartists argued for annual Parliaments on the grounds that MPs need to be tied to the views of the people. Some argue, conversely, for longer terms of office, so that politicians are able to take the longer view. The fact that most countries have settled on periods of four or five years indicates that this is probably the right compromise position. Two terms of office would take a government to eight or ten years – which seems to be about the maximum period that a prime minister or president can maintain public support. Tony Blair gave way after a decade; Margaret Thatcher lost power after 11 years, as did Charles de Gaulle. American presidents are limited to two terms plus the remainder of a four-year term if a vice-president takes office more than halfway through (as Lyndon Johnson did when John Kennedy was assassinated in 1963); a potential maximum of ten years.[1] The Chinese, too, now replace their leaders every decade.

These three essentials are a modest list, but there is plenty of scope for flexibility – indeed, different reforms may be needed for different countries. Readers will have their own views on what needs to be changed, but most will probably agree on the minimum three conditions above.

GETTING GROWTH

Before any reforms are discussed, we need to recognize that the biggest factor behind voter dissatisfaction is probably the economy. Democracy suffered its biggest setback in the 1930s when Western economies fell into depression. Most people couldn't give two hoots whether they vote under PR or first-past-the post, for one chamber of Parliament or two, or whether their vote counts at the local level or at the national one. They just want a job and the prospect of a rising standard of living for themselves and their children. If they don't get that, they will be dissatisfied even if their elected leaders are a combination of Florence Nightingale, Nelson Mandela and Abraham Lincoln.

If Western economies combine low growth with rising inequality, dissatisfaction is bound to rise. And, as previous chapters have indicated, Western economies have painted themselves into a corner, where they have accumulated high debts (and big promises of future benefits) at a time when growth prospects look dismal. There is no instant solution to these problems, not least because of demography: baby boomers are retiring and the workforce will be static or shrinking over the next few decades, conditions that make it very difficult to generate growth. Western voters also have to understand that they need to pay high taxes if they want good social services, and that the world does not owe them a living. Countries that have high debts and persistent trade deficits end up being controlled by creditors and lose the right to control their destiny. They need to reform themselves before that happens.

So we have to prioritize. The original idea behind the welfare state was as a safety net for those unable to find jobs, either because of a downturn in the economy or because of disability or old age. We have created instead a vast system of transfer payments: around two-thirds of all American government spending is in the form of benefit pro-grammes in one form or another.[2]

This bill has to be reduced and it should be done, not by targeting the poor, but by closing tax loopholes and reducing subsidies that benefit the better off (middle-class welfare). If there is evidence that higher effective tax rates (thanks to the elimination of loopholes) are driving companies and entrepreneurs abroad, then the marginal rates of tax should be cut. But given the size of the deficits we are trying to close, let us see the evidence for that supposition before we act on it.

The budget cannot be balanced immediately and to attempt to do so would be economically foolish. We should commit to long-term reforms that will reduce the burden of spending – the pension age must rise and health spending should be controlled by limiting choice. There are faults in Britain's National Health Service but it delivers better life expectancy than the US system, at much lower cost.

While interest rates are low, governments should take advantage, just as most companies would use cheap funding to invest for the future. My suggestion is that public spending be refocused towards infrastruc-ture, which can both boost the long-term productive potential of the economy and can create jobs in the short term. Insulating homes, for example, will employ a lot of people and reduce energy use. More jobs and less inequality may reduce resentment towards minorities and thus reduce the potential vote for the far left and the populist right.

This agenda looks like a challenge for both the right and the left. If we want to maintain the safety net for the poor, cuts are going to have to be made elsewhere, in the tax breaks that are being enjoyed by the middle classes. Britain's coalition government has made a start by cut-ting child benefit for the better off; there is much to do in other countries, such as the elimination in the US of the 'carried interest' loophole (that benefits private-equity and hedge-fund managers). It does not help that those on the right seem more concerned with pro-tecting such tax breaks than shrinking the deficit (and also have a pre-Enlightenment approach to scientific issues), while those on the left, understandably wary of hurting the poor, seem reluctant to accept any role in the shrinking of government.

In Europe, economies have to be made more efficient and competi-tive if the demographic problems are to be faced: the old cartels and restrictive practices have to be dropped. Europeans will have to work longer if they want to maintain their standard of living: by 2050 the retirement age will have to reach 70. Again, this does not mean abandoning the welfare state. But only if the economy is efficient will we be able to afford a safety net for the poor.

A stronger economy will also reduce the temptation to blame 'outsiders', whether they be immigrants or those of a different religion. Developed economies have become multi-ethnic and multicultural, and they have gained many benefits from being so; often those who are most eager to work or form businesses are those who make the effort to cross national borders. While it is perfectly legitimate for societies to debate how many more immigrants they should let in, Europe is not going back to the homogeneous 1950s; the US, of course, has always been a nation of immigrants.

IDEAS FOR CHANGE

While the West is tackling those economic challenges, there are some alterations that could be made to the political system. Ideas for reform tend to fall into a number of categories. One involves change to the electoral process itself – replacing first-past-the-post systems with proportional representation, for example, or making more use of referenda. Another involves greater localism – taking more decisions down to the district level – and internationalism – adding a democratic element to international bodies. And then there is reform of party funding: limiting campaign spending or replacing it with government subsidies.

Of all these elements, the power of money seems the most corrosive to the health of democracy in the long term. One person, one vote is the fundamental principle of democracy – but most citizens are aware that some votes have a lot more weight than others.

In many walks of life, we try to limit the idea of a conflict of interest: a doctor should not be paid by a drug company; a policeman should not be paid by those he investigates; journalists should not write about companies in which they own shares. When politicians are paid by the state, they are effectively paid by all voters. But when they have to solicit money to finance their campaigns, they turn to rich people and interest groups. Naturally that creates the temptation to favour the interest of those providing the funding. If such a temptation did not arise, donors would be far less willing to part with their cash. The idea that politicians are in hock to special interests is a significant cause of voter disillusionment. The data from Larry Bartels, cited in Chapter 10, showing that politicians pay no attention at all to the views of poor voters, indicate that voters are right to be disillusioned. Those Italian voters who have supported the insurgent campaign of Beppe Grillo seem to have been motivated, in large part, by a feeling that the entire political class is corrupt.

Western European countries have tried to address this problem in various ways: by providing all funding through the state, by limiting the amount of campaign spending, and by insisting on transparency (revealing the names and amounts of all donations). While objections can be made to all these approaches, they still seem far better than the US system, which results in unlimited spending with only limited transparency. Nor does all this campaign spending result in the provision of reliable information upon which the voters can make a judgement. Anyone who has lived in or visited the US will be aware of the depressing avalanche of negative TV advertisements in election season – twisting the words of an opponent to make him or her sound out of touch or hypocritical. These ads are designed to destroy the opponent, not to construct a rational argument for a set of policies.

Changing these rules will not be easy, given that the US Supreme Court has ruled that campaign spending benefits from the free-speech definition of the First Amendment to the Constitution. Voters have the time-consuming options of changing the justices or changing the Constitution. But until one or the other is done, the reputation of US politics will remain in the doghouse.

What about changing the voting system? Given that the dissatisfaction described in this book is true of countries with PR systems as well as those with first-past-the-post, it seems unlikely that a change from one to the other will make much difference. Britain had a referendum on the issue in 2011 and a switch to PR was defeated. This may have been down to the unpopularity of the party most in favour of it – the Liberal Democrats – at the time the referendum was held.

The irony was that the pro-PR camp argues that the system fosters more consensus and coalitions – but for once, the first-past-the-post election of 2010 had produced a coalition anyway.

In the current circumstances, PR systems may give more clout to the extreme parties, an outcome that in the long run might prove dangerous for democracy. Throughout their histories, both the British and American first-past-the-post systems have largely managed to exclude outright communists and fascists from gaining seats in Parliament or Congress.

What about localism? Can we turn more decisions over to local people? Most countries have a tier of local government which deals with mundane issues like rubbish collection and street cleaning. Yet although these subjects affect voters directly, the public demonstrates even less enthusiasm for voting in local elections than in national polls. Localism would also involve assigning more taxation power to the local level, something not all residents would welcome.

Another issue is devolution – Scotland is due to vote on leaving the UK in 2014, and Catalonia may opt for a referendum on leaving Spain. Such votes could be seen as a further sign of the decline of national democracy – if voters feel that their traditional governments have little to offer them, partly because of economic turmoil, they may hope for a better deal by striking out on their own and becoming independent. It seems likely that both sets of voters will settle instead for more devolved powers – although devolution creates its own problems. The so-called West Lothian question, named for the constituency of Tam Dalyell, the MP who raised the issue in the 1970s, still applies. Is it right that Scottish MPs can vote on purely English issues at Westminster but English MPs cannot vote on purely Scottish issues in Edinburgh? It may seem a technical point, but it strikes at the heart of democracy – what gives an elected representative the right to decide?

A further problem has already been discussed. Some issues are inevitably national (the building of new motorways or power stations) whereas others are international (terrorism, global warming). Local voters might easily obstruct the actions needed to deal with these issues. Problems may also arise if local voters want services that require more spending from the national government. But within that financial constraint, there seems plenty of scope for local people to make decisions on things that matter to them. Whether local roads should have speed bumps or reduced speed limits; whether parent-run schools can be opened; whether licensing hours can be extended and so on. Of course, some of these decisions are already made by local councils. This, however, may be an instance where the Athenian principles of direct, rather than representative, government can be applied. Attempts to increase local participation have focused on creating new elected representatives, such as Britain's police and crime commissioners, but voter turnout has been dismal.

Give people the chance to vote online, and on issues that matter to them, and the turnout may be significantly higher. There would clearly be some security issues (such as identity theft), but if every voter on the electoral roll can be given a sign-on address and password, it should surely be possible to hold fair elections. Banks and credit card companies deal with these security issues every day, and there is much more incentive for fraudsters to attack such networks than there is for them to interfere in a vote on, say, refuse collection.

In their book *Intelligent Governance for the 21st Century*,[3] the Californian political activists Nicolas Berggruen and Nathan Gardels describe an elaborate structure that combines democracy, local involvement and expert guidance. They propose that a hypothetical country with 80 million inhabitants would be subdivided into units of just 2,000 voters. Each district would select 10 delegates to a local council by a system of proportional representation. Those delegates would select one member as a further delegate to a 20-member regional council, which would in turn elect one member to a 20-member provincial council, which would in turn select one of their members to be part of a 100-strong national Parliament.

The admirable aim is to make decisions real for people by making voting local. But one can foresee all kinds of problems with this structure, even setting aside the problem that 2,000 citizens does not equal 2,000 voters (children are citizens, but not voters). Would you find 10 volunteers willing to act as delegates in every 2,000 voter-bloc (let alone sufficient volunteers to create an interesting contest)? The authors state that 'candidates would have to obtain a minimum number of signatures and have demonstrated community leadership and experience or obtained a minimum level score on a comprehensive civic/issues test to stand for election'. That would narrow the field even further.

And what will turnout be like? Voters will be choosing a delegate to choose *another* delegate to choose *another* delegate to choose an MP – all of which seems more remote from actually choosing an MP or Congressman, and hardly a process likely to inspire enthusiasm.

After all this effort, the body formed would just comprise the lower house of Parliament. The upper house would be appointed in part by the lower house, in part by the chief executive (who is in turn elected by the lower house), and in part by a quadrumvirate, or collective presidency, of elder statesmen. This quadrumvirate would schedule frequent referenda to put the policies of the government to public approval, with mandatory voting.

This elaborate structure is designed to import into the modern system both the idea of Plato's guardians (the wise men who can govern in our collective interest) and James Madison's unelected Senate, the cool heads who will not succumb to popular passions. But apart from its over-elaborate nature, it does not seem to solve completely some of the key issues of democracy. Suppose the voters rejected in a referendum some, but not all, of a government's policies: for example, the revenue-raising element but not the spending element? Suppose the voters rejected a measure to protect minority rights?

And how would the system deal with the old issue of *Quis custodiet ipsos custodes* ('who guards the guards')? The wise men in charge will be deemed wise because they are members of the established elite; any test of citizenship or expertise will be a test of established knowledge. They will have a subconscious bias in favour of the status quo. New ideas may come from maverick thinkers who may not be deemed to be 'qualified' by the system. More fundamentally, it is not clear how, under the Berggruen/Gardels proposal, voters would exercise their most fundamental right: to throw the rascals out. They would have to rely on their 10 local delegates to affect events further up the chain. This could lead to even greater disillusionment.

One can see the various elements that Berggruen and Gardels are juggling in terms of the elements discussed in the previous chapter – aggregation, the balance between accountability and efficiency, the lack of voter trust. The voters' choices would be aggregated by the experts in the Senate and quadrumvirate, which would make the system more efficient, while accountability (as well as voter enthusiasm) would be achieved by the use of referenda and the devolved nature of elections.

But the system seems ludicrously over-complicated. Part of this may be down to the authors' backgrounds: they struggled to reform the mess that is California's government, where interest groups often put forward referenda for public vote. In that context, a council of wise men, who had to approve all ballot measures and make sure they are framed in a clear way, seems like a good idea.

Berggruen and Gardels may also be on to something with their ideas for a reformed Senate. Second chambers present countries with a particular problem – what are they really for? The British House of Lords looks like an absurd anachronism, even though its hereditary element is much reduced. Its origins lie in the old concept that Parliament should represent the classes of estates of the country. France had its first and second estates – the nobility and the clergy; Britain combined the two, which is why bishops still sit in the Lords.

The power of the Lords was broken at the beginning of the twentieth century in a rebellion over a Lloyd George Budget that taxed the rich. King George V was persuaded to go along with a threat to create new peers until the Lords gave way. In 1958 the number of hereditary peers started to be diluted by life peers, who were allowed to assume the title of Lord and to sit in the upper house, but not to pass the honour down to their children.

This reform created a potential new life for the Lords, as a chamber of experts who can scrutinize and advise on government legislation, like a newspaper sub-editor looking for typos and grammatical infelicities. While there undoubtedly are experts in the Lords – retired generals, businessmen, scientists – these are generally outnumbered by retired politicians. A peerage is seen as a reward for a long-serving party member, especially one who lost his seat at a recent election.

This unsatisfactory outcome has led to calls for the House of Lords to become a fully, or mostly, elected chamber. But that is opposed by many in the House of Commons who think an elected second chamber would be a challenge to the lower house's authority. Reform has stalled as a result. A 'revising' chamber is all very well, but what gives its members the right to revise? Since the lower house in most democracies represents all voters, there is no 'other interest' on whose behalf the upper house acts. One possibility is that the upper house could be designed to give regions more of a say – which is why each US state has two senators. Germany, meanwhile, has the Bundesrat, the upper house which represents the 16 regional states, or *Länder*. Members of the Bundesrat are delegates of the state Parliaments rather than directly elected. In this respect, Bundesrat members are similar to the original US senators who were appointed by the individual states, rather than elected directly. Their independence should allow them to take a detached view.

Australia has a Senate that represents the various states and territories – based on direct elections rather than appointments. The Senate has fairly broad powers except on the issue of financial bills, which it cannot amend. In large countries like Australia or the US, this regional/national balance seems perfectly valid and should not be adjusted. But what about smaller countries? Britain could in theory get by without the House of Lords, since it does not make that much difference to the workings of the government. That would leave the judiciary, both within and outside the country (e.g. the European Court of Human Rights, the International Criminal Court), as the only constitutional check on the power of elected officials (the press performs this function unconstitutionally, but in a highly erratic way).

Perhaps the upper house in non-federal countries could be reconstituted as a genuine forum of experts. Some would be from academia; some from the professions; some from trade unions, and so on. To prevent the house from becoming too much of a club for vested interests, some members could be drawn from the public, perhaps on the basis of competitive examination. Candidates could be asked questions on politics, law, mathematics and economics to ensure they have a well-rounded view of the issues.

The upper house could review decisions made by the lower house; where the two houses could not agree, the issue could be put to the voters in a referendum. The wording of that referendum would have to be agreed by the two houses. Where they could not agree, the final wording could be set by a panel of judges, such as a Supreme Court.

The upper house could also act as a further check on the operations of the non-elected bodies, such as central banks or quangos. Because the upper house would be comprised of experts, it would have greater technical know-how than normal politicians. If the upper house felt that a quango was exceeding its authority, or had pushed through some ridiculous regulation, it could alert the lower house, requiring the democratically elected body to debate and vote on the issue within, say, three months. This would apply, for example, to radical departures in central bank policy, as well as other bodies: central banks can do a lot of harm as well as good. In other words, the upper house could be a powerful force, but would not take decisions without the approval of the electorate or the democratic chamber. It would act more like the US Senate envisaged by the founding fathers.

DIRECT DEMOCRACY

Why not let the people bypass the politicians (and the unelected bodies) altogether by having them vote via referenda? California's experience demonstrates the problems that direct democracy can cause. One issue is aggregation. Passing a budget is a messy business. Over the long run, revenues and spending must be in rough balance, meaning that unpopular decisions must occasionally be made. But it also means that budgets must be passed as a whole: if individual items are cherry-picked for cancellation or amendment, the numbers will not add up. California's Proposition 13, passed in 1978, limited taxes but without defining which spending items had to be cut as a consequence.

Over time, Proposition 13 was followed by more than one hundred other initiatives which combined to undermine California's budget by promising a tax cut or a spending increase, without suggesting how such largesse could be paid for. Two-thirds of those initiatives passed.[4] The state suffered a budget crisis in 2010, briefly giving it the worst credit rating of any state in the nation, at A minus.[5] A surplus emerged in 2013 after taxes rose, but few were confident it would last.

Voters have not traditionally approved budgets in any formal sense. They leave their representatives to make the messy decisions and then re-elect or fire them if they don't like the result. In a Parliamentary system, the budget is at the heart of a government's programme: defeat on a budgetary issue can cause the fall of an administration. The voters can blame the government for the budgetary policies they do not like, although in a coalition government parties may get the blame for policies that were not part of their platform.

When it comes to direct democracy, it should not be possible to put tax or spending packages to voters in separate referenda. If the two houses of Congress or Parliament did not agree on the annual budget, the entire deal should be put to the voters for approval. Rejection by the electorate would require an alternative budget to be prepared, but with the same balance between tax and spending (so as to prevent the voters from approving endless give-aways). These revenue assumptions should be subject to checking by an independent body such as the Congressional Budget Office or Britain's Office for Budget Responsibility.

The danger with this system is that the public might be forced to vote too often. But I think that the threat of a referendum might concentrate the minds of the lower house and indeed the government. Subsidies to special interests might be harder to push through if the government feared that the upper house would reject the notion, and the public might be asked to rule on any disputes.

Switzerland, which regularly polls its citizens via referenda, is rather better run than California. But a 2009 poll that banned the construction of minarets (the towers attached to mosques) in Switzerland showed that the majority can vote to restrict the rights of a minority. Some argue that the ban runs counter to the Swiss Constitution, which protects freedom of religion. Even if this does turn out to be the case, it only serves to illustrate the issue: if a constitution can overturn the result of a referendum, then referenda cannot be the only answer to the democratic problem.

More generally, referenda can be subject to the same problems of turnout as other elections. If the issue is complex, or concerns the interests of only a small number of people, few voters may be bothered to turn out. Those who do may be disproportionately interested in the subject – the potential recipients of a tax break or subsidy, for example. Unless campaign finance is restricted, interested parties will have every incentive to publicize their cause, with the result that voters fail to get a balanced view. In short, referenda on their own are not the answer to democracy's problems.

THE ONLINE ANSWER

Beppe Grillo, the Italian comedian who burst to prominence in the 2013 election, has used social media to attract supporters, blogging extensively and attracting 1 million people into 'liking' his Facebook page[6] and 1.16 million people to follow his tweets.[7] He is far from alone in this; in both 2008 and 2012 the Obama Presidential campaign was seen as much more successful in connecting to his online followers than were his Republican opponents. In some ways, Grillo's success is a response to the failure of the old parties, particularly in Italy where economic growth has been dismally slow; he campaigns against political corruption, calls for lower salaries for elected representatives, argues for measures to redistribute wealth and for more direct democracy, in the form of referenda and online polls.[8]

But Grillo's campaign illustrates one of the potential problems with direct democracy. He called for a referendum on Italy's membership of the euro zone. Were he to get close to political power, the destabilizing potential of a referendum, and a euro zone exit, would probably have huge negative economic effects; Italian bank depositors, fearing devaluation of their savings, might rush for the exits, triggering a banking crisis; bond investors would fear the same, driving up the cost of government borrowing; while foreign companies would avoid direct investment in Italy, fearing they might put euros in and get devalued lire out.

Nor is there an easy way to reconcile direct democracy with human rights. Were the public to vote for the return of hanging, or the expulsion of immigrants, would the policy be followed through? And if some topics were deemed out of bounds for direct democracy, who would decide where the boundary should lie? Some non-democratic element would be needed.

Douglas Carswell, the Conservative MP, is an enthusiast for the idea of 'idemocracy', as he dubs it in a recent book.[9] As Mr Carswell rightly notes, the Internet has transformed many businesses, giving consumers the ability to find the cheapest deals and the products that most closely match their needs. Why couldn't government be transformed in the same way? Yet he doesn't really address the practical difficulties of giving citizens more choice in national government services. Take one example from his book: 'Try suggesting to the teachers in a British state school that your child ought to learn Spanish, not French . . . It's not on offer.'

However, there is an obvious reason for that lack of flexibility. The school might not have a teacher who is qualified to teach Spanish. And what if other pupils wanted tuition in Italian, or Serbo-Croat or Japanese? Governments have to make decisions about how many teachers should be trained in particular disciplines: this inevitably constrains the curriculum choices that pupils can have. If British pupils want a school that offers them a wide range of course options, they generally have to go private. They then get what they pay for.

It would be possible to buy in language services from a commercial provider. But if the teaching were face to face this might be a very expensive option. And if the teaching were online, the school would still need to have someone present in the classroom to monitor the pupils: it generally helps if that teacher is able to answer any questions which the pupil might have. Other public services would face the same issues. When it comes to health care, consumers might all want to see the very best surgeons or attend GP surgeries at 7 p.m. in the evening. But all their needs cannot be met simultaneously.

Public service provision generally has to balance the three Cs: coverage, cost and choice. You can cover all the people, as the British NHS does, but if you want to keep the cost down, you have to limit consumer choice. Not everyone can have the most expensive treatment; not everyone can be treated immediately. The pre-Obamacare US health system gave consumers more choice, but at a high cost and without covering the entire population for non-emergency treatment.

That is not to say that public services could not be more responsive to the needs of citizens; clearly, they are too bureaucratic. Mr Carswell is right in declaring that the public sector still has a lot to learn from the private sector. If a private business offers a service that is unappealing to consumers, it will go out of business. There is also merit in his suggestion for making Parliamentary deliberations more responsive to public opinion, by allowing debates to be triggered on an issue if a set limit of signatures have been collected. There is scope, of course, for abuse of such a system and for trivia to be put forward.

But such a problem could be eliminated if the proposals were subject to the approval of an independent panel: motions to praise football teams and rock stars could – thankfully – be weeded out.

To avoid empty chambers on such occasions, these debates could be subject to mandatory attendance by representatives, with outside experts on the issue perhaps invited to address the assembled politicos. It might be quite instructive for, say, the US Senate to be forced to listen to the issues surrounding drug legalization, or for French MPs to hear about the problems businessmen face in dealing with that country's regulations.

WARDING OFF EXTREMISTS

How to deal with the American problem of bitter division between the parties? One driving force, particularly on the Republican side, is the primary system. A candidate who fails to kowtow to the religious right, or to fiscal conservatives, has real problems in winning the Republican nomination. Mitt Romney had to describe himself as 'seriously conservative' when running for the Republican nomination in 2012; he then tacked back to the centre in the actual race. His aide, Eric Fehrnstrom, remarked in March of that year that 'I think you hit a reset button for the fall campaign. Everything changes. It's almost like an Etch A Sketch. You can kind of shake it up, and we start all over again.' The danger is that the candidate can get trapped by the promises made in his extreme phase – and that such reversals of policy only add to voter cynicism.

In 2010 a Tea Party revolt in the Republican Party meant that establishment candidates were unseated in favour of eccentric nominees such as Christine O'Donnell in Delaware and Sharron Angle in Nevada. The former had to go on TV to declare that she was not a witch. The latter favoured a policy of withdrawal from the United Nations, the banning of all abortions even in the cases of rape and incest, the privatization of Medicare and the phasing out of Social Security. Although O'Donnell and Angle lost, there was still a shift to the right in the Republican make-up, with many moderate voices choosing not to run again. An analysis of roll-call votes by Messrs

Thomas Mann and Norman Ornstein[10] found that 'Political parties today are more internally unified and ideologically distinctive than they have been in over a century.'

Primaries in the US are normally confined to party members, so the most ideologically committed voters are the most likely to turn out. Similarly, an ideological commitment is probably more likely to make people volunteer for, and fund, a politician's campaign. One answer to weeding out the extremists is to move to open primaries, in which all citizens can vote – although this leaves parties open to mischief-making by their opponents, voting for the most bizarre candidate to make the rival party unelectable. However, open primaries are already used in presidential races and seem to have favoured more moderate candidates – John McCain, for example, seems to have been favoured by open voting in the race for the 2008 Republican nomination.

Another answer is the elimination of gerrymandering, the deliberate redrawing of constituency boundaries to favour a chosen party. The result is the creation of a lot of safe seats for one party or another: this both reduces voter enthusiasm and helps to promote the election of extreme candidates, who can focus their appeal on the party faithful. In the US, as in many other countries, the boundaries can be set by politicians of the state concerned; there was a notorious example of gerrymandering in Texas in 2003. The answer is to move to an independent commission, as in Australia or Britain.

Some hope that in the United States a third-party candidate might emerge and prove a unifying influence. The US party system was fairly fluid up until 1860 when Abraham Lincoln led the newly formed Republicans to victory. But a combination of the first-past-the-post system and the advantages of incumbency have locked the main two parties in place ever since 1912, when Teddy Roosevelt came in second as a third-party Progressive candidate. After the Second World War southern states voted for a few states' rights candidates (i.e. they were anti-civil rights), such as Strom Thurmond and George Wallace. In 1980 John Anderson briefly registered over 20% of the vote in opinion polls, before fading to 7% on election day. In 1992 Ross Perot, a businessman, led in the national polls in June and secured 19% of the actual vote, but failed to win a single state in the electoral college.

Michael Bloomberg, the billionaire who won three terms as Mayor of New York, looked into running as a third-party candidate in 2008, but decided against it. Messrs Mann and Ornstein[11] state that 'there is simply no reliable evidence to support the belief that voters would flock to a straight-talking, centrist, independent or third-party candidate'. Even if a third-party candidate were to win office, they would still have to face the problem of governing with a Congress in which they would have no natural allies.

INTERNATIONAL RELATIONS

Democracy started in the ancient Greek cities and became entrenched in nation states. It now has an international component in the not very inspiring form of the European Parliament, where representatives from the 27 member states meet and debate in Brussels and Strasbourg. The dual headquarters of the Parliament, the result of French lobbying, adds to the cost and to the general public sense that the whole institution is an expenses-driven junket.

The Parliament has, on occasion, held the European Commission to account and has revised a myriad of laws. Given Europe's violent twentieth-century history, we should be thrilled that its representatives are talking and not fighting. But the Parliament was imposed by the elite on the public rather than the other way round; it is not viewed with any widespread enthusiasm. Nor is it the basis for a European government, which of course is the function of parliaments in other states. At least, however, the European Parliament exists. At the global level, there is only the General Assembly of the United Nations, where there is one nation, one vote. While the assembly can make symbolic gestures, such as recognizing the Palestinian state in 2012, it has no real power.[12]

In economic terms, the most influential bodies are the International Monetary Fund and the World Bank. Their structures still reflect the balance of power when they were established at the end of the Second World War, and are clearly inappropriate for the twenty-first century. The convention by which the Europeans get to choose the head of the

IMF (two successive French politicians) and the Americans choose the head of the World Bank is absurdly anachronistic.

As well as opening up the leadership to the best candidates from all nations, the developing world clearly has to get more votes. Given the parlous state of finances in the developed world, the negotiating power is shifting away from the West. Eventually, developing countries may find themselves bailing out ageing European economies. At that stage, reform will occur.

In my last book, I suggested that there may come a point in the next 10 years or so when the global financial system gets remade, probably in response to a crisis in the dollar or in the US Treasury market. America would then be in a weaker position, relative to the developing world. Of course, this shift in power will not be to the liking of Western democracies. But in the long run, the answer to creditor power is not to be in hock to creditors.

Some of my suggestions may already strike readers as impractical and any proposal to remake the UN risks going too far off into la-la land. World government is not an imminent possibility – although it might one day be more popular than it is now. It was once seen as a noble aim: back in 1947, 56% of Americans agreed with the statement that 'the UN should be strengthened to make it a world government'.[13]

But we have to take more decisions on a collective basis. Let me make a suggestion as to how the world will eventually come to terms with reconciling national states, democracy and global problems. It lies with the same mechanism the US founding fathers dreamed up – the electoral college.

When the US Constitution was being drawn up, there was immense mutual suspicion among the states of a federal authority, just as there is immense suspicion of global bodies today. The small Yankee farmers of the northeast feared being outvoted by the plantation owners of the south, and vice versa. The Senate was one way of getting round this fear: each state, however small, had two votes. Since a global Parliament seems a complete pipedream, the Senate model is only useful as a model at a national level. But the electoral college might be more helpful. The idea behind it was that presidents should not be directly elected by the voters, but by a group of wise men who could assess the candidates carefully. The practical implication of the electoral college, as repeated elections have shown, is that candidates need to focus on the swing states, rather than the big states (like California and New York) where lots of people live.

Any global voting system (such as the UN) needs to balance the need for a broad spread of support against the massive power of the most populous nations. Each state could be given a vote total, with the smallest nations getting one each and China and India getting the most. In effect, the smallest nations would be over-represented. Any proposal for a global policy would need a two-thirds majority via this voting method: neither America's economic power nor China's size of population would be decisive. Every nation's vote would count, for every nation might be the swing vote.

What would make the large nations cede any power at all? The most likely reason is to deal with the 'free rider' problem. This crops up not just with global warming (why cut back on your emissions if other people will feel most of the benefit?) but with other issues such as tax. The big nations cannot crack down on tax avoidance if companies are free to operate from tax havens. They cannot crack down on terrorism if small states give them shelter. They may not be able to safeguard their computer networks if small nations allow hackers free rein. These issues require global action, which is why big nations may have to give up some sovereignty to cope with them.

THE LAST VOTE

Even if the political system were reformed or improved along the lines suggested in this chapter, none of it would matter if voters still regarded the whole system with distaste. That is why this book is addressed, not at national leaders or at academics, but at the general reader. The fault is not in our stars, or in our politicians, but in ourselves. Wake up, in other words. Politicians have made mistakes; some of them have been greedy and corrupt. But by and large they have followed the priorities we have set them. If they have failed to balance the budget, it is because voters have refused to recognize that they cannot have high benefits without high taxes. If politicians have failed to produce economic growth, it may be that we, the voters, have resisted reform too strongly, preferring peace and quiet for existing homeowners to the construction of new houses or transport links, for example.

It is easy to be an armchair football supporter and shout abuse from the comfort of your sofa. If you believe politicians have an easy life, think about whether you would willingly swap your life for theirs, with the associated round-the-clock meetings, media intrusion and public opprobrium. Most of us would opt to avoid the limelight. If you think politicians are corrupt, then write, demonstrate and vote for reform of the system.

Those of us who work in the media can play our part. It is easy to be cynical about the actions and motives of politicians, but we need to remember that we have 'power without responsibility', as Stanley Baldwin remarked when attacked by the press barons of the 1930s. Criticism of governments is necessary, but it needs to be considered criticism, not abuse; constructive criticism, not mindless demagoguery. Every journalist has made a mistake under the pressure of a deadline, something that ought to make writers more tolerant of the mistakes made by government officials under far greater pressure.

It is up to us to understand there is no magic bullet that will suddenly solve all our problems; no ideal system we can copy. But the very least we can do is take an interest in the issues that affect our everyday lives and the world in which we live. And when we do examine those issues, let us make sure we are honest about the trade-offs concerned. If you want taxes to be lower, which spending programmes would you cut? (And make sure the sums balance when you make your proposal.) If you want more social spending, which taxes would you raise? If you want a crackdown on tax fraud, do you pay your builder in cash to avoid VAT? Before you favour a policy that applies to others, make sure you would be happy if it applied to you.

The more we get involved, the less chance special interests have to tilt the system against us, and the less chance extremists have to take over political parties and to win seats in low turnouts. The more we protest against decisions made behind closed doors, the more we will force politics into the open.

The decline of democracy has been a slow, unspectacular process, which is why many people have not noticed it. Thankfully, there is no equivalent of Hitler threatening to do away with the system, no mass army at the border that might overthrow our state. But indifference and cynicism act like water on a rock, wearing away democracy year after year. If we cease to care who wins our vote, we may cease to care whether we vote at all.

Having the vote is a great privilege, one still only available to half the world's population. Even in most countries where it seems long established, full adult suffrage has only been around for a hundred years or so. So don't be cynical about it. Take your responsibilities seriously. Study the problems that face us, and the policies each party proposes. Don't vote because one person looks better on TV, or because you heard something bad about the candidate on the Internet.

We can no longer act as if each vote is our first vote. But we can act as if each vote might be our last. Which leaders are likely to act in the long-term interest of the nation? Which leaders are just advancing short-term gimmicky solutions? Which are just sowing hatred against foreigners or minorities? If we treat each vote as our last, we will think twice about voting for extremists or joke parties. We might be stuck with them.

It is our democracy and our vote. We should use it wisely. If democracy meets its demise, we will only have ourselves to blame.

Afterword

On 18 September 2014 Scotland held a referendum on independence from the UK. Almost 85 percent of the electorate voted, a record turnout since mass suffrage was introduced in 1918. The campaign, while occasionally rowdy, generated much enthusiasm; those in the Yes campaign accepted their defeat with sadness, but no violence. In a sense, it was a triumph for democracy.

But countries cannot hold independence referenda very often. Traditional electoral contests arouse far less enthusiasm. The chances are that, when it comes to a general election in May 2015, the Scottish turnout will be much lower (it was 64 percent in 2010), as it will be throughout the rest of the UK. Indeed, turnout in national elections across the western world has been falling for forty years.

The Scottish campaign may also have been a symptom of democracy's wider problems. A powerful driver of the Yes campaign was the alienation felt by many voters towards the 'Westminster elite': the mainstream political parties (and even the BBC as the perceived voice of the establishment). In Scotland, then, this alienation manifested itself in the form of a desire for separation; in other countries, it has shown itself in the form of voters switching en masse from centrist to extreme parties on the right and the left.

Those Scots who voted Yes wanted their government to be much more local: based in Edinburgh, not London. More specifically, they did not want to be ruled by Conservatives, who few Scots had voted for in the national elections (only one Conservative out of a total of fifty-two Scottish MPs was elected in 2010). In essence, they did not accept the legitimacy of a British government that was dependent on English voters for its majority.

This points to another problem facing democracy. For it to work properly, voters must accept that the outcome of a poll is fair. Democracy requires the existence not just of an elected government but an opposition that can take charge should the views of the voters change. And it requires voters to feel that either party can represent their interests. Ukraine is an extreme example of what happens when this turns out not to be the case: both pro-Russian and pro-EU sections of the electorate refuse to accept that a government from the other camp can fairly represent their interests.

So why not get round this problem by making all government as local as possible? The Scottish referendum raised the question of whether devolution should be extended not only to Scotland, but to English regions and cities too. But there has to be a limit to this process: for instance, local residents may want to enjoy the benefits of power stations but refuse to have one sited in their area; the same goes for prisons and oil refineries. At some point, a national government must step in and make the decision.

Furthermore, many issues facing the modern world are global, not local – terrorism, climate change, tax evasion and so on. These issues need international co-operation to solve, in the process requiring local populations to surrender some degree of sovereignty. Attempts to tackle such global issues also tend to result in backroom deals being done between governments, in a messy process that often involves bleary-eyed compromises being made at two in the morning after hours and days of negotiations. These compromises are rarely submitted to democratic approval, even where the countries in question have all elected their governments as a result of democratic processes; to do so would be too time-consuming and fraught with risk. If one country's voters rejected a deal made by a hundred countries, would the whole deal have to be unpicked? The European Union has struggled, and failed, to deal with this problem.

There is plenty of evidence that voters do not like such internationally agreed solutions, whether it is Greeks protesting against EU-imposed austerity, Britons moaning about decisions made by the European Court of Human Rights, or Americans refusing to sign up for global deals on climate change or war crime prosecutions. The Scottish independence campaign was a sign of the continued power of nationalism in a globalized world. What was expressed peacefully in Scotland may be expressed much more violently in other countries.

Furthermore, economic change is global in scope, whether it is technological progress that makes some jobs obsolete (think driverless cars), financial shocks that are transmitted round the world, or supply change disruptions such as the Japanese earthquake and nuclear accident in 2011.

In the face of these pressures, politicians are caught in the middle. They are forced by a competitive electoral process to pretend they have all of the answers but they are often shown, in office, to be at the mercy of global events. The gap between their rhetoric and the reality only increases voter cynicism.

That cynicism has already been displayed on several occasions since the first edition of this book was published. Even though the euro crisis has abated and most economies have emerged from recession, radical parties of the right and left did extremely well in the European parliamentary elections of May 2014. In France, Marine le Pen of the Front National topped the with 25 percent of the vote; in Britain, UKIP achieved 27 percent. In Greece, the Trotskyist Syriza party and the neo-fascist Golden Dawn received 40 percent of the vote between them. Even in Germany, where Angela Merkel's popularity held firm, a fascist won a seat. All told, some 30 percent of seats in the European parliament are now held by eurosceptic and anti-establishment parties.

Elsewhere in the world, the forward march of democracy, so confidently assumed at the start of the Arab Spring, has been reversed. Egypt is once more being ruled by the army, as is Thailand; Libya is in chaos, the Isis fundamentalist group has occupied swathes of territory in Iraq, and is also involved in Syria's bloody civil war. Russia and China are edging together, potentially forming a powerful bloc against what they see as the arrogant democracies of the west.

Why has so much been going wrong with democracy? Sluggish economic growth is clearly the biggest problem; real incomes have been squeezed in much of the western world. More broadly, democracy has been losing its core appeal, which was built on three characteristics: efficiency, equality and liberty.

Efficiency. When the largely aristocratic regimes of Europe blundered into the First World War, few countries were full democracies.

As millions were slaughtered and illusions of military glory turned to dust, the idea that hereditary elites were best-placed to rule society was made to look ridiculous. In addition, soldiers who were asked to die for their country claimed a right to choose their government. Democracy seemed like the answer: the right to choose our leaders on merit, rather than by accident of birth.

As early as the 1930s, however, the idea that democracies were efficient came under challenge. Faced with the Great Depression, it seemed that authoritarian leaders like Hitler (with rearmament and road-building) or Stalin (with his five year plan and industrialization) were most likely to put their unemployed, impoverished citizens back to work. By comparison, the grey men who ran 1930s democracies seemed ineffectual.

Nowadays, ask people which governments in the world are most efficient and they will probably name China or Singapore, neither of which are full democracies. Such governments can plan for the long-term, whether that involves building the right infrastructure or delivering the education for a twenty-first-century workforce. Our democracies, it seems, are too beholden to the electoral cycle; there is no incentive for a politician to deliver a big infrastructure project that will pay off over twenty years, if it risks losing him the next election. Yet attempts to get round this problem by passing decisions to technocrats are of course inherently anti-democratic.

Equality. In the late nineteenth and early twentieth centuries, many working-class citizens who campaigned for universal suffrage assumed that, if they had a say in electing a government, it would be more inclined to look after their interests. That seemed to be the case, particularly after the Second World War, when European countries developed their welfare states, complete with free health care and unemployment benefits. At the other end of the income scale, high taxes were hitting the rich. The period from the 1940s to the 1980s, known as the 'Great Compression', was one in which inequality reduced significantly.

But since the 1980s, for reasons explained earlier in the book, inequality has widened again. The central bank response to the 2008 crisis, which has involved propping up the asset markets, may have made matters worse. The rich own assets, but the poor don't. One study found that the income of the top 1 percent of Americans rose 31 percent in real terms between 2009 and 2012, while that of the bottom 99 percent rose less than 1 percent.

The rise of the far-right (and far-left) in European polls must be partly driven by a sense that the governing class rules on behalf of the elite, not the ordinary man, as illustrated by the failure of the latter's standard of living to advance. In the US, the same emotion has helped the rise of the tea party. And many Scottish Yes voters seem to have been motivated by a desire for greater social justice.

Liberty. The appeal of democracy was not just economic. Democratic regimes seemed to offer much greater liberty than authoritarian countries; indeed, this factor enabled them to overcome communism. They built a wall in Berlin to keep East Germans in, not to keep West Germans out. But the notion of the west as a bastion of liberty has been undermined in recent years, most recently by the extent to which intelligence agencies have been monitoring our phone calls and e-mails, including those of friendly allies. No longer is there a black-and-white contrast between the west and the rest.

Restoring voters' confidence in democracy probably requires progress on all three fronts. And that may take a long time. It is hard to make democracies more efficient if there is such a low opinion of the political elite and if there appears to be gridlock because of the rise of extremism; look at the US, where sheer stubbornness in Congress twice brought the government close to default on its debt.

It may also be hard to tackle inequality since macro-economic forces are driving in that direction. Since this book was written, economists like Erik Brynjolfsson and Andrew McAfee of the Massachusetts Institute of Technology have argued that the workforce is dividing in two, with a small number of participants reaping the big rewards from technological advance and the rest surviving on the scraps. If that trend develops, citizens will be tempted to look for someone to blame. The target may well be minority populations; a further threat to liberty.

This book has tried to set all these pressing issues in context, both in terms of the history of societies and in the sense of democracy as an idea. While we date democracy to ancient Athens, its use as a system for governing countries covers only a fraction of human history. If we believe that our democracies are destined to endure, this fact alone should give us pause.

Despite all democracy's problems, there is hope. Wherever I have gone to speak about the themes of the book, I have found that people do care about the future of democracy and want things to improve: let us hope there is enough of a critical mass of such people that the system can be rebooted. Indeed, even showing an interest by reading this book is a start. The next step is to get involved – and, above all, to vote.

Notes

INTRODUCTION

1. *The Economist* Intelligence Unit, Democracy index, 2011.
2. See http://www.publicpolicypolling.com/main/2013/01/congress-less-popular-than-cockroaches-traffic-jams.html.
3. Cited in *The Independent*, 4 September 2012, p. 5.
4. Catherine Fieschi, Marley Morris and Lila Caballero, 'Recapturing the Reluctant Radical: How to Win Back Europe's Populist Vote', *Counterpoint*, September 2012. The quoted sentence refers specifically to Finland but I think can be applied to other countries as well.
5. First published by the Free Press in 1992; published in Britain by Penguin Books.
6. *The Third Wave: Democratization in the Late Twentieth Century*, University of Oklahoma Press, 1993.
7. *Ill Fares the Land*, Penguin, 2010.
8. Dominic Sandbrook, *Seasons in the Sun: The Battle for Britain 1974–1979*, Penguin, 2013.
9. ibid.
10. *Capitalism, Socialism and Democracy*, Harper & Bros., 1942.
11. op. cit.
12. Editorial page comment, 11 September 2012.
13. See http://www.unrisd.org/80256B3C005BCCF9/%28httpAuxPages%29/AE49CC52BEFC658EC1256EFA002D44FB/$file/RPB3e.pdf
14. Strictly speaking, Wilson used this term only in respect of Austria-Hungary. When it came to colonies, he spoke only of a balance between the claims of existing governments and the 'interests of the populations concerned'. But it was hard to limit the idea of self-determination once established.
15. Already monetary policy (the setting of interest rates) is out of the hands of voters, as we shall discuss later in the book.

16. *The Economist* Intelligence Unit, Democracy index, 2011.

17. See http://www.yougov.polis.cam.ac.uk/?p=4138

18. Taken from 'Democracy on Trial: What Voters Really Think of Parliament and Our Politicians', presented to the Reuters Institute for the Study of Journalism by Peter Kellner, March 2012. http://d25d2506 sfb94s.cloudfront.net/cumulus_uploads/document/w3436dvzzd/Democ racy%20Results%20120124%20GB%20sample%20%282%29.pdf.

1. A TURBULENT HISTORY

1. *Setting the People Free: The Story of Democracy*, Atlantic Books, 2005.

2. *Athens on Trial: The Antidemocratic Tradition in Western Thought,* Princeton University Press, 1994.

3. *Politics*, Kindle edition.

4. *The Republic*, translated by Desmond Lee with an introduction by Melissa Lane, Penguin, 2007.

5. John Stuart Mill, *Considerations on Representative Government*, Harper & Bros., 1862.

6. See 'Democracy on Trial: What Voters Really Think of Parliament and Our Politicians', presented to the Reuters Institute for the Study of Journalism by Peter Kellner, March 2012.

7. *The Federalist*, essay no. X.

8. ibid.

9. Mill, *Considerations on Representative Government*.

10. Gallup poll, http://www.gallup.com/poll/27847/Majority-Republicans-Doubt-Theory-Evolution.aspx. There may be a framing problem here as slightly more (49%) believed in evolution than did not (48%).

11. *The Federalist*, essay no. XXXIX.

12. The story may well be apocryphal, but it's a good metaphor.

13. *The Federalist*, essay no. LI.

14. Indeed, the Republicans controlled the House of Representatives, where seats are in proportion to population. Direct comparisons are complicated because the Senate is elected a third at a time.

15. Mill, *Considerations on Representative Government*.

16. Second edition, Pober, 2010, pp. 284–5.

17. The Butler lecture to the Reuters Institute for the Study of Journalism, March 2012.

18. Quoted by Neil Harding in *Democracy: The Unfinished Journey*, Oxford University Press, 1992.

19. *Models of Democracy*, third edition, Polity, 2006.

20. Penguin Classics, 2007. Be warned: you need to be an Atlas to lift it. It weighs in at 1,184 pages.
21. Mill, *Consideration on Representative Government*.

2. THE GRAND DISILLUSION

1. *The Economist* Intelligence Unit, 'Democracy under Stress'.
2. The data are from International IDEA and are an unweighted average of all the democracies that were generally considered to be in the Western camp during the Cold War (so no Eastern European countries are included, except for East Germany after reunification). The countries concerned are Australia, Austria, Belgium, Canada, Cyprus, Denmark, Finland, France, Germany, Greece, Iceland, Ireland, Israel, Italy, Japan, Liechtenstein, Luxembourg, Malta, Monaco, the Netherlands, New Zealand, Norway, Portugal, Spain, Sweden, Switzerland, the UK and the US. All numbers are for voter turnout except for the US, where IDEA does not have data until 1968; accordingly, the US figures are for turnout as a proportion of the voting-age population. This makes the totals rather lower, but the trend is the same; failure to register is, in any case, a sign of apathy. See the chart on US Presidential elections (Fig. 2.2) for a guide to voter turnout as well.
3. Some countries that do have compulsion still fall well short of 100% turnout.
4. The Presidential election turnout was much higher, at 80% of registered voters and 71% of those of voting age. The latter number was more than 5 percentage points below the 2007 turnout.
5. In his book *Patterns of Democracy: Government Forms and Performance in Thirty-Six Countries*, Yale University Press, 1999.
6. Taken from 'Democracy on Trial: What Voters Really Think of Parliament and Our Politicians' presented to the Reuters Institute for the Study of Journalism by Peter Kellner, March 2012.
7. ibid.
8. Andreas Kluth, 'The People's Will', *The Economist*, April 2011.
9. An Illinois city's ballot question from 2012.
10. ibid.
11. Bagehot, 'For the Birds', *The Economist*, 29 September 2012.
12. *The New Few: or a Very British Oligarchy*, Simon & Schuster, 2012.
13. Bagehot, 'For the Birds', *The Economist*, 29 September 2012.
14. *Bowling Alone: The Collapse and Revival of American Community*, Simon & Schuster, 2000.

15. After Groucho Marx, who said 'I would never join any club that would have me as a member.'

16. Andreas Kluth, 'The People's Will', *The Economist*, April 2011.

17. Jacob S. Hacker and Paul Pierson, *Winner-Take-All Politics: How Washington Made the Rich Richer and Turned Its Back on the Middle* Class, Simon & Schuster, 2010.

18. See http://www.heritage.org/federalbudget/federal-revenue-sources.

19. See http://www.usgovernmentrevenue.com/statelocal_revenue_2012 USrn.

20. See http://www.hm-treasury.gov.uk/junebudget_diagrams.htm.

21. 'What Have We Learned about Fiscal Policy from the Crisis?', *In the Wake of the Crisis: Leading Economists Reassess Economic Policy*, edited by Olivier Blanchard, David Romer, A. Michael Spence and Joseph E. Stiglitz, MIT Press, 2012.

22. *The Rise and Decline of Nations: Economic Growth, Stagflation and Social Rigidities*, Yale University Press, 1982.

23. Bryan Caplan, *The Myth of the Rational Voter: Why Democracies Choose Bad Policies*, Princeton University Press, 2007.

24. Interview with author, 27 September 2012.

25. The best example is probably Thomas Frank's *What's the Matter with Kansas: The Resistible Rise of the American Right*, Henry Holt, 2004.

26. Larry M. Bartels, *Unequal Democracy: The Political Economy of the New Gilded Age*, Princeton University Press, 2008.

3. THE TRIUMPH OF AN IDEA

1. 'The Italian City-Republics', in *Democracy: The Unfinished Journey 508 BC to AD 1993*, edited by John Dunn, Oxford University Press, 1992.

2. *A Free Nation Deep in Debt: The Financial Roots of Democracy*, Princeton University Press, 2003.

3. The declaration is regarded with great reverence by Americans. But there were signs of future trouble in one passage, which declares that King George 'has endeavoured to bring on the inhabitants of our frontiers, the merciless Indian Savages, whose known rule of warfare, is an undistinguished destruction of all ages, sexes and conditions'.

4. *The Federalist*, essay no. XXXIX.

5. Fareed Zakaria, *The Future of Illiberal Democracy*, W. W. Norton & Co., 2007.

6. *Democracy in America*, originally published in two volumes in 1835 and 1840.

7. *The Idea of a Party System: The Rise of Legitimate Opposition in the United States 1780–1840*, University of California Press, 1969.

8. *The Age of Revolution*, Weidenfeld & Nicolson, 1962.

9. *Democracy and Its Critics*, Yale University Press, 1991.

10. *Democracy in America*, Kindle edition.

11. 'Why Did the West Extend the Franchise? Democracy, Inequality and Growth in Historical Perspective', *The Quarterly Journal of Economics*, November 2000.

12. *The Age of Capital 1848–1875*, Abacus Books, 1977.

13. George Dangerfield wrote a book of that title in 1935. It is still in print in the twenty-first century.

14. New Nationalism speech, 1910, see http://www.whitehouse.gov/blog/2011/12/06/archives-president-teddy-roosevelts-new-nationalism-speech

15. *The Third Wave: Democratization in the Late Twentieth Century*, University of Oklahoma Press, 2012.

16. Initially de Gaulle was granted emergency powers by Parliament; it was only later that he was elected president. He revamped the constitution to give the president more powers.

17. Lena Edlund and Rohini Pande, 'Why Have Women Become Left-Wing? The Political Gender Gap and the Decline in Marriage', Columbia University, 11 October 2001.

18. Ronald Inglehart and Pippa Norris, 'The Developmental Theory of the Gender Gap: Women's and Men's Voting Behaviour in Global Perspective', *International Political Science Review*, October 2000.

19. http://fivethirtyeight.blogs.nytimes.com/2012/11/15/gay-vote-seen-as-crucial-in-obamas-victory.

4. AN ECONOMY BECALMED?

1. Adam Przeowrski and Fernando Papaterra Limongi Neto, 'Modernization: Theories and Facts', cited in Fareed Zakaria, *The Future of Freedom: Illiberal Democracy at Home and Abroad*, W. W. Norton & Co., 2007.

2. For a detailed and depressing account, read Frank Dikötter, *Mao's Great Famine: The History of China's Most Devastating Catastrophe 1958–1962*, Bloomsbury, 2010.

3. 'What if the Turkeys Don't Vote for Christmas?', *The Times*, 12 May 2012.

4. See Barry Eichengreen, *Golden Fetters: The Gold Standard and the Great Depression*, Oxford University Press, 1995.

5. The New Deal, although involving a lot of government activity, did not really qualify as Keynesianism since President Roosevelt was inconsistent,

sometimes appearing to favour a balanced budget. The biggest stimulus to the US economy came from the devaluation of the dollar against gold, which headed off deflation. The most successful Keynesians were the Nazis, who boosted the economy through spending on rearmament and roads. But Hitler was simply impatient to build up his armed forces, rather than following an economic plan.

6. Andreas Kluth, 'War by Initiative', *The Economist*, 20 April 2011.

7. It is quite surprising that they did not, given all the other things they managed to trade.

8. The Financial Instability Hypothesis, http://www.levyinstitute.org/pubs/wp74.pdf

9. The role was defined by Walter Bagehot, a former editor of *The Economist*, in his book *Lombard Street*, Wiley Investment Classics, 1999.

10. For the full text, see http://blogs.wsj.com/economics/2011/09/20/full-text-republicans-letter-to-bernanke-questioning-more-fed-action/

11. Subtitled *Eight Centuries of Financial Folly*, Princeton University Press, 2009.

12. 'It Ain't Necessarily So', *The Economist*, 13 October 2012.

13. Author of the books *Atlas Shrugged* and *The Fountainhead*, and the founder of objectivism, the belief that the moral purpose of a man's life is his own happiness (but not someone else's; she rejected altruism, one of the central tenets of Christianity). She is a hero figure for some on the American right.

14. Except to make the obvious point that it can't be more than 100% of GDP.

15. For the data, taken from UN population projections, see http://www.economist.com/blogs/buttonwood/2012/02/demography

16. Source http://www.focus.com/fyi/productivity-wars-europe-vs-usa/

17. Subtitled *The End of Western Affluence*, Yale University Press, 2013.

18. 'Austerity and Anarchy: Budget Cuts and Social Unrest in Europe 1919–2008' by Jacopo Ponticelli and Hans-Joachim Voth, December 2011.

19. In fact, most benefits are financed on a pay-as-you-go basis with current workers paying for the cost of previous generations. That system starts to break down if one generation is smaller than the last.

5. THE DEAD WEIGHTS OF DEMOCRACY

1. *The Rise and Decline of Nations*, Yale University Press, 1982.

2. The original piece appeared as a *National Journal* article in 1992. Later he turned the thesis into a book, updated as *Government's End: Why Washington Stopped Working*, Public Affairs, 1999.

3. Rauch, *Government's End*.

4. 'Children of the Corn: The Renewable Fuels Disaster', American Enterprise Institute, 4 January 2012.

5. 'Big Sugar Wins in the Senate', 13 June 2012, www.cato-at-liberty.org

6. www.americanprogress.org

7. Margaret Thatcher managed it in Britain. But the deduction was capped at £30,000 per loan and she was able to let inflation erode the allowance until it became relatively insignificant. The US deduction is uncapped.

8. See   http://www.asaecenter.org/AboutUs/Index.cfm?navItemNumber= 51733

9. In a nice irony, many Tea Party supporters will have voted for the Republican Mitt Romney, whose main achievement as governor of Massachusetts was a health care scheme almost identical to the Obama plan.

10. For a rundown on the Kochs' activities, see http://www.newyorker.com/ reporting/2010/08/30/100830fa_fact_mayer

11. Amazon, Google and Starbucks are struggling to defend their tax avoidance, *The Guardian*, 13 November 2012.

12. For international figures, see http://www.economist.com/blogs/ buttonwood/2011/03/taxation_policy_2

13. Graham Stewart, *Bang! A History of Britain in the 1980s*, Atlantic Books, 2013.

14. http://www.ukpublicspending.co.uk/

15. http://www.usgovernmentspending.com/

16. 'Debt and Democracy', working paper presented at the Legatum Institute, 21 May 2012.

17. *Democracy in America*, Kindle edition.

18. See http://www.economonitor.comdolanecon/2011/07/31/how-smart-fiscal-rules-keep-swedens-budget-in-balance/

19. Organization for Economic Cooperation and Development – a club of 34 wealthy countries committed to democracy and the free market, including the US, the UK, France, Germany, Italy, Japan and South Korea.

20. 'Incapacity Benefits in the UK: An Issue of Health or Jobs?' http://www. social-policy.org.uk/lincoln/Beatty.pdf

21. ibid.

22. The benefits kick in at different ages.

23. Toke S. Aidt and Peter S. Jensen, 'Tax Structure, Size of Government and the Extension of the Voting Franchise in Western Europe 1860–1938', 3 April 2008, in *International Tax and Public Finance*, June 2009.

24. Belgium, Denmark, France, Germany, Italy, the Netherlands, Norway, Sweden, Switzerland and the UK.

25. Toke S. Aidt, Jayasri Dutta and Elena Loukoianova, 'Democracy Comes to Europe: Franchise Extensions and Fiscal Outcomes 1860–1938', October 2004, in *European Economic Review*, 2006.
26. *The End of Politics and the Birth of iDemocracy*, Biteback Publishing, 2012.
27. 'The Economic Role of the State in the 21st Century', *Cato Journal*, vol. 25, no. 3, 2005.
28. ibid.
29. http://www.forbes.com/2009/11/19/republican-budget-hypocrisy-health-care-opinions-columnists-bruce-bartlett.html
30. 'China Scolds US over S&P Credit Downgrade', http://www.bbc.co.uk/news/world-us-canada-14430598
31. *The Rise and Fall of the Great Powers: Economic Change and Military Conflict from 1500 to 2000*, Random House, 1988.
32. Published by Profile, 2012. The subtitle is *The Origins of Power, Prosperity and Poverty*.
33. Some historians argue that the reluctance to pay taxes dates all the way back to the days of the Ottoman Empire, when tax avoidance was a form of passive resistance by the Greeks.

6. GOING TO EXTREMES

1. 'The Sources of Extremism', *Journal of Democracy*, October 2012.
2. The irony of this was that the EU did not insist on a levy on insured depositors – those with under €100,000. That condition was put in by the Cypriot government because the alternative would have been a bigger levy on uninsured depositors, many of whom were wealthy Russians. But the protests focused on the EU, not the Russians.
3. EC briefing note, http://ec.europa.eu/economy_finance/articles/governance/2012-03-14_six_pack_en.htm
4. 'Warnings from History', *Journal of Democracy*, October 2012.
5. A second poll was needed because the parties failed to form a coalition after the first.
6. In Spain, General Franco also relied on fascist support. But his rule is really more in the long and disgraceful tradition of conservative military dictatorships.
7. Matthew Goodwin, 'Right Response: Understanding and Countering Populist Extremism in Europe', Chatham House report, September 2011.
8. Transatlantic Trends Topline Data, 2010, figures from the Chatham House report.

9. Belgium, Denmark, France, Germany, Greece, Ireland, Italy, Luxembourg, the Netherlands, Portugal, Spain and the UK. Taken from the Chatham House report.

10. Dr Matthew Goodwin and Professor Jocelyn Evans, *From Voting to Violence? Far Right Extremism in Britain*, Searchlight Educational Trust, 2012. Technically speaking, 88% disagreed with the proposition that Islam was *not* a threat to Western civilization.

11. 'Intolerance, Prejudice and Discrimination: A European Report', quoted in the Chatham House study, 2011.

12. 'Recapturing the Reluctant Radicals', 2012, www.counterpoint.uk.com

13. 'Immigrants as Scapegoats', *The Economist*, 6 October 2012.

14. 'Greece, in 2012: Fascists Beating Up People while the Police Look On' by Yiannis Baboulias, *The Guardian*, 13 October 2012.

15. It may still be there as you read this. www.livingingreece.gr/strikes.

16. 'Populism in Europe: The Netherlands' by Jamie Bartlett, Jonathan Birdwell and Sarah de Lange, Demos thinktank, September 2012.

17. 'Recapturing the Reluctant Radicals', www.counterpoint.uk.com.

18. Goodwin and Evans, *From Voting to Violence?*

19. ibid.

20. 'The Rise of UKIP: What Does It All Mean?' by Dr Rob Ford, University of Manchester, http://www7.politicalbetting.com/index.php/archives/2012/12/04/the-rise-of-ukip-what-does-it-all-mean/

21. http://ukip.org/media/pdf/UKIPlocalManifesto2012.pdf

22. Goodwin and Evans, *From Voting to Violence?*

7. CLOWNS TO THE LEFT, JOKERS TO THE RIGHT

1. It wasn't jet lag or a dream. See http://www.guardian.co.uk/commentis-free/cifamerica/2011/feb/02/egypt-fox-news

2. He has since left.

3. 'The Foxification of News', *The Economist*, 7 July 2011. CNN viewership fell to third behind MSNBC, which shifted to a liberal echo of Fox News programming.

4. *The Paranoid Style in American Politics* by Richard Hofstadter, Jonathan Cape, 1966.

5. ibid.

6. ibid.

7. 'The State of the News Media 2012', the Pew Research Center's Project for Excellence in Journalism.

8. ibid.

9. Quoted in *Democracy Under Attack: How the Media Distort Policy and Politics* by Malcolm Dean, Policy Press, 2012.

10. *The Economist* Intelligence Unit, 'Democracy Under Stress'.

11. See http://www.gallup.com/poll/1654/honesty-ethics-professions.aspx

12. 'How Luther Went Viral', *The Economist*, 17 December 2011.

13. See http://www.gbuwh.co.uk/ for those who are interested.

14. *Going to Extremes: How Like Minds Unite and Divide Us*, Oxford University Press, 2009.

15. Jacob S. Hacker and Paul Pierson, *Winner-Take-All Politics: How Washington Made the Rich Richer – And Turned Its Back on the Middle Class*, Simon & Schuster, 2010.

16. 'The Polarisation of the Congressional Parties', http://voteview.com/political_polarisation.asp

8. TAKING A LIBERTY

1. Subtitled *Illiberal Democracy at Home and Abroad*, W. W. Norton, 2007.

2. *The Age of Revolution: 1789–1848*, first published in 1962. The late Mr Hobsbawm did not generally use the world 'bourgeois' as a compliment.

3. For a case study, see http://www.bbc.co.uk/history/ww2peopleswar/stories/11/a3332611.shtml

4. See http://www.worldlii.org/eu/cases/ECHR/1978/1.html

5. See http://www.guardian.co.uk/world/2012/oct/05/mau-mau-veterans-win-torture-case

6. 'A Savage War of Peace: Algeria 1954–1962', *The New York Review of Books*.

7. See http://www.internmentarchives.com/showdoc.php?docid=00055&search_id=19269&pagenum=2

8. Early news reports blamed Islamic terrorists. In fact, the bombing was carried out by Timothy McVeigh, a supporter of right-wing militia movements. Although he was raised a Catholic and took the sacrament before his execution, he was not dubbed a 'Christian terrorist'.

9. See the Seton Hall report http://law.shu.edu/publications/guantanamoReports/guantanamo_report_final_2_08_06.pdf. The report found that only 8% of detainees could be classed as Al Qaeda fighters. The vast majority of detainees (86%) were captured by Pakistani or Afghan forces in return for cash bounties.

10. The various memos are available from *The New York Times* website at http://www.nytimes.com/ref/international/24MEMO-GUIDE.html.

11. See 'Waterboarding: A Tortured History', http://www.npr.org/templates/story/story.php?storyId=15886834.

12. See the Senate report on the issue, http://www.reuters.com/article/2012/04/27/us-usa-congress-torture-idUSBRE83Q07J20120427.

13. See http://www.europarl.europa.eu/sides/getDoc.do?type=REPORT&reference=A7-2012-0266&language=EN.

14. 'In the Name of Security', see www.hrw.org.

15. ibid.

16. *Democracy in America*, vol. II.

17. *The Better Angels of Our Nature*, Allen Lane, 2011.

18. The law was later blocked by a Federal court. Its proponents admitted that they knew of no case where Sharia law had been used.

19. *The End of History and the Last Man*, Free Press, 1992.

20. 'Is It a Crime to Take Pictures?', http://news.bbc.co.uk/1/hi/uk/7888301.stm.

21. 'Why do Police Seize Photographers' Cameras?', http://www.guardian.co.uk/media/greenslade/2010/aug/10/news-photography-police.

9. EUROPE DIVIDED

1. 'An Ever Deeper Democratic Deficit', *The Economist*, 26 May 2012.

2. Subtitled *The Euro Crisis and Why Politicians Don't Get It*, Biteback Books, 2012.

3. Technically, it needs to run a primary surplus; that is, its revenues need to exceed its expenditure, before interest costs. But in the case of Greece, it was nowhere near surplus on any measure.

4. Not to be confused with the European Court of Human Rights, based in Strasbourg, which has 47 member states and has nothing to do with the EU.

5. See 'A Concise Encyclopaedia of the European Union' at http://www.euro-know.org/europages/dictionary/q.html.

6. 'An Even Deeper Democratic Deficit', *The Economist*, 26 May 2012.

7. 'Italian Politics: So, What Next?', *The Economist*, 24 November 2012.

8. Countries where the debt-to-GDP ratio is over 60% have to aim for 0.5%; those where the ratio is significantly below 60% can go as high as 1%.

9. Sebastien Dullen, 'Reinventing Europe: Explaining the Fiscal Compact', European Council on Foreign Relations, www.ecfr.eu.

10. John Glover, 'ECB Collateral Moves Re-Open "Soup Kitchen" for Struggling Banks', *Bloomberg*, 7 September 2012.

11. It is all on the ECB website at http://www.ecb.int/mopo/eaec/fiscal/html/index.en.html.

12. Some maintain that a hole in the central bank's balance sheet wouldn't matter; it is just an accounting item. It seems likely that the authorities would worry that the concept of a notionally bust ECB would undermine confidence in the euro. But so many strange things have happened that it is always possible everyone will carry on regardless.

13. 'Democracy is the Loser in the Battle to Save the Euro', *The Financial Times*, 11 September 2012.

14. 'Euro Update: The Perils of Pointless Pain', 26 September 2012, krugman.blogs.nytimes.com.

15. Pryce, *Greekonomics*.

16. 'State of Denial', *The Economist*, 27 October 2012.

17. 'Spain's Regional Governments: How They Got into Trouble', http://www.bbc.co.uk/news/business-18951575.

18. 'Catalans Want Referendum on Independence' poll, http://uk.reuters.com/article/2012/10/28/uk-spain-catalonia-poll-idUKBRE89R0AN20121028.

19. 'Adjustment in the Euro Zone', *The Economist*, 17 November 2012.

20. He was also one of the *soixante-huitards*, the French student protesters of 1968, when he was known as 'Danny the Red'.

21. 'There is No Alternative to a Federal Europe', www.social-europe.eu

10. ALL MEN ARE CREATED UNEQUAL

1. *The New Few: Or a Very British Oligarchy*, Simon & Schuster, 2012.

2. Zanny Minton Beddoes, 'World Economy Survey', *The Economist*, 13 October 2012.

3. *The State of Working America*, Economic Policy Institute, 12th edition.

4. Joseph Stiglitz, *The Price of Inequality: How Today's Divided Society Endangers Our Future*, W. W. Norton & Company, 2012.

5. ibid.

6. *Winner-Take-All Politics: How Washington Made the Rich Richer – and Turned Its Back on the Middle Class* by Jacob Hacker and Paul Pierson, Simon & Schuster, 2010.

7. 'How England's Country Houses Recovered Their Glory' by Harry Mount, *The Daily Telegraph*, 9 July 2011.

8. Data from Professor Danny Dorling of Sheffield University, as reported in 'Inequality Worst since the Second World War', *The Guardian*, 27 June 2012.

9. 'American Incomes before and after the Revolution', by Peter Lindert and Jeffrey Williamson, 2011, NBER WP 17211.

10. Hacker and Pierson, *Winner-Take-All Politics*.

11. 'The Rich and the Rest', *The Economist*, 12 October 2012.

12. 'The Reproduction of Privilege' by Thomas B. Edsall, www.campaignstops. blogs.nytimes.com

13. 'Like Father, Not Like Son', *The Economist*, 12 October 2012.

14. 'Divided We Stand: Why Inequality Keeps Rising', OECD report, 2011.

15. This is a truism. Alas, it doesn't tell us the precise point at which higher taxes start to lead to lower revenues.

16. *Unintended Consequences: Why Everything You've Been Told About the Economy is Wrong,* Portfolio/Penguin, 2012.

17. Thomas L. Hungerford, 'Taxes and the Economy: An Economic Analysis of the Top Tax Rates Since 1945', available at http://democrats.waysand-means.house.gov/sites/democrats.waysandmeans.house.gov/files/Updated%20CRS%20Report%2012%3A13%3A12.pdf.

18. 'How Progressive is the US Federal Tax System? A Historical and International Perspective', *Journal of Economic Perspectives*, vol. 21, no. 1.

19. Hacker and Pierson, *Winner-Take-All Politics*.

20. 'How Progressive is the US Federal Tax System?'

21. *The Submerged State: How Invisible Government Policies Undermine American Democracy* by Suzanne Mettler, University of Chicago Press, 2011.

22. ibid.

23. ibid.

24. Lawrence Mishel and Natalie Sabadish, 'CEO Pay and the Top 1%: How Executive Compensation and Financial-Sector Pay have Fuelled Income Inequality', Economic Policy Institute, May 2012.

25. Hacker and Pierson, *Winner-Take-All Politics*.

26. Paul Krugman, 'Oligarchy, American Style', *The New York Times*, 3 November 2011.

27. Thomas Philippon and Ariell Reshef, 'Wages and Human Capital in the US Financial Industry, 1909–2006', National Bureau of Economic Research, working paper 14644.

28. See http://www.opensecrets.org/lobby/top.php?indexType=c.

29. Co-written with James Kwak. The subtitle is 'The Wall Street Takeover and the Next Financial Meltdown'.

30. 'A Fistful of Dollars: Lobbying and the Financial Crisis' by Deniz Igan, Prachi Mishra and Thierry Tressel, IMF working paper, December 2009.

31. These loans disappeared into the alphabet soup of CDOs and RMBs, which proved to have such fatal flaws.

32. 'RBS "Gamble" on ABN Amro Deal' by Simon Bowers and Jill Treanor, *The Guardian*, 12 December 2011.

33. Talking on Radio 4's *Today* programme, 14 August 2010.

34. Called *What's the Matter with Kansas* in the US and subtitled *How the Conservatives Won the Heart of America*, published by Henry Holt in the US and Vintage in the UK.

35. *The Rise and Decline of Nations*, Yale University Press, 1982.

36. See http://www.opensecrets.org/lobby/index.php

37. *The Submerged State*.

38. Figures from Opensecrets.org, the website of the Center for Responsive Politics.

39. ibid.

40. *One Way Forward*, e-book by Lawrence Lessig.

41. Hacker and Pierson, *Winner-Take-All Politics*.

42. *Unequal Democracy: The Political Economy of the New Gilded Age*, Princeton University Press, 2010. Mr Bartels defines 'poor' as the income of the 20th percentile and 'rich' as the 80th percentile. Of course, Congress plays as big a part as the president in setting economic policy and the Democrats were in charge of one, or both, houses for much of the period.

43. *Considerations on Representative Government*.

44. Bartels, *Unequal Democracy*.

45. ibid.

46. Source: www.opensecrets.org from the Center for Responsive Politics.

47. 'Did Newt Gingrich Just Coordinate with His SuperPac?', theatlanticwire.com.

48. For details, see http://www.ukpolitical.info/Expenditure.htm.

49. Details are on the Electoral Commission website at http://www.electoralcommission.org.uk/elections/election-spending/party-campaign-expenditure.

50. *Democracy in America*, vol. 1.

51. The Center for Responsive Politics, http://www.opensecrets.org/pres12/index.php

11. DEFINING THE PROBLEM

1. *The Sunday Times*, 1 January 2012.

2. 'Legitimacy Rests on Restoring Opportunity', *The Financial Times*, 18 October 2012.

3. 'The Debt Democracy', available at http://www.chiltoncapital.com/assets/feb-12---the-debt-democracy.pdf

4. *The Third Wave: Democratization in the Late Twentieth Century*, University of Oklahoma Press, 1993.
5. 'Stuck With Him', *The Economist*, 12 October 2012.
6. Some cite this coup attempt as justification for Mr Chavez's actions. However, he was hardly a democratic purist. He attempted his own coup, against an elected government, in 1992.
7. 'Tilting the Pitch', *The Economist*, 5 July 2012.
8. ibid.
9. 'More than 100 Quangos Axed by Coalition, Say Ministers', http://www. bbc.co.uk/news/uk-politics-19338344.
10. 'Too Much of a Good Thing', 6 October 2011.
11. See the Tax Policy Center's analysis at http://www.taxpolicycenter.org/ taxtopics/bowles-simpson.cfm.
12. For the data, see http://www.imf.org/external/np/sec/memdir/members.aspx.
13. http://www.huffingtonpost.com/ian-fletcher/gov-buddy-roemer-free-trade_b_1026078.html.
14. See Mark Mazower, *Governing the World: The History of an Idea*, Allen Lane, 2012.
15. *The Globalization Paradox: Why Global Markets, States and Democracy Can't Coexist*, Oxford University Press, 2011.
16. ibid.
17. 'The Curious Strength of the NRA', *The Economist*, 16 March 2013.
18. *Capitalism, Socialism and Democracy*, second edition, Martino Publishing, 2011.
19. 'Old School Ties', *The Economist*, 20 March 2012.
20. Although living standards have stagnated for the poor in recent decades, as the last chapter noted.
21. *On Democracy*, Yale University Press, 2000.
22. Some would argue that Mr Paulson's background made him more inclined to rescue the banks. But it is possible to ascribe a cynical motive to all his actions; for example, when he let Lehman Brothers go bust, a Goldman competitor was eliminated.

12. SOLUTIONS

1. This term limit arises from the Twenty-second Amendment, passed after Franklin Roosevelt won four consecutive terms in office.
2. Source: http://www.nytimes.com/interactive/2012/02/12/us/relying-on-government-benefits.html
3. Subtitled *A Middle Way between West and East*, Polity Press, 2013.

4. Andreas Kluth, 'The Withering Branch', *The Economist*, 20 April 2011.

5. 'California Has Nation's Worst Credit Rating, Pew Study Finds', *Sacramento Bee*, 26 September 2011.

6. See http://www.prospectmagazine.co.uk/blog/beppe-grillo-five-star-movement-social-media.

7. As of early April 2013, see https://twitter.com/search?q=beppe%20grillo&src=typd.

8. See http://www.reuters.com/article/2013/03/07/us-italy-vote-grillo-insight-idUSBRE92608G20130307

9. *The End of Politics and the Birth of iDemocracy*, Biteback Press, 2012.

10. *It's Even Worse Than It Looks: How the American Constitutional System Collided with the New Politics of Extremism*, Basic Books, 2012.

11. ibid.

12. See http://www.guardian.co.uk/world/2012/nov/29/united-nations-vote-palestine-state

13. Mark Mazower, *Governing the World: The History of an Idea*, Allen Lane, 2012.

Bibliography

Aaronovitch, David, *Voodoo Histories: How Conspiracy Theory Has Shaped Modern History*, Vintage Books, 2010

Acemoglu, Daron and Robinson, James A., *Why Nations Fail: The Origins of Power, Prosperity and Poverty*, Crown Publishers, 2012

Aristotle, *Politics: A Treatise on Government*, Kindle edition of 1912 translation by William Ellis, published by J. M. Dent

Bartels, Larry M., *Unequal Democracy: The Political Economy of the New Gilded Ages*, Princeton University Press, 2008

Berggruen, Nicholas and Gardels, Nathan, *Intelligent Governance for the 21st Century: A Middle Way between West and East*, Polity Press, 2013

Blanchard, Olivier, Romer, David, Spence, A. Michael and Stiglitz, Joseph E. (joint eds.), *In the Wake of the Crisis: Leading Economists Reassess Economic Policy*, MIT Press, 2012

Caplan, Bryan, *The Myth of the Rational Voter: Why Democracies Choose Bad Policies*, Princeton University Press, 2007

Carswell, Douglas, *The End of Politics and the Birth of iDemocracy*, Biteback Publishing, 2012

Dahl, Robert A., *Democracy and Its Critics*, Yale University Press, 1989

Dahl, Robert A., *On Democracy*, Yale University Press, 2000

Dean, Malcolm, *Democracy Under Attack: How the Media Distort Policy and Politics*, Policy Press, 2012

Dikötter, Frank, *Mao's Great Famine: The History of China's Most Devastating Catastrophe 1958–62*, Bloomsbury, 2010

Dunn, John, *Setting the People Free: The Story of Democracy*, Atlantic Books, 2005

Dunn, John (ed.), *Democracy: The Unfinished Journey*, Oxford University Press, 1992

Eichengreen, Bary, *Golden Fetters: The Gold Standard and the Great Depression*, Oxford University Press, 1995

Eijk, Cees van der and Franklin, Mark N., *Elections and Voters*, Palgrave Macmillan, 2009

Elliott, Larry and Atkinson, Dan, *Going South: Why Britain Will Have a Third World Economy by 2014*, Palgrave Macmillan, 2012

Frank, Thomas, *What's the Matter With America? The Resistible Rise of the American Right*, Secker & Warburg, 2004

Freeland, Chrystia, *Plutocrats: The Rise of the New Global Super Rich and the Fall of Everyone Else*, Allen Lane, 2012

Fukuyama, Francis, *The End of History and the Last Man*, Penguin Books, 1992

Hacker, Jacob S. and Pierson, Paul, *Winner-Take-All Politics: How Washington Made the Rich Richer and Turned Its Back on the Middle Class*, Simon & Schuster, 2010

Hamilton, Alexander, Jay, John and Madison, James, *The Federalist Papers*, originally published by J. and A. McLean, 1788

Held, David, *Models of Democracy*, third edition, Polity Press, 2006

Hobsbawm, Eric, *The Age of Revolution: Europe 1789–1848*, Weidenfeld & Nicolson, 1962

Hobsbawm, Eric, *The Age of Capital: 1848–1875*, Weidenfeld & Nicolson, 1975

Hofstadter, Richard, *The Idea of a Party System: The Rise of Legitimate Opposition in the United States, 1780–1840*, University of California Press, 1969

Hofstadter, Richard, *The Paranoid Style in American Politics*, Jonathan Cape, 1966

Horne, Alastair, *A Savage War of Peace: Algeria 1954–1962*, New York Review of Books Classics, revised edition, 2006

Huntington, Samuel P., *The Third Wave: Democratization in the Late Twentieth Century*, University of Oklahoma Press, 1992

Johnson, Simon and Kwak, James, *13 Bankers: The Wall Street Takeover and the Next Financial Meltdown*, Pantheon, 2010

Judt, Tony, *Ill Fares the Land: A Treatise on Our Present Discontents*, Penguin Books, 2010

Judt, Tony, *Postwar: A History of Europe since 1945*, Vintage Books, 2010

Judt, Tony, *Reappraisals: Reflections on the Forgotten Twentieth Century*, William Heinemann, 2008

Kennedy, Paul, *The Rise and Fall of the Great Powers: Economic Change and Military Conflict from 1500 to 2000*, Fontana Press, 1989

King, Stephen D., *When the Money Runs Out: The End of Western Affluence*, Yale University Press, 2013

Lessig, Lawrence, *One Way Forward*, Byliner Original, 2012

Lijphart, Arend, *Patterns of Democracy: Government Forms and Performance in Thirty-Six Countries*, Yale University Press, 1999

Mann, Thomas E. and Ornstein, Norman J., *It's Even Worse Than It Looks: How the American Constitutional System Collided with the New Politics of Extremism*, Basic Books, 2012

Mazower, Mark, *Governing the World: The History of an Idea*, Allen Lane, 2012

Mettler, Suzanne, *The Submerged State: How Invisible Government Policies Undermine American Democracy*, University of Chicago Press, 2011

Mill, John Stuart, *Considerations on Representative Government*, Kindle edition, originally published 1861

Morris, Ian, *Why the West Rules – For Now: The Patterns of History and What They Reveal about the Future*, Profile Books, 2010

Mount, Ferdinand, *The New Few: Or a Very British Oligarchy*, Simon & Schuster, 2012

Olson, Mancur, *The Rise and Decline of Nations*, Yale University Press, 1982

Ormerod, Paul, *The Death of Economics*, Faber and Faber, 1994

Pinker, Steven, *The Better Angels of Our Nature: The Decline of Violence in History and Its Causes*, Penguin Books, 2010

Plato, *The Republic*, translated by Desmond Lee, Kindle edition of a Penguin classic, originally published 1955

Pryce, Vicky, *Greekonomics: The Euro Crisis and Why Politicians Don't Get It*, Biteback Publishing, 2012

Putnam, Robert, *Bowling Alone: The Collapse and Revival of American Community*, Simon & Schuster, 2000

Rauch, Jonathan, *Government's End: Why Washington Stopped Working*, Public Affairs, 1999

Reinhart, Carmen and Rogoff, Kenneth, *This Time Is Different: Eight Centuries of Financial Folly*, Princeton University Press, 2009

Roberts, Jennifer Tolbert, *Athens on Trial: The Antidemocratic Tradition in Western Thought*, Princeton University Press, 1994

Robinson, Eric W. (ed.), *Ancient Greek Democracy: Readings and Sources*, Blackwell Publishing, 2004

Rodrik, Dani, *The Globalization Paradox: Why Global Markets, States and Democracy Can't Coexist*, Oxford University Press, 2011

Ryan, Alan, *The Making of Modern Liberalism*, Princeton University Press, 2012

Sandbrook, Dominic, *Seasons in the Sun: The Battle for Britain 1974–1979*, Allen Lane, 2012

Schumpeter, Joseph A., *Capitalism, Socialism and Democracy*, second edition, Martino Publishing, 2011

Stewart, Graham, *Bang! A History of Britain in the 1980s*, Atlantic Books, 2013

Stiglitz, Joseph E., *The Price of Inequality: How Today's Divided Society Endangers Our Future*, W. W. Norton, 2012

Sunstein, Cass R., *Going to Extremes: How Like Minds Unite and Divide*, Oxford University Press, 2009

Tetlock, Philip E., *Expert Political Judgment: How Good is It? How Can We Know?*, Princeton University Press, 2005

Tocqueville, Alexis de, *Democracy in America*, volumes I and II, translated by Henry Reeve, Kindle edition

Zakaria, Fareed, *The Future of Freedom: Illiberal Democracy at Home and Abroad*, W. W. Norton, 2007

Index